691-4574

THE RUSSIAN PIANO CONCERTO

VOLUME I
The Nineteenth Century

RUSSIAN MUSIC STUDIES
Malcolm Hamrick Brown
Founding Editor

THE RUSSIAN PIANO CONCERTO

VOLUME I
The Nineteenth Century

JEREMY NORRIS

INDIANA UNIVERSITY PRESS
Bloomington and Indianapolis

Norris, Jeremy, date
    The Russian piano concerto / Jeremy Norris.
        p.   cm. — (Russian music studies)
    Includes discographies, bibliographical references, and indexes.
    Contents: v. 1. The nineteenth century
    ISBN 0-253-34112-4 (v. 1 : cl : alk. paper)
    1. Concertos (Piano)—19th century—History and criticism.
    2. Music—Russia—19th century—History and criticism. I. Title.
    II. Series: Russian music studies (Bloomington, Ind.)
ML1263.N67   1994
784.2'62'0947—dc20   93-11565

    1 2 3 4 5   99 98 97 96 95 94

To my parents,
James and Enid Norris

Contents

Preface
ix

Introduction
I

I
The European Heritage
5

2
The Piano Concertos of Anton Rubinstein
21

3
The Piano Concertos of the Nationalists
and the Eclectics
54

4
The Piano Concertos of Peter Tchaikovsky
114

Conclusion
186

Notes
189

Contents

Chronological List of Works Analyzed
205

Selected Bibliography
208

Discography, compiled by David Griffioen
211

Index
224

Preface

When I embarked on this project, ringing in my ears was Abraham Veinus's gentle warning: "A musicologist, one hopes, can be something other than a dreary janitor of music history tidying a magnificent cathedral where none comes to pray." Consequently, I have tried to avoid an overly academic approach, choosing instead a course based on the letters, diaries, and other writings of Russians who composed concertos, principally to discover why they composed them, under what circumstances, and in what way these motives and circumstances manifested themselves in their music. In so doing, Veinus's cathedral is no longer silent, but reverberates with the sound of personal recollections, opinions, and observations. Other voices are also heard: the voices of relatives and friends of the composers, their publishers, their critics. As the janitor/musicologist, I found myself too busy to be dreary, for this great wealth of primary material had to be put in order and analyzed—together with the music in question—with the aim of shedding new light on the composers' intentions.

The general plan of the study is chronological, though as is clear from the Contents, I have dealt with Rubinstein and Tchaikovsky separately because of their more substantial contributions to Russian concerto literature. This results in a number of minor chronological anomalies—with Rubinstein's last concerto (in E-flat, Op. 94, 1875) being discussed before Balakirev's first attempt of 1855, Scriabin's Concerto in F-sharp minor, Op. 20, (1986–97) before Tchaikovsky's celebrated Concerto No. 1 in B-flat minor, Op. 23 (1875), etc.—but they are outweighed by the obvious advantage of analyzing Rubinstein's and Tchaikovsky's concertos collectively. Moreover, despite my determination to remain impartial, I must ask the reader's forgiveness for having devoted more space and attention to what are generally considered the finer concertos composed in Russia during the nineteenth century. Whether this is a *modus operandi* to be condemned or approved I have never been able to discover, though certainly many greater writers than myself have adopted this practice as a lifelong principle.

More problematic has been the matter of transliteration, invariably a thorn in the side of writers dealing with subjects in languages based on alphabets other than the Latin. As a general principle, I have used the Library of Congress system, particularly in the Notes and Bibliography. However, for Russian names in the text I have turned to more traditional transliterations for both known and unknown persons for the sake of consistency if not for linguistic accuracy. For instance, to discuss Tchaikovsky and then to mention Tchaikovsky's friend Stoiovskii gives the impression of writing about persons of two different nationalities! Only in cases of irresolvable confusion—the half dozen or so acknowledged transliterations of the publisher Beliaev (Belaiew, Belayev, Belaiev, even Byelyayeff!)—have I resorted to the Library of Congress system for clarity. Translations from Russian sources, incidentally, are my own unless indicated otherwise in the Notes.

Again, to avoid confusion, all dates have been given according to the Russian Julian, or Old Style, calendar, which in the nineteenth century lagged behind the European Gregorian, or New Style, calendar by twelve days.

For assistance in the preparation of this volume, my thanks go to Edward Garden, who cast a stern eye over the early drafts, and to Jarmila Hickman, Laurence Marshall, and Terence Warburton for their useful and sometimes invaluable help. I would also like to express my gratitude to the following persons:

A. F. Leighton Thomas, the editor of *Music Review*, and Gordon Watson for granting permission to use a revised version of my article on Rubinstein's piano concertos (published in *Music Review* in 1985), as the second chapter of the present volume.

Basil Ramsey, the editor of the *Musical Times*, for allowing me to incorporate my discoveries concerning Balakirev's Piano Concerto, first published in the *Musical Times* in July 1990.

The publisher Victor Gollancz Ltd. for permission to use the musical example cited on page 129, taken from David Brown, *Tchaikovsky*, Vol. II.

Acknowledgments are also due to the music publishers who have kindly granted permission to reproduce extracts from copyrighted scores:

Excerpts from Rachmaninov, Concerto No. 1 and *Etude-Tableau*, Op. 33, No. 5, are reproduced with permission from Boosey & Hawkes Music Publishers Ltd.

Excerpts from Tchaikovsky, Piano Concertos Nos. 1 and 2, and Scriabin, Piano Concerto, Op. 20, are quoted courtesy of Edition Eulenburg/Schott.

Excerpts from Mussorgsky, *Pictures at an Exhibition*; Chopin, Scherzo in C minor, Op. 39; and Borodin, Scherzo in A; and from the Piano Concertos of Grieg, Rimsky-Korsakov, and Tchaikovsky are reproduced by kind permission of Peters Edition Ltd., London.

Excerpts from Chopin, Etudes, Op. 10 and Op. 25 are quoted with permission of Stainer & Bell.

THE RUSSIAN
PIANO CONCERTO

VOLUME I
The Nineteenth Century

Introduction

The literature of the piano concerto is a vast, heterogeneous affair containing examples in every conceivable mood and style, from the aristocratic concertos of Koželuch, Vanhal, and Mozart to the jazz-inspired compositions of Copland, Gershwin, and Jarrett; from the transcendentally virtuosic concertos of Kalkbrenner, Henselt, and Prokofiev to the "infantile" concertos of Margola and Raphling; from the exotic creations of Schulhoff, d'Indy, and de Falla to the neoclassical austerity of Stravinsky. Almost every composer of instrumental music attempted a piano concerto, though few made concerto composition central to their creativity, and fewer still invested in it their finest music. The reasons for this lie in the intrinsic nature of the concerto itself, above all in the expressive limitations imposed by the ubiquitous element of display and in the compositional difficulties inherent in the joining together of two disparate forces. After Mozart—the first and probably the greatest composer to consider the piano concerto on a par with other forms—the concerto languished in the shadow of the symphony, which offered greater technical and expressive freedom. Subsequently, self-expression never convincingly found a foothold in the Romantic concerto as it did in the symphony. A few composers, such as Brahms, Dvořák, and Rachmaninov, came close to conveying in their concertos sentiments of a symphonic nature, but even in these masterworks such sentiments are expressed in perceptibly broader strokes than in a symphony—with one eye cocked on public reaction as it were—and these ideas are often reiterated and underlined so as to leave no room for misunderstanding. Furthermore, the expression of subjective emotions was often compromised by the "theatrical" aspect of the Romantic concerto, for the drama unfolding between the two protagonists on the concert platform and the virtuosic means with which this contest is fought often distract the listener from the sentiments expressed by the music and obscure the channel of communication between composer and audience. Not all nineteenth-century composers, however, nurtured ambivalent feelings toward the concerto. For many, in particular the composer-virtuosi of the so-called Biedermeier period (c. 1810–35), including Herz, Moscheles, Hunten, and Kalkbrenner, the concerto represented an ideal vehicle for displaying their technical prowess, if not compositional ability; and soon genuine self-expression as a creative impulse became virtually extinguished by the weight and proliferation of superfluous virtuosity and spectacular effects. The "Biedermeier" composers' domination of the European concert halls—so vociferously condemned by Schumann in *Neue Zeitschrift für Musik*—was short-lived, for, rescued by Mendelssohn and consolidated by Schumann, the piano concerto regained its respectability toward the 1850s, though it was rarely taken up by composers with more serious musical intentions until several decades later. Nineteenth-century piano concertos were frequently composed with a specific performer in mind—again, hardly an apposite stimulus for self-expression—and the end product was almost invariably tailor-made to gratify the virtuosic rather than the expressive abilities of the performer. Among Russian composers, Tchaikovsky, for example, wrote his Second Piano Concerto in G major, Op. 44, for Nikolai Rubinstein and his Third Piano Concerto in E-flat, Op. 75, for the French pianist Louis Diémer.

The musical outcome of such lukewarm and disinterested inspiration, as with the earlier "war horses" of the "Biedermeier period," is generally disappointing. Neither can one expect profundity of creative thought from the piano concertos based on material originally intended for other works but rejected on the grounds of unsuitability or inferiority (Tchaikovsky's Third Concerto, in E-flat, and his *Concert Fantasia*, Op. 56, for example). Then there are piano concertos composed merely for the sake of writing something, usually to fill gaps resulting from creative lassitude. Again, among Russian composers, Tchaikovsky figures prominently with his Second Concerto.

Just as the piano concerto proved not entirely suitable for the expression of profound emotions, so it struggled to convey, for more or less the same reasons, sentiments of a nationalist character. Few composers, Russian or otherwise, succeeded in writing genuinely fine nationalist concertos. In addition to the conceptual and compositional difficulties involved in composing piano concertos—in particular, the tonal balance and distribution of thematic material between soloist and orchestra—they were confronted with the task of employing often modally conceived folk material in large-scale structures based on Western European tonal schemes. Though Glinka's *changing background* technique proved effective in varying repeated statements of a folk melody on a small scale (as displayed in his orchestral fantasia *Kamarinskaya*), in a concerto situation, aspiring nationalist composers were faced, sooner or later, with elaborating and developing what are often stubborn and intransigent thematic chunks. Not surprisingly, most so-called nationalist concertos employ folk material only in the finale "after the serious business of the concerto is done," to quote Veinus[1] (usually a congenial rondo requiring little if any thematic development), and these folk melodies are usually incorporated merely to provide a dash of national color or a taste of the exotic and unfamiliar. Genuine national concertos on the other hand, that is to say, concertos that contain folk characteristics as an intrinsic part of their musical vocabulary, are less common because of the enormous musical and technical problems already hinted at. However, the finer examples in the literature, including the piano concertos of Dvořák, Grieg, and Rimsky-Korsakov, are so immersed in their native folk idiom that these difficulties resolve themselves as a matter of course in fresh and often breathtakingly beautiful ways. Occasionally, the concertos' basic material is so rich in national elements that the direct quotation of folk material is not even deemed necessary. Indeed, the employment of folk material does not necessarily signify greater national color, as a comparison of two celebrated piano concertos—Tchaikovsky's Concerto in B-flat minor and Grieg's Concerto in A minor—reveals. But as already noted, such concertos are rare. Nationalism, in fact, found a more sympathetic reception in symphonic works in which virtuosity is of secondary importance to programmatic content, for example, in the symphonic poem; and it blossomed into full flower in musical-literary genres such as opera and song. Unfortunately, these genres—the most profound expression of nationalist ideals and arguably the finest musical creations of nationalist composers in general—are still little known to Western European audiences because singers and public alike are reluctant to confront unfamiliar languages, particularly of Slavic origin. As far as Russian is concerned, this has led to the curious situation in which composers are generally better known by their less-representative works. Opera, for example, was central to the creativity of both Tchaikovsky and Rimsky-Korsakov, yet both are still considered in the West as master orchestral composers who occasionally, and apparently without significant success, dabbled in operatic fields.

The development of the nineteenth-century piano concerto—in addition to practical and compositional considerations—was also influenced by the role and status of the instrument itself and the general attitude of contemporary composers toward piano composition. In Germany and Austria, the piano enjoyed considerable popularity from the earliest days of its evolution, and both the solo and the concerto repertoires of these countries are rich and varied. In Russia, on the other hand, because of the slow and limited diffusion of the instrument, the lack of a tradition of piano composition, and the strong bias toward opera inherited from the French and Italian theatre companies, few piano works of significance were composed during the nineteenth century. Furthermore, the piano was considered primarily a component of the aristocratic salon. Almost all Russian composers wrote salon music, from the dilettante efforts of Engalichev, Laskovsky, and Glinka to the "pot-boilers" of Tchaikovsky, Lyadov, and Blumenfeld. Even Rachmaninov found himself writing facile, innocuous pieces for the *fin-de-siècle* Russian salon "just to balance his account."[2]

Serious piano composition, that is, works composed specifically for concert performance, began with Anton Rubinstein during the 1850s, but his contribution, though substantial, is of little musical significance. However, with the publication of Balakirev's magnificent essay in transcendental virtuosity, the Oriental fantasy *Islamey*, in 1869, and five years later, Musorgsky's splendidly eccentric *Pictures from an Exhibition*, Russian piano music began to establish itself on the European musical scene. But these were isolated occurrences; Balakirev dissipated his energies guiding the *Moguchaia Kuchka* (The Mighty Handful), and Musorgsky only turned to the piano to compose song accompaniments and miniatures during pauses between his more ambitious operatic projects. It was only during the closing decade of the nineteenth century, with the appearance of Scriabin's Piano Sonata in F minor, Op. 6, in 1892 and Rachmaninov's *Fantasy* (First Suite) for two pianos, Op. 5, in 1893 that Russian composers resumed the exploration of the piano's technical and expressive capabilities initiated by Balakirev and Musorgsky. Scriabin and Rachmaninov were soon joined by a host of minor composers, including Lyapunov, Glazunov, and Arensky, and the tradition of Russian piano composition was consolidated once and for all by Prokofiev.

The composition of piano concertos in Russia roughly coincided with these sporadic bursts of interest in the piano as a solo instrument, though rarely do these concertos match their solo counterparts in quality. The two finest Russian piano concertos composed during the nineteenth century— Tchaikovsky's deservedly popular Concerto in B-flat minor and Rimsky-Korsakov's unjustly neglected Concerto in C-sharp minor—were penned by composers who were not expert performers and who had only a minor interest in the piano as an expressive instrument.

I
The European Heritage

The Russian piano concerto could not have had more inauspicious beginnings. Unlike the symphonic poem and indirectly, the symphony—genres for which Glinka, the so-called Father of Russian Music provided an invaluable model: "Well? It's all in *Kamarinskaya*, just as the whole oak is in the acorn," wrote Tchaikovsky[1]—the Russian piano concerto had no such indigenous prototype. All that existed to guide and inspire early nineteenth-century Russian composers was a small handful of dilettante concerto-style works and fantasies for "fortepiano or harpsichord," composed for the entertainment of the Russian aristocracy. Their influence on the evolution of the Russian piano concerto was negligible, for none were published and few have survived. Certainly Anton Rubinstein's concertos—the first Russian piano concertos to see their way into print—offered something more substantial, as Tchaikovsky acknowledged in his celebrated Piano Concerto in B-flat minor, Op. 23, but by this time the century was approaching its final quarter.

The reasons for the Russian piano concerto's delayed incipience are both many and complex, but almost all are derived from two crucial factors: Russia's cultural and geographical isolation, and the country's lack of an indigenous tradition of symphonic music. Whereas other Slavic peoples, in particular, the Poles and the Czechs, have always maintained close links with Western Europe, Russian contacts, until the eighteenth century, had been more or less limited to isolated incidents, such as the employment of an Italian organist, Giovanni Salvatore, by Ivan III toward the end of the fifteenth century and the gift of a clavichord by Elizabeth I to the court of Fyodor Ivanovich in 1586. During the eighteenth century, however, the Russian Imperial Court, eager to recreate the splendor and opulence of its Western European counterparts, particularly Versailles, engaged foreign instrumentalists to perform and train Russian musicians. On 5 August 1702 the Court received its first official visit by foreign musicians—a German wind band invited by Peter I—organized through the agency of Popp Bros., Hamburg. Soon afterward, foreign ambassadors brought both musicians and instruments, and during the reigns of Anna, Duchess of Courland (1730–40), and Catherine II (1762–96), French and Italian music and musicians began to dominate the concert halls and salons of the Imperial Court and the palaces of the aristocracy. Italian opera *buffa* and *seria* and French *opéra comique* were the most popular forms of musical entertainment, but chamber music was also performed by members of the theatre orchestras.

Russian composers active during this period were encouraged to study abroad and assimilate contemporary Western European composition. Dmitri Stepanovich Bortnyansky (1752–1825) lived in Italy for ten years (1769–79) and studied with Baldassare Galuppi;[2] Daniel Nikitich Kashin (1769–1841) worked in Bessarabia with Giuseppe Sarti; and Evstignei Ipatovich Fomin (1761–1800) studied at Bologna with various teachers between 1776 and 1785, including Buini, Padre Martini, Sartori, and Mattei. Those who remained in Russia endeavored to master the art of composition by studying the imported French and Italian music. Inevitably, most Russian compositions dating from this period are little more than pale imitations of their European counterparts. Nevertheless, a few demonstrate a spark of individuality, if not originality; and one or two even hint at the emergence of a national character, though the employment of folk material is generally primitive and superficial. Russian symphonic composition of this period is probably best represented by the overture, in particular the overtures to the earliest nationalist operas; *The Miller—Magician, Cheat and Matchmaker* (with songs compiled and arranged by the violinist Sokolovsky, revised by Fomin in 1791), Mikhail Matinsky's *The St. Petersburg Bazaar*, and V. A. Pashkevich's *The Misfortune of Having a Carriage* (all of which were composed in 1779). Significant also are the program overtures to melodrama and tragedy, such as Fomin's *Orfeo and Euridice*, produced in St. Petersburg in 1791–92.

Russian composition on a smaller scale toward the end of the eighteenth century was dominated by variations, and many were based on folk melodies. Probably the earliest examples are the two sets for "clavicembalo o pianoforte" by Vasili Fedorovich Trutovsky (c. 1740–1810), published in 1780. Some of the finer keyboard variations of this period were composed by Lev Stepanovich Gurilëv (1770–1840) and Kashin. Though the overall style of these variations is clearly derived from early Classical fortepiano music, folk elements are evident in their dancelike characteristics, modal harmony, and occasional passages influenced by the *gusly*—a stringed folk instrument similar to a psaltery. Variations for other instruments were less common. The court violinist Khandoshkin composed "Six Old Russian Songs with additional variations for violin and viola" (1783), and many variations appeared for harpsichord or fortepiano "con violino obbligato."

It was also during this period that the earliest Russian piano concertos were written, though none have survived to the present day. Composed specifically for performance at the Imperial Court and the palaces of the aristocracy, they were probably of chamber dimensions, despite their generic title; and to judge from contemporary Russian instrumental works, they were most likely heavily influenced by Western European music.

Whether Bortnyansky's piano concerto was typical is impossible to determine, as the manuscript has never come to light. Gerald Seaman suggests that "in all probability it resembled the 'Concert Symphony' [*Sinfonia Concertante*] written by Bortnyansky in 1790 and took the form of a Sextet in which the leading part was played by a 'fortepiano organisé' i.e. a piano equipped with organ registers."[3] A general idea of the lost concerto can be gleaned therefore from a study of the *Sinfonia Concertante* (in B-flat major). Like the Quintet in C (for piano, harp, violin, viola da gamba, and cello, composed in 1787), it dates from the period of Bortnyansky's employment as Kapellmeister at the court of the Grand Duke and heir-apparent Paul Petrovich, in St. Petersburg, between 1780 and 1796. It was composed, as were many of Bortnyansky's chamber works, for performance at the palaces of Gatchina and Pavlorsk and was dedicated to "son Altresse impériale Madame La Grande Duchesse de Russie par D. Bortniansky 1790"[4] and scored for "Le Fortepiano Organisée, L'Arpe, deux violons, viola de gamba, Basson et Violoncelle." The *Sinfonia Concertante* is eclectic in style and combines melodic elements derived from Italian opera *buffa* with obvious rhythmic and structural characteristics of German *Galanter Stil*. Both influences are evident in the delicately scored *Allegro maestoso* opening movement, the thematic material of which is based predominantly on the repetition of brief melodic fragments alternating with variants (see Ex. 1-1).

Though they are hardly developed in a conventional sense, these fragments are employed with a degree of technical proficiency rivaling that of Bortnyansky's teacher Galuppi. They surpass all future Russian instrumental composition until the chamber works of Alexander Alexandrovich Alyabev (1787–1851) and Glinka some thirty years later. Bortnyansky's slim, elegant *Sinfonia* displays little if any Russian character, though, curiously, a variant of the French folk song "Dodo l'enfant do, l'enfant dormira bientôt" is introduced into the thematic material of the first movement.[5] It is initially announced by the piano in the closing section of the exposition and rises to prominence in the development and coda, where it is subjected to some degree of elaboration (see Ex. 1-1b). Coincidentally, Debussy, more than a century later, constructed the opening

Ex. 1-1. Bortnyansky, *Sinfonia Concertante*, first movement: a. first subject, mm. 1-4; b. second subject, mm. 41-44.

and closing sections of his sparkling piano solo *Jardin sous la pluie* (from *Estampes*) on this folk song, and like Bortnyansky, he exploits the melody in both major and minor keys.

The second movement of the *Sinfonia Concertante, Larghetto,* is less inspired. Its somewhat insipid elegiacal theme tends to pall after a while, and although the more complex central episode, heralded by an attractive bassoon solo, attempts to recreate the first movement's vivacious interplay between concertante instruments, the movement as a whole lacks sufficient contrast to be entirely satisfactory (see Ex. 1-2).

The *Allegretto* finale is in the form of a rondo and is characteristically conceived in a lighter vein. The Russian musicologist Yuri Keldysh considers its themes reminiscent of Ukrainian folk dance (Bortnyansky was, in fact, Ukranian) and draws attention to the similarity between the principal theme, Ex. 1-3a, and the refrain from the first aria from Bortnyansky's nationalist opera *Syn-sopernik* (The rival son),[6] shown in Ex. 1-3b. However, the movement suggests more the influence of Western European rococo or galant composition, particularly the early chamber music of Haydn and Mozart.

During the early years of the nineteenth century, the process of musical cross-fertilization between Russia and Western Europe ceased to be the

Ex. 1-2. Bortnyansky, *Sinfonia Concertante,* second movement, mm. 1-4.

Ex. 1-3. Bortnyansky: a. *Sinfonia Concertante,* third movement, mm. 1-4; b. *Syn-sopernik,* refrain from first aria, mm. 1-4.

prerogative of the culturally hermetic palaces of the aristocracy. The so-called Napoleonic period (1807–12) of the reign of Alexander I encouraged many Russian noblemen to travel abroad, and in the European capitals they came into contact with people of social and cultural backgrounds other than their own. The consequences of these encounters were far-reaching, for they stimulated dormant sentiments of nationalism and at the same time drew attention to the appalling backwardness of the Russian people as a whole. Taking advantage of the temporary lifting of repressive measures implemented during the reign of Paul I (who was assassinated in 1801) and the apparent, though short-lived moderacy of the new tsar, Alexander I, Russian intellectuals formed secret societies and circles to discuss proposals for reform. Images of the dark and dangerous times that followed culminating in the Decembrist Revolt of 1825, are found in contemporary Russian literature, most notably in the writings of Gogol and Pushkin. One searches in vain, however, for parallel sentiments in Russian symphonic music, then very much in its infancy.[7]

Also significant for the development of early Russian composition was the exploitation of the newly opened channels of communication between East and West by European piano manufacturers,[8] singers, composers, conductors, and—most important for the Russian concerto—composer-virtuosi such as Field, Steibelt, Hummel, Henselt, and Liszt. Apart from introducing to Russians musical forms and styles then prevalent in Western Europe, they demonstrated recent developments in instrumental technique and established new levels of professionalism.

Despite the stimulating presence of foreign musicians, music making in Russia continued to be an almost exclusively aristocratic pastime and remained centered around the palaces of St. Petersburg and Moscow. However, serf orchestras began to be established on private estates, and music salons became increasingly fashionable in the larger towns and cities. Concert societies such as the Musical Academy (Moscow, 1800) and the St. Petersburg Philharmonic Society (1802) were founded, and musical activities were further stimulated by a growth in publications such as the journals *Severnaia arpa* (Northern harp) and *Zhurnal otechestvennoi muzyky* (Journal of national music), the latter published by Kashin between 1806 and 1809. However, during the reign of Alexander I, music criticism was discouraged, and unfavorable reportage of the Imperial theatres was actually forbidden. It was only with the appearance of Feofil Tolstoy in 1852, writing under the pseudonym Rostislav in the journal *Severnaia pchela* (Northern bee) that serious music criticism began to assert itself. Nevertheless, the standard was generally low, as journalists were "encouraged" by their editors to overlook negative aspects of a work or a performance and to write with enthusiasm whenever possible.

The years immediately following the Napoleonic invasion in 1812 were crucial in Russia's cultural development, for never before had her relationships with Western Europe been so intense. Many Russian noblemen spent years in France and Germany as part of the armies of occupation, and their experiences abroad made them more conscious than ever before of the comparative backwardness of their homeland and its agonizingly slow progress toward cultural emancipation. On their return to Russia they saw the organization of music making entirely controlled by, and almost exclusively intended for, aristocratic amateurs, with little if any provision for ordinary Russians. To their credit, however, these amateurs were considerably more earnest in their musical activities than their "powdered wig" counterparts in the eighteenth century. Among the more notable were the scholars Ulybyshev and Prince Odoevsky; the composers Alyabev, Verstovsky, Glinka, and Dargomizhsky; and performers such as the Wielhorski brothers and L'vov.

These early pioneers of Russian musical culture, some of whom were wealthy enough to maintain their own choirs, orchestras, and even opera companies, organized charity concerts and founded societies and circles for music appreciation, including the Society of Music Lovers, established during the 1840s. As these activities were primarily undertaken for the pleasure of the aristocracy, whose preferences lay with foreign music, performances of contemporary Russian music were rare. Furthermore, the performers themselves were predominantly foreign and were usually recruited from the choirs and orchestras of the Imperial chapel and theatres. For the ordinary Russian, therefore, there were few opportunities to attend concerts of "serious" music and even fewer for Russian composers to have their works performed in public. Growing indignation at the blatant discrimination against Russian music and musicians encouraged the organizing of "alternative" concert societies. One such society, curiously named the Musical Exercises of the Students of the Imperial University, was founded during the 1840s by a university inspector, A. I. Fitzum von Ecstedt. It featured an orchestra of mainly nonmusic students and amateurs, conducted by Carl Schuberth. Its repertoire included contemporary Russian music, most probably operatic overtures by Alyabev, Verstovsky, and Glinka. There were no rehearsals, despite the Society's proviso "in the best possible performance"; and the concerts must have been excruciating, saved only from total disaster by the small handful of professional players seconded from theatre orchestras. Despite taking place on Sunday mornings during the winter months, the concerts were well attended. Nevertheless, the Society's existence was precarious, being entirely financed from tickets sold at the door.

Considering the primitiveness of Russian musical life during the early years of the nineteenth century, it is perhaps surprising that Steibelt and Field, two of the most influential foreign musicians to have ventured to Russia during this period, decided to settle there permanently—Steibelt in St. Petersburg from 1809 until his death in 1823, and Field in St. Petersburg from 1803 to 1822, and then in Moscow, where he died in 1837. Actually, it was this very "primitiveness" which attracted them, along with the opportunity of earning large sums of money by teaching enthusiastic, wealthy aristocrats and the possibility of even greater riches by assailing their untutored, aristocratic ears with spectacular program-concertos such as *Voyage sur le Mont St. Bernard* (Steibelt's sixth concerto, in G minor, composed in 1816) and *L'incendie par l'orage* (Field's fifth concerto, in C major, dating from 1817). Both realized the advantages of being strangers in a strange land, and Steibelt, in particular—by all accounts a rather unscrupulous individual—was eager to exploit the situation to the full.

Steibelt's compositions have all but been forgotten, and his once-celebrated pianistic effects (such as his famous tremolo), when studied in the cold light of day, are little more than conventional scale, tremolo, and arpeggio figurations enhanced by unusually generous applications of the sustaining pedal, which was still a fairly recent development.[9] Nevertheless, his influence on the evolution of musical culture in Russia is inestimable, for through his entrepreneurial skills and spectacular performances, he created the need for symphonic concerts on a regular basis for the entertainment of both aristocrats and ordinary Russians. The repercussions of Steibelt's activities, though born of self-interest, were widespread and touched every corner of Russian musical life. Orchestral players, who formerly depended on the silk purses of the Imperial court, found themselves involved with impresarios and agencies.

The commercialization of symphonic concerts also induced dramatic changes in the style and content of the music itself. To attract new audiences, novelties, special effects, and musical representations of recent historical events became part and parcel of the composer-virtuoso's box of tricks, and gratuitous virtuosity gradually superseded genuine musical creativity. A typical example is Steibelt's concerto *Voyage sur le Mont St.-Bernard*, which incorporates a storm sequence and utilizes a large orchestra including bass trombone, piccolo, drums, and even a triangle. Steibelt also composed for Russian audiences the *Grand Concerto Militare dans le genre des grecs* for piano and two orchestras (1820)—shrewdly dedicated to Alexander I—and various miscellaneous novelties, such as the *Destruction of Moscow, Naval Combat,* and the *Martial Sonata,* capitalizing on the wave of Russian patriotism following the Napoleonic Invasion.

Steibelt had been a thorn in Field's side since 1809, when the German composer arrived in St. Petersburg to take over Boieldieu's post of director of the French Opera. When Steibelt achieved a resounding success with his *Voyage* concerto, Field, in a classic example of one-upmanship, retaliated with his fifth concerto, *L'incendie par l'orage*, thus blatantly adding a third element, fire, to Steibelt's portrayal of wind and water.[10] Field rarely indulged in spectacular virtuosity, however, for he was by nature less of a showman than Steibelt. He eschewed Steibelt's melodramatic gestures and technical artifice, and his aspirations as a composer were sincere. Field wrote concertos primarily for his own use, not as a means to an end, as they were with Steibelt; rather, they were the genuine expression of musical ideas in a form which Field knew intimately.

Field's concertos reveal three principal influences: the concertos for harpsichord or fortepiano by Tommaso Giordani (1730–1806), an Italian composer-impresario who organized concerts for the young Field in Dublin (1792) and London (1794); the piano concertos of Jan Ladislav Dussek (1760–1812), a celebrated pianist and composer active in London's musical scene during the 1790s, Field's formative years; and the piano sonatas of Field's celebrated teacher Muzio Clementi. From Dussek, Field acquired the *cantilena* melodies and widely spaced arpeggio accompaniment figurations that formed the basic material of his once-famous nocturnes and nocturne-style interludes of the piano concertos.[11] Field's celebrated *fioritura* melodic embellishment, on the other hand, suggests the influence of Giordani, whose concertos abound in vocalistic elements derived from his principal musical activities of opera composer, singer, and impresario. Lastly, it was Clementi who rounded out Field's pianistic style with such virtuosic devices as rapid passages in thirds, sixths, and octaves.

Field composed seven piano concertos, many of which he performed regularly both on tour and in St. Petersburg (where he made his debut in March 1804, playing the Concerto No. 1 in E-flat). Several were published in St. Petersburg between 1812 and 1821, and the first three became very popular throughout Europe. Field's impact on the contemporary Russian musical scene is evident in the many imitative dilettante piano compositions dating from this period, the most popular form being solo variations on folk melodies and Russian song (pseudo–folk song).[12] However, Field was unable to make much of an impression on the development of the Russian piano concerto for the simple reason that there were so few concerto composers to impress, though structural and pianistic similarities are evident in three early Russian works for piano and orchestra that have survived from this period: the piano concerto by Field's pupil Ivan Feodorovich Laskovsky (1799–1855); Alyabev's Concertstück on themes by Steibelt; and the piano concerto by Iosif Iosifovich Genishta (1795–1853), which is preserved in the library of the Moscow State Conservatory. Another concerto which has survived from this period, by a composer of German origin who lived and worked in Russia, Ivan Genrikhovich Cherlitsky, takes Field's Third Concerto, in E-flat, as a model. Composed in 1818, Cherlitsky's concerto is constructed in two long and brilliant movements—an *Allegro* in sonata form and a rondo finale—and displays features of Field's virtuosic style.

Field's concertos also incorporate structural innovations which were adopted and further developed by later, more-celebrated composers. His Second Concerto, in A-flat (c.1811)—thought to be a model for Chopin's Concerto in F minor Op. 21—contains a lengthy *fugato* in its rondo finale, which may have suggested a similar procedure to Balakirev in both the first and third movements of his Concerto in E-flat. Tchaikovsky, like Cherlitsky, may also have been persuaded to adopt a two-movement scheme for his *Concert Fantasia*, Op. 56, from his acquaintance with Field's Third Concerto. However, Field's most influential composition for piano and orchestra, as far as the Russian piano concerto is concerned, is his Seventh Concerto, in C minor, his only piano concerto in a minor key. It was first performed on Christmas Day 1832, published two years later, and praised by Schumann in *Neue Zeitschrift für Musik*.[13] It was to have a considerable influence on the Piano Concerto, Op. 4, also in C minor, by Anton Rubinstein's teacher Alexandre Villoing, which in turn was to serve as a model for Rubinstein's earliest attempt at concerto composition: the Piano Concerto in D minor, 1849 (later revised as the Octet, Op. 9).

Villoing's concerto was the first piano concerto composed in Russia to be performed abroad and was frequently played by Rubinstein during his European tours of 1840–43. Field's influence is evident not only in Villoing's early Romantic coloring and lyricism but also in the expansiveness and virtuosity of the piano writing, which foreshadows developments in both Rubinstein's and Tchaikovsky's pianistic style (see Exx. 2-1 and 2-2). Structurally, Villoing's concerto reveals the influence of another concerto by Field, No. 5 in C major (*L'incendie par l'orage*), in that its *Adagio*, like the corresponding movement in Field's concerto (subtitled "Hymn of Thanksgiving"), serves as an introduction to the rondo finale. However, Beethoven's *Waldstein* Sonata, Op. 53, may have given Villoing the initial idea for such a scheme (Genishta's concerto also displays characteristics of Beethoven's music in its first and second movements). Further inspiration appears to have been provided by an epigraph of verses from Lamartine, dedicated to Byron, printed on the title page of Villoing's score.

Although as a composer, Field exercised only marginal influence on the painfully slow development of the early Russian piano concerto, his activities as pianist and teacher were to have a profound effect on piano playing in Russia. He had inherited his brilliant technique and rich sonorous tone from his teacher Clementi, who acquired these qualities through many years of playing and manufacturing English instruments. On hearing John Field, Glinka remarked, "He did not seem to strike the keys, instead, his fingers fell on them like large drops of rain scattered like pearls on velvet."[14]

Field was also a gifted teacher. Among his many pupils were Alexander Gurilëv, Laskovsky, Glinka, and most important for the development of piano playing in Russia, the expatriate Frenchman Alexandre Dubuque (1812–98). For a brief period, Balakirev was his pupil and studied Hummel's Concerto in A minor with him using Field's fingering. Dubuque was evidently an exceptional teacher, for although Balakirev had only ten lessons with him and was only ten years old at the time, he attributed his pianistic talent solely to Dubuque's teaching: "If I have any technical ability at all, I am indebted for this to A. I. Dubuque, who taught me the principles of correct technique and fingering on the pianoforte."[15]

This particular branch of the pedagogic tradition established by Field terminated with Balakirev, for although Balakirev was an excellent pianist, he concentrated on composition and devoted most of his time and energies on the musical development of others.[16] Nevertheless, his dazzling Oriental fantasy, *Islamey* (1869), dedicated to Nikolai Rubinstein, established a threshold of technical difficulty which arguably surpasses anything written by Liszt. It encouraged later composers, including Ravel and Lyapunov, to experiment further in the field of transcendental virtuosity.

Dubuque's pupils Villoing and Nikolai Zverev (1832–93) were also outstanding teachers; Villoing's pupils included the Rubinstein brothers and V. I. Safonov (who taught Medtner, Scriabin, and Lhevinne), and among Zverev's pupils were Siloti, Rachmaninov and Scriabin. Fig. I shows the principal pedagogical relationships in the Russian piano playing tradition, which was initiated by Field. With the death of Scriabin in 1915 and the turbulent events following the Revolution two years later, which forced many of the finest Russian pianists into exile, this fabulous tradition lost impetus and continuity, though Goldenweizer and Igumnov, both of whom remained in Russia, continued to teach its methods to new generations of Soviet pianists, and the émigrés Lhevinne, Siloti, and Hofmann passed on its secrets to young American pianists.

The concertos of Field, Steibelt, and, later, Johann Nepomuk Hummel (1778–1837), who visited Russia in 1822, introduced to Russian audiences the post-Beethoven, early-Romantic piano concerto. It arose between 1810 and 1835, during the so-called Biedermeier period of European culture.[17] Stylistically, the "Biedermeier" concerto[18] was created from a fusion of Mozartian lyricism—drawn principally from the slow movements of Mozart's later piano concertos—with contemporary developments in pianistic virtuosity, notably in Clementi's sonatas and Dussek's piano concertos. Mozart's *cantilena* became embellished with operatic *fioriture* in the manner of Paganini and Spohr; and the virtuosic elements derived from Clementi and Dussek were expanded and developed, encouraged by, among other factors, recent advances in piano technology.[19]

In the concertos of Mozart and Beethoven, lyricism and virtuosity are employed in a myriad of combinations, the proportions of which are minutely calculated in accordance with the musical significance of the phrase or passage in question. Often, lyrical ideas are apotheosed in a virtuosic manner, or brilliant passagework is fashioned from the thematic material which underpins it. In the "Biedermeier" concerto, on the other hand, there is usually a clear distinction between lyricism and virtuosity. Occasionally, as in Weber's concertos, this distinction suggests the further influence of opera and represents a conscious attempt to introduce new elements into the concerto.[20] In the majority of "Biedermeier" concertos, however, the separation of lyrical and virtuosic elements reflects a lack of sustained musical inspiration and an inability to think in symphonic terms.

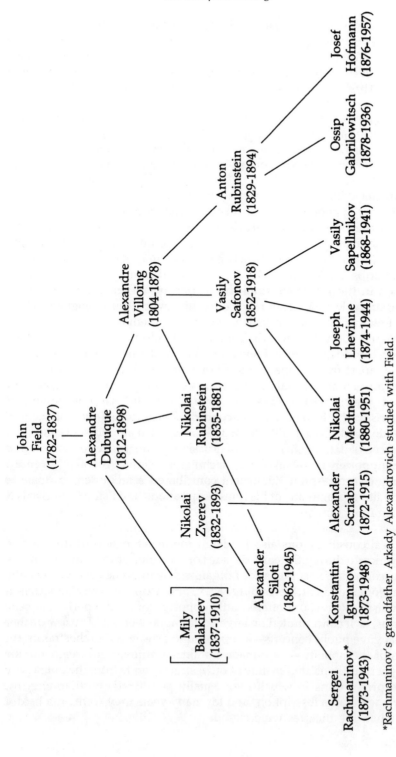

Fig. I. Pedagogical relationships in Russian piano playing

*Rachmaninov's grandfather Arkady Alexandrovich studied with Field.

"Biedermeier" composers paid little heed to the "patchwork" quality of their concertos; their prime concern was to bring into the concert hall the passion and excitement of the theatre, with themselves as protagonists. Virtuosity eventually dominated all other considerations, including good taste. As Abraham Veinus wrote:

> The uncreative virtuoso is content to put his fingers to work and his musicianship to sleep. . . . They give us more sound than sense, more manual dexterity than emotional depth, more trickery than true technique. They are the Neros who fiddle while our patience burns.[21]

Fortunately, Russian audiences were spared the worst excesses of the "Biedermeier" phenomenon, for Steibelt, Hummel, and Field were craftsmen. Despite the occasional aberration, they composed musically attractive, if unremarkable concertos. A few achieved considerable popularity, and three in particular—Field's Second Concerto, in A-flat, and Hummel's two concertos, in A minor, Op. 85 (1816), and B minor, Op. 89 (1819)—remained in the repertoire until the early 1900s. Their influence on the contemporary Russian piano concerto, however, was negligible, for as noted, few Russian composers felt confident enough to tackle such a large and complex form. Besides, their interests lay elsewhere, generally along paths well trodden by their French and Italian teachers. Bortnyansky, for example, apart from a small handful of chamber works, concentrated on church music; and Alyabev, Glinka, Verstovsky, and Dargomizhsky achieved their finest results in opera. Nevertheless, one important characteristic of the "Biedermeier" concerto—the incorporation of a dance-like rondo finale based on folk or folk-oriented material[22]—became part and parcel of later generations of Russian piano concertos and found ardent supporters in Tchaikovsky, Rachmaninov, and Prokofiev. Even the generally eclectic Anton Rubinstein contributed a folk-oriented finale to concerto literature, in one of his finest inspirations, the Piano Concerto No. 4, in D minor, Op. 70.

Practical considerations also hindered the development of the Russian piano concerto during the early decades of the nineteenth century. Particularly discouraging was the lack of organized symphonic concerts, even in such major cities as St. Petersburg, Kiev, and Moscow. The Philharmonic Society in St. Petersburg offered little opportunity for the performance of concertos, as it concentrated on large-scale choral works.[23] The few orchestras that gave public concerts—as opposed to private serf orchestras on the estates of the nobility—were made up almost entirely of foreigners, and their repertoire consisted mainly of orchestral excerpts from the operas and theatre productions in which they usually performed. Furthermore, the concerts were on subscription, and for many years they were only held at Lent, when the theatres were closed.

Apart from the lack of opportunities for the performance of newly composed piano concertos, also discouraging was the extremely variable quality of orchestral players during the early 1800s, both in Russia and in Western Europe. This did not greatly concern composers of "Biedermeier" concertos, for in their pursuit of spectacular pianistic effects, which brought the soloist to the fore to an unprecedented degree, the orchestra was often relegated to a mere accompanying role.[24] Indeed, in some concertos, for instance, Woelfl's Op. 20 (1801) and Dussek's Op. 70 (1810), the orchestral part is even inscribed "ad libitum"; and it was frequently the practice to perform the soloist's part unaccompanied, as Field often did in St. Petersburg and Moscow, and as Chopin did, when he performed his F minor Concerto in Paris in 1831.[25] Not surprisingly, the cadenza, which in the eighteenth-century concerto represented the eagerly awaited moment in which the soloist cast off the shackles of the orchestra, was deemed superfluous in the "Biedermeier" concerto and had been jettisoned as early as 1799, in Steibelt's Third Concerto and Field's First Concerto. In fact, Field made no provision in any of his concertos for a cadenza, though he took the innovative step, adumbrating Rachmaninov by nearly a century, of introducing an accompanied written-out cadenza (*cadenza a tempo*) in his Fifth Concerto, *L'incendie par l'orage*.

All the more salient characteristics of the "Biedermeier" concerto—the exaggerated emphasis on display, the reduction in the role of the orchestra, the alternation of lyrical and virtuosic sections—are also found in the many variations, fantasias, and potpourris for piano and orchestra composed during the early decades of the nineteenth century. Notable among the concerto-style variations are Moscheles' Variations on "Au clair de la lune," Op. 50 (1821); *Variations on a Swedish Air*, Op. 52, by Beethoven's pupil Ferdinand Ries; and the Variations on a Theme from *Don Giovanni*, Op. 2, by Chopin (1827). Moscheles also wrote several fantasias for piano and orchestra, including *Souvenirs d'Irlande*, Op. 69 (1826), *Anklänge aus Schottland*, Op. 75 (1826), and *Souvenirs de Danemarc*, Op. 83 (1830), the first two of which inspired Chopin's *Fantasia on Polish Airs*, Op. 13 (1829). Though Field contributed to the genre with his *Variations on a Russian Theme*, published in 1823, the majority of his Russian colleagues, discouraged by the near impossibility of having orchestral works performed, concentrated on writing variations for solo piano. The few Russians who did aspire to symphonic composition had to have the financial resources to maintain their own orchestras or be so highly motivated as to undertake the difficult task of organizing concerts for the performance of their works. Alyabev, being of the Russian aristocracy, was one of the fortunate few who had an orchestra at his disposal. He was thus able to embark on various large-scale projects for orchestra, including four symphonies and several concerto-style works for various solo instruments, such as the unpublished "Concertstück on Themes by Steibelt" for piano and orchestra (the manuscript of which is preserved in the State Central Museum of

Musical Culture in Moscow). Unfortunately, a crushing dilettantism accompanied the composition of these works, and Alyabev achieved finer results in his songs, of which there are over a hundred.[26]

There also existed for a time, a piano concerto by the blind composer Alexei Dmitrievich Zhilin (176?–c.1850). Zhilin, like Alyabev, was a Russian nobleman, and his compositions, according to Seaman,[27] reflect the influence of his more-celebrated compatriot Glinka, in particular, the structure of Glinka's variations.

Important among less-privileged Russian composers who attempted concerto composition was Kashin, the son of one of General G. I. Bibikov's serfs. Kashin became director of Bibikov's orchestra during the 1790s and was quick to take advantage of the opportunities offered by the post, as demonstrated by the many concerts he organized and in which he took part as conductor, composer, and pianist. Though Kashin left Bibikov's service after being given his freedom in 1798, his concert activities continued unabated, as did his interest in Russian folk music. In the early 1800s, after a second visit to Italy, he returned with renewed vigor to the study and collecting of folk song, and between 1806 and 1809, he published twelve issues of *Zhurnal otchestvennoi muzyky* (Journal of national music). He later produced a three-volume anthology of Russian folk song, *Russkie narodnye pesni*, published in Moscow in 1833–34. Kashin apparently composed several piano concertos, though none have survived. The earliest, which was first performed by the composer in Moscow and dates from 1790, was written down immediately after Kashin's return from his first visit to Italy; it vies with Bortnyansky's for being the first piano concerto composed by a Russian. However, as both concertos are no longer extant and the precise date of composition of Bortnyansky's is unknown, the matter remains unresolved. Considering his profound interest in folk music, Kashin's concertos were more probably composed in the form of fantasias or potpourris on Russian folk songs than as *bona fide* concertos. Certainly the few works by Kashin that have survived are richly furnished with folk themes and folk like material.[28]

It is doubly unfortunate that the piano "concertos" by Kashin—which according to contemporary newspaper reports, he performed in public—were never published. Apart from their historical interest, they might collectively have formed the foundations, albeit primitive, of a tradition of Russian nationalist concerto composition nearly half a century before its actual incipience, Balakirev's patchy and immature efforts dating from the 1850s. But Kashin's concertos were probably never heard outside of Moscow and the fact that they remained in manuscript suggests that they had a very limited influence on contemporary Russian composition.

Whatever the weakness of Kashin as a composer, he was undoubtedly an outstanding personality and driving force in the musical life of Moscow during the early decades of the nineteenth century. He was probably the first true Russian nationalist, not only in his lifelong passion for folk music, as demonstrated by his folk song collections and the incorporation of folk elements in his music, but also in his efforts to provide ordinary Russians with the possibility of studying music and attending concerts.[29] Though the influence of Kashin was slight, he helped to prepare the ground, as it were, for the creation of the Russian national school of music during the 1860s, under the aegis of Balakirev, Lomakin, and the art critic and historian Vladimir Stasov.

During the early 1830s, a less-expensive though equally dramatic musical entertainment gradually superseded the old "war horses" of Kalkbrenner, Woelfl, and the like: the solo fantasia on operatic themes. The orchestra had reached a point where, to all intents and purposes, it was no longer considered essential, hence the ignominious tag "ad libitum" inscribed on the orchestra parts of several concertos of the period. The operatic fantasia represented the next logical stage in the evolution of the piano "spectacular." The iconoclastic implications of these changes had little significance for the development of the Russian piano concerto, as there was no tradition to interrupt. Besides, innovations and changes in Western European music usually reached Russia a generation later; Villoing penned his Fieldian concerto during the 1840s and Balakirev was happily writing works for piano and orchestra in the "Biedermeier" style as late as the 1850s.[30]

With the publication of Mendelssohn's Piano Concerto in G minor, Op. 25, in 1832, the concerto resumed a healthier aspect and returned to the congenial balance between soloist and orchestra perfected by Mozart and last convincingly adopted in Beethoven's Concerto No. 5, in E-flat (1810). At the same time, Mendelssohn also proposed important structural innovations which were to influence profoundly the overall design of the concerto to the present day. In essence, they involve the linking of movements and the elimination of the opening movement's orchestral exposition. They were taken up and developed further by Mendelssohn's contemporaries, in particular, Moscheles, in his last three piano concertos—No. 6, *Fantastique*, in B-flat, Op. 90 (1833); No. 7, *Pathetique*, in D minor, Op. 93 (1835–36); and No. 8, *Pastorale*, in D major, Op. 96 (1838)—and Liszt, in his piano concertos in E-flat (1849–56) and A major (1849–61).

In Russia, however, few composers were willing or able to follow Mendelssohn's example. Glinka and Dargomizhsky were not expert pianists and, in any case, were busy composing nationalist operas. Balakirev, despite two unfinished youthful attempts during the 1850s, soon found himself fully occupied guiding the "Mighty Handful" and even failed to complete his last effort, the more-mature though uneven Piano Concerto in E-flat, begun in 1861.

So the fate of the Russian piano concerto lay in the hands of Anton Rubinstein. It seemed at first that he was eminently suited to the task, for he was considered the finest pianist of his generation and was also highly respected as a composer. Through his frequent tours abroad he came into contact with many of the most influential musicians on the international scene, including Liszt, Berlioz, and Saint-Saëns, and was certainly aware of recent developments in the piano concerto. However, Rubinstein's musical aesthetic was limited, as were his talents as a composer and his ability to assimilate and utilize new ideas. Though Rubinstein was influenced by Mendelssohn's refined and elegant piano style, he was unable to grasp the significance of Mendelssohn's important structural innovations until much later (see pp. 24–25). Hence the conventional three-movement designs of all five of Rubinstein's piano concertos. The influence of his compositions on the development of the Russian piano concerto was nevertheless decisive, for despite the poverty of musical invention displayed in the majority of his concertos, the Fourth, in D minor, Op. 70, an altogether finer conception, was to become the model for Tchaikovsky's epoch-making Piano Concerto in B-flat minor, Op. 23. With the phenomenal success of Tchaikovsky's concerto, the future of the Russian piano concerto was assured, and later generations of Russian composers had, at last, a tradition to follow.

2

The Piano Concertos of Anton Rubinstein

There are artists who devote a lifetime to one composition in order to make it perfect. There are others who throughout their lives create innumerable compositions which are, however, far from being perfect. These last seem to me more logical. There cannot be absolute perfection in a man's composition. However, in imperfect compositions one could find enough beauty worthy of appraisal. There is something sympathetic in the fertility of creativity because it is naive. At the same time, the faith that one could create something perfect carries in it the seal of conceit.

—Anton Rubinstein

Few were better qualified to make a statement of this kind than Anton Grigorevich Rubinstein (1829–94), himself no stranger to conceit.[1] Although the issue is eloquently and persuasively argued, it is clearly little more than a veiled attempt to justify his own excessive production and lack of self-criticism. As early as 1853, before Rubinstein had established himself as a composer and long before his more important works had been written, one astute critic had already noted his shortcomings:

One could say that each of his works contains surprising moments but rarely is the impression of the whole fully satisfactory; some motif or other makes one feel bored; there is lack of clarity, and too much monotony. . . . In my opinion, Mr. Rubinstein writes too much and too quickly. That is his greatest enemy.[2]

The following year, Liszt independently reached similar conclusions. Though usually magnanimous and encouraging to fledgling composers, he felt compelled to inform Rubinstein of them:

I respect your compositions and I find much to praise in them . . . with a few critical observations. Your excessive productivity does not afford you spare time to disclose more individuality in your compositions and complete them. It has been justly said that it is not sufficient to *make* a composition, one should *complete* it.[3]

Evidence of Rubinstein's frustratingly lackadaisical attitude toward the finer and final stages of composition—which resulted in a scar of carelessness that ran its course through almost all his music—is found in his correspondence. In a letter to his publisher, Bartholf Senff, dated 5 June 1874, for instance, Rubinstein admitted to having great difficulty with two of his compositions (the Fourth Symphony and the Fifth Piano Concerto) and doubted whether he would be able to finish them before the winter. However, in a letter to his mother written just four months later, it appears that Rubinstein had managed to complete both works well within the deadline and had even found time to undertake other large-scale musical projects: "I am very satisfied with my summer (from the work point of view); the piano concerto, symphony, concerto for cello and sketches for an opera have all been finished."[4]

Such haste of conception and lack of objective self-criticism—reflected, incidentally, in the flawlessness of his manuscripts—is apparent in all Rubinstein's works for piano and orchestra, with the exception of the Fourth Concerto, in D minor, Op. 70, his finest contribution to the genre. Undoubtedly, the uncharacteristic care taken by the composer in the concerto's composition and subsequent revisions eliminated many of the flaws that marred his other works for piano and orchestra. The Fourth Piano Concerto, dedicated to the German violinist and composer Ferdinand David, was composed in 1864 and was arranged and published for two pianos in 1866. In 1869 Rubinstein undertook several revisions which he considered "not particularly important"; further changes incorporated into the second edition (1872) involved performance indications, piano texture, and orchestration of the second half of the first movement coda.

Rubinstein's five existing piano concertos, though central to his creativity and composed over a period of 24 years, reveal little in the way of musical or technical development. Like Beethoven's five concertos, for example, they exhibit a steady growth in both structural dimensions and complexity of the soloist's part. In Beethoven's concertos this growth was the natural and spontaneous outcome of developments in the composer's musical evolution; but in Rubinstein's concertos, the grandeur of expression and virtuosity are usually insincere, created merely for effect independent of the underlying musical ideas.

Rubinstein's earliest attempts at concerto composition—the lost concertos in F major[5] and C major dating from 1848—probably leaned heavily, stylistically, on the Fieldian Piano Concerto in C minor by his teacher Villoing, which Rubinstein frequently performed as a child prodigy during his European tours of 1840–43. Certainly, Rubinstein's third attempt, a four-movement Concerto in D minor, dating from 1849 (later arranged as an octet for piano, violin, viola, cello, double bass, flute, clarinet, and horn and published as Op. 9), reflects Villoing's influence. This is immediately apparent in the soloist's initial entry (Ex. 2-1). The similarity between Rubinstein's piano writing (Ex. 2-1a) and Tchaikovsky's employment of octaves in the opening section of his Concerto in B-flat minor is also striking (Ex. 2-2). In view of the considerable influence of Rubinstein's Fourth and Fifth concertos on Tchaikovsky's First Concerto (discussed on pp. 43–49), it is possible that the Octet also figured among the works examined by Tchaikovsky during the conception of his First Concerto.

Rubinstein's first piano teacher was his Prussian-born mother, Kaleria, who had little imagination as far as repertoire was concerned. The pianistic influence of Villoing and of such contemporary composer-virtuosi as Herz, Moscheles, Czerny, Hummel,[6] and Kalkbrenner was certainly present, but the principal influence on Rubinstein in his formative years was the music he studied with Siegfried Dehn in Berlin,[7] in particular, the works of

Ex. 2-1.   a. Rubinstein, Octet, Op. 9, first movement, opening piano statement; b. Villoing, Piano Concerto in C minor, Op. 4, first movement, opening piano statement.

Ex. 2-2. Tchaikovsky, Piano Concerto in B-flat minor, Op. 23, first movement, mm. 36-38.

Schumann and Mendelssohn. Indeed, so potent was the impact of German music on the young Rubinstein that, for the remainder of his life, he was unable to break away from its influence, despite several determined attempts in later years to compose in a consciously nationalist style.[8] Although Rubinstein admired and performed magnificently Schumann's music—an enthusiasm kindled perhaps by Schumann's favorable review of Rubinstein's first published piano piece, a study entitled *Ondine*[9]—it was the less-complex, more-accessible compositions of Mendelssohn that Rubinstein turned to for musical ideas while composing his Concerto (later Octet) in D minor. Typically, Rubinstein's poverty of harmonic resourcefulness and melodic invention manifests itself even in passages inspired by musical ideas of others (see Ex. 2-3).

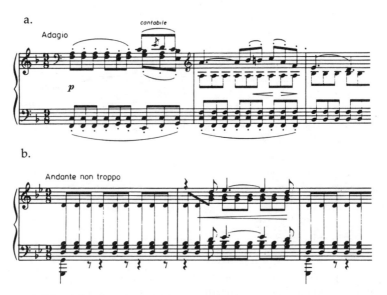

Ex. 2-3. a. Mendelssohn, *Song Without Words*, Op. 53, No. 4, mm. 1-3; b. Rubinstein, Octet, Op. 9, third movement, mm. 1-3.

Rubinstein's dependence on Mendelssohn's music did not pass unnoticed by his contemporaries. For example, the composer and critic Alexander Serov wrote:

> How unfortunate that our era still cannot free itself from the influence of tedious Mendelssohnism and that precisely those aspects of that great talent that are weak and harmful for art . . . have found such a zealous and prolific disciple in Rubinstein![10]

Liszt was of the same opinion, but he believed that Rubinstein would eventually develop his own creative individuality:

> I don't want to preach to Rubinstein—he can sow his wild oats and fish deeper in Mendelssohn waters, and even swim away if he likes, but sooner or later I am certain he will give up the apparent and the formalistic for the organically real. . . .[11]

Rubinstein never quite fulfilled Liszt's hopes. For a time he did indeed continue to "fish in Mendelssohn waters," but afterward, instead of evolving a musical style of his own, he once again turned to the music of others, including Liszt's, for ideas and inspiration. In Rubinstein's piano concertos, the influence of Beethoven, in particular, his Fourth Concerto, in G major, Op. 58, is evident both in the balance and distribution of thematic material between piano and orchestra and in the general design of the soloist's part. Occasionally, sections and even entire movements are constructed on ideas "borrowed" from Beethoven's music. For instance, the beautiful dialogue between piano and orchestra in the *Andante con moto* of Beethoven's Fourth Concerto served as a model for the second movement of Rubinstein's First Concerto in E minor, Op. 25. Among the blatant examples of plagiarism is the soloist's entry in Rubinstein's Fifth Concerto, in E-flat, which is lifted from the first movement of Beethoven's Fourth Concerto. The filched material is incorporated in precisely the same position as it occupied in the work from which it was taken (see Ex. 2-4). Rubinstein's acquaintance with Beethoven's piano sonatas also proved advantageous while searching for ideas for the opening theme of his First Concerto (see Ex. 2-5).

Rubinstein's most significant borrowings from Liszt are also found in the Fifth Concerto, the most derivative of all Rubinstein's works for piano and orchestra. Indeed, they are so well preserved that, as in Lyadov's *Variations on a Theme of Glinka*, Op. 35 (unashamedly based on selected piano works by Chopin), and Lyapunov's *Transcendental Studies* (modeled on Liszt's studies of the same title), it is possible to identify the actual piece from which the borrowing has occurred. The soloist's chordal writing in the closing section of the first movement exposition, for example, was probably inspired by the *Allegro deciso* section of Liszt's Piano Concerto in A[12] (see Ex. 2-6).

Ex. 2-4.   a. Rubinstein, Piano Concerto No. 5, in E-flat, Op. 94, first movement, mm. 35-38; b. Beethoven, Piano Concerto No. 4, in G, Op. 58, first movement, mm. 76-79.

Ex. 2-5.   a. Beethoven, Piano Sonata in E-flat, Op. 31, No. 3, fourth movement, mm. 64-70; b. Rubinstein, Piano Concerto No. 1, in E minor, Op. 25, first movement, mm. 219-22.

It was, however, Liszt's solo piano compositions that were the richest source for Rubinstein's Fifth Concerto. In particular, Liszt's Transcendental Etude *Mazeppa* furnished him with ideas for both the first movement (Ex. 2-7a,b) and the second (Ex. 2-7c,d); and Liszt's *Tarantella*[13] suggested the pianistic layout for the opening theme of the finale (also, incidentally, a tarantella;[14] see Ex. 2-8).

The finale also contains extended passages based on Liszt's Paganini

Ex. 2-6. a. Liszt, Piano Concerto No. 2, in A,☐ mm. 1-3; b. Rubinstein, Piano Concerto No. 5, in E-flat, Op. 94, first movement, mm. 264-67.

Etude No. 5, *La Chasse* (see Ex. 2-9), and a lengthy cadenza constructed entirely on the arpeggio figurations of Liszt's Paganini Etude No. 4. As if anxious to disguise the source of his inspiration, Rubinstein redistributed the arpeggios over two staves, transposed the original material into a lower register, and altered the notation from thirty-second notes to sixteenths. In performance, however, the passages are practically identical (see Ex. 2-10). Ascending and descending chromatic scales also figure prominently in the central episode of the finale and may have been inspired by Liszt's Transcendental Etude No. 12, *Chasse-neige* (Ex. 2-11). Alternatively, they may have been modeled on passages in the fourteenth variation of Alkan's *Le festin d'Esope*, Op. 39, No. 12. As Rubinstein dedicated his Fifth Concerto to Alkan, it is almost certain that he was acquainted with, and perhaps, influenced by Alkan's most celebrated work for piano (published in 1857).

Rubinstein's dependence on Liszt's music is curious in view of his low opinion of Liszt as a composer:

> I know his faults (a certain pomposity of manner for one thing), but always esteemed him as a great performer . . . a performer-virtuoso indeed, but no composer. I shall doubtless be devoured piecemeal for giving such an opinion. . . .[15]

Nevertheless, Rubinstein was clearly attracted by Liszt's inexhaustible pianistic imagination, and though loath to admit it, probably recognized an affinity between his own compositions and Liszt's in regard to their heady

Ex. 2-7. a. Liszt, *Mazeppa*, mm. 95-96; b. Rubinstein, Piano Concerto No. 5, in E-flat, Op. 94, first movement, mm. 273-75; c. Liszt, *Mazeppa*, mm. 169, 178-80; d. Rubinstein, second movement, m. 134.

mixture of virtuosity, sentimentality, and, particularly in Rubinstein's case, an ambivalence toward salon music. Rubinstein was also profoundly influenced by Liszt as a performer:

> There was at that time a manner of virtuosity—Liszt headed this movement. In my own playing I imitated Liszt. I adopted his mannerisms, his movements of the body and the hands, the throwing back of his hair, and in general, all the fantastic devices which accompanied his playing.[16]

Ex. 2-8. a. Liszt, *Tarantella,* from *Année de Pèlerinage,* mm. 74-76; b. Rubinstein, Piano Concerto in E-flat, third movement, mm. 1-4.

Ex. 2-9. a. Liszt, *La Chasse,* mm. 8-12; b. Rubinstein, Piano Concerto No. 5, third movement, mm. 25-29.

From a structural point of view however, Rubinstein showed little interest in Liszt's experiments in multisectional concerto designs and thematic transformation:

> His desire for novelty (à tout prix) gave him the idea of forming whole compositions of one and the same thing. Sonata, Concerto, Symphonic Poem, all with one theme only—an absolutely unmusical proceeding.[17]

Typically, however, in later years Rubinstein changed his mind—as he did toward nationalist music—for all three of his miscellaneous works for piano and orchestra: the Fantasy in C major, Op, 84, the Russian Capriccio in C minor, Op. 102, and the Concertstück in A-flat, Op, 113, are con-

Ex. 2-10.   a. Liszt, Paganini Etude No. 4, mm. 1-3; b. Rubinstein, Piano Concerto No. 5, third movement, mm. 707-709.

Ex. 2-11.   a. Liszt, *Chasse-neige*, m. 49; b. Rubinstein, Piano Concerto No. 5, third movement, mm. 557-59.

structed in a manner similar to Liszt's concertos; and one work, the Fantasy, is even monothematic.

Rubinstein's five piano concertos, on the other hand, are more conventional in design and are all tripartite in construction. For the most part, they reveal a rather unexpectedly fine grasp of concerto structure and an adept handling of the problems of balance between soloist and orchestra. Following Mendelssohn's example, Rubinstein abandoned the orchestral exposition after the completion of his First Piano Concerto, in E minor.[18] In his Second Piano Concerto, in F major, he introduced the soloist into the transition between the first and second subjects, and the latter is subsequently assigned to the piano. A neat compromise, indeed, for although the movement is condensed and the possible tedium of a second exposition is avoided, the air of expectancy generated by the delay in the soloist's entry is nevertheless preserved.

In the Third Piano Concerto, in G major, Op. 45, dedicated to Moscheles,[19] the emancipation of the soloist is taken beyond the then accepted guidelines of conventional concerto writing. Indeed, the exposition of the first movement suffers from "a kind of musical malaria," to quote John Culshaw (in reference to Liszt's concertos), "a tendency to break out in cadenzas at every possible opportunity."[20] In fact, continuous interruptions of the piano cause the first subject to resemble more a large-scale introduction than the opening section of a concerto's exposition. Perhaps the unorthodox treatment of soloist and orchestra adopted by Rubinstein was intended to represent, in musical terms, a dream—noted in his book *Gedankenkorb* (Thought basket)—experienced by the composer shortly before he began work on the concerto:

> I once had an unusual dream of a church in which were gathered various orchestral instruments. Into the church entered a piano, which aggressively demanded that it too should be accepted as one of them. The instruments of the orchestra subjected it to questioning and asked it to produce various timbres and melodies. But in the end they found it lacking and thus not suitable. The piano fell into despair and complained but then, having gathered all its strength, impudently declared itself an independent orchestra and sneered at the other instruments. Annoyed, they pointed out to it that it could not even imitate them and they threw it out of the church.
>
> I was trying to describe this dream in sounds and I even wanted to add a program. However, I finally decided not to carry out this idea, having come to the conclusion that, despite having a program written out beforehand, one might hear one thing and then, later, something quite different.[21]

Despite the musical possibilities offered by this dream-program, the Third Concerto is almost devoid of interesting or enduring ideas. Furthermore, the writing for soloist is clumsy, unimaginative, and far from convincing in its efforts to support the second-rate thematic material. This is particularly evident in the soloist's principal statement of the opening theme, where the piano takes over material previously announced by the orchestra: probably the moment in the dream when the piano "having gathered all its strength, impudently declared itself an independent orchestra. . . ." (see Ex. 2-12).

It is only in the Fourth Piano Concerto that Rubinstein achieved a well-balanced distribution of material between soloist and orchestra. In the first movement, the first-subject group and the transition are divided equally between the two forces; and in the second-subject group the first theme is allocated to the piano, the second, to the orchestra. Far from being

Ex. 2-12. Rubinstein, Piano Concerto No. 3, in G, Op. 45, first movement, mm. 41-44.

fragmentary in effect, the close antecedent-consequent relationship between the two melodies creates a tightly organized thematic block which admirably fits into the structure of the first movement exposition.

Though Rubinstein rejected contemporary innovations which influenced concerto structure as a whole, he nevertheless implemented, with varying degrees of success, certain modifications within the concerto format itself. Perhaps inspired by a procedure adopted by Mozart in his Piano Sonata in D major, K. 311, Rubinstein recapitulates the thematic material of the first and last movements of the Third Concerto, and of the second movement of the Fifth Concerto, in reverse order. A further modification, employed in almost every sonata-form movement in Rubinstein's concertos, is the abridgement of the recapitulation. This is most frequently achieved through a reduction or exclusion of transitional material between first and second subject groups, or, as in Chopin's piano sonatas, Opp. 35 and 58, and Beethoven's Op. 31, Nos. 1 and 2, by the elimination of subject material that has been prominent in the development or is likely to be so in the coda.

In the more extreme examples of abridgment, the line of demarcation between the altered recapitulation and the coda is often difficult to determine. In the finale of the First Concerto (in E major), for instance, what appear to be fragments of a recapitulation could be interpreted as constituents of an extended coda grafted onto the development. The somewhat bizarre tonal scheme of this section gives us no clue as to Rubinstein's intentions as his subject material is recapitulated in the unrelated keys of F and A-flat major respectively. Whether Rubinstein consciously incorporated these modifications in order to streamline his concertos, or whether they are due to carelessness and impatience, is difficult to ascertain.

An additional modification undertaken by Rubinstein was the introduction of a lengthy piano solo fugato in the first movement of the Second Concerto. This was by no means a new development; several composers, including John Field, had already incorporated fugatos into their concertos. Indeed, it was probably Field's Second Concerto, in A-flat,[22] which suggested the idea to Rubinstein in the first place. More importantly, Rubinstein's concerto, in turn, may have similarly influenced a later and superior piano concerto by one of his Russian contemporaries. While working on the preliminary sketches of his new piano concerto (in E-flat major), Balakirev asked the music critic and historian Vladimir Stasov, in a letter dated 14 July 1860, to send him the scores of Litolff's Fourth Concerto, Chopin's Third Scherzo, and the recently published Second Concerto of Rubinstein. As Edward Garden points out, Balakirev "was always willing to study Rubinstein's scores, even if only as examples of what to avoid."[23] All three works requested by Balakirev were to have some influence on his new concerto (see pp. 60–64). As far as Rubinstein's concerto is concerned, it was the idea of incorporating a piano solo fugato into the fabric of a concerto movement which particularly attracted Balakirev. However, whereas Rubinstein confined his 56-bar fugato, based on the first subject, to the first half of the cadenza, Balakirev, seeing further possibilities in the contrapuntal treatment of his theme—in this instance, the second subject—makes the fugato, perhaps inadvisedly, the central idea of the development.[24]

Although, as noted earlier, Rubinstein rejected on principle the structural experiments of his contemporaries—in particular, Liszt and Moscheles—with multisectional single-movement concertos, he was not unaware of the importance of thematically unifying large-scale compositions. In his Third Concerto, inspired perhaps by Beethoven's Fifth Concerto,[25] Rubinstein introduces material from earlier movements into the finale. Though this is the only substantial example of thematic recall in his concertos, it is employed on a massive scale; no fewer than five different quotations from the previous two movements are assembled in an episode which replaces the closing section of the recapitulation:

(1) *Adagio:* three bars from section B of the second movement (E-flat major)
(2) *Andante:* four bars from section A of the second movement (E-flat major)
(3) *Moderato con moto:* eight bars of second-subject group theme *a* of the first movement (C minor)
(4) (continuation): eight bars of second-subject group theme *b* of the first movement (A-flat major)
(5) Cadenza (solo piano): exact statement of cadenza material from the exposition (first-subject group) of the first movement.

Rubinstein makes no attempt to bind together these disparate chunks of material. Neither does he endeavor to incorporate them into the surrounding movement. What he presents us with, in effect, are musical flashbacks, but flashbacks that bear no relation to the plot unfolding around them. Consequently, what was intended to be a glorious résumé of the first and second movements becomes a curious musical aberration that ruins the otherwise boisterous and effective finale and leaves the listener confused and disoriented.

A more convincing and widespread feeling of unity in the concertos is created by similarities in Rubinstein's thematic material (see Exs. 2-13, 2-14, 2-15, and 2-16). Whether these similarities—which take the form of short motifs (indicated by *(a)* and *(b)* in these examples)—are preconceived and consciously introduced into the concertos' principal thematic material to generate a feeling of unity, or are merely the consequence of the sameness of much of Rubinstein's bland and often characterless melodic writing, is difficult to determine. Besides, thematic similarities are sometimes found in more than one composition (see Ex. 2-17).[26]

Genuine thematic transformation is far less common in Rubinstein's music. One instance occurs in the finale of the First Concerto, where the languid introductory theme reappears as the strident, martial second subject (shown in Ex. 2-18). Other examples of thematic transformation are found in the finale of the Fourth Concerto, in D minor. The opening theme

Ex. 2-13. Rubinstein, Piano Concerto No. 1, in E minor, Op. 25, first movement: a. first subject, mm. 1-4; b. first subject, subsidiary theme, mm. 17-20; c. transition theme, mm. 41-45; d. second subject (rhythmically simplified to clarify the melodic contours), mm. 219-23; e. *Salon* interlude, mm. 147-53.

a.

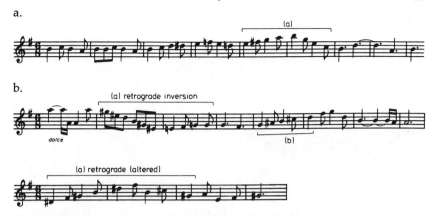

Ex. 2-14. Rubinstein, Piano Concerto No. 3, in G, Op. 45, first movement: a. first subject, mm. 6-14; b. second subject, mm. 89-96; second subject (b), mm. 121-24.

Ex. 2-15. Rubinstein, Piano Concerto No. 4, in D minor, Op. 70, second movement: a. Section A, principal theme, mm. 13-20; b. Section B, principal theme, mm. 41-48; c. Section C, mm. 105-12.

of the concerto (Ex. 2-19a), one of Rubinstein's finest melodies, serves as the prototype for the principal theme of the finale (Ex. 2-19b) and for much of the movement's subsidiary material (Exx. 2-19c–g).

The transformations are ingenious and convincing, and the attractive dancelike melodies that emerge are presented without the slightest hint of artifice. A perceptible Russian flavor also pervades much of the Fourth Concerto's finale, though Rubinstein avoids the kind of obvious folk characteristics that condemned his earlier efforts at nationalist composition to obscurity (see above, note 8). Nevertheless, extraordinary attempts were

Ex. 2-16. Rubinstein, Piano Concerto No. 5, third movement: a. Section A, principal theme, mm. 1-8; b. principal theme, mm. 25-26; c. Section B, principal theme, mm. 189-204.

Ex. 2-17. Rubinstein: a. Piano Concerto No. 4, first movement; b. Impromptu, Op. 75, No. 4; c. Romance, Op. 44, No. 1; d. Piano Concerto No. 1, second movement.

made by Soviet musicologists to attribute folk characteristics to Rubinstein's music in general. A. D. Alekseev, for example, believes that Rubinstein's compositions are based on two principal stylistic elements: Russian (e.g., urban songs and romances) and Oriental (peasant folk music): "Contrary to general opinion, the second element was widely expressed in Rubinstein's music."[27] General opinion, however, may in fact be better informed, for neither Rubinstein's music nor his attitude toward folk song support Alekseev's view: "Russian folk songs are exclusively melancholy and monotonous," wrote Rubinstein. "This monotony has been a stumbling block for composers."[28] He even attributed the initial failure of

a.

b.

Ex. 2-18. Rubinstein, Piano Concerto No. 1, in E minor, Op. 25, third movement: a. mm. 1-16; b. mm. 167-74.

Glinka's operas to their folk song content. In the piano concertos there is little evidence of Russian folk material, spurious or otherwise. In fact, the only example of folk song employed by Rubinstein is of Italian origin—a "Tarantella napolitaine populaire" found in the central episode of the finale of the Fifth Concerto (Ex. 2-20).

Curiously, the Russian musicologist L. A. Barenboim attributes the folk-like characteristics of the Fourth Concerto's finale to the influence of the *krakowiak,* a dance of Polish origin. However, he hastens to point out that the *krakowiak* was "widely accepted in Russian towns and was played by orchestras at aristocratic and merchants' dances as well as performed by amateur pianists during students' evenings or meetings of the intelligentsia."[29] Furthermore, together with the waltz and the quadrille, this dance "became popular in the city suburbs and was performed along with peasant folk dances in the factory workshops accompanied by accordions."[30] Barenboim also believes that the alternating chords at the close of the finale's principal subject and their subsequent development in the transition (Ex. 2-19g) were inspired by the accordion and that the "shouts and the stamping of the dancers" are represented by *sforzando* chords in the orchestra. César Cui's impression of the Fourth Concerto's finale is also curious: "[It is] something like those wild dances that Gluck and Righini composed . . . something like the 'alla Turca' one finds in Mozart." Nevertheless, Cui considered the finale original, though "strange and lacking in artistry owing to its crude dancing character."[31]

The Fourth Concerto is Rubinstein's finest work for piano and orchestra and can be justly considered the first significant contribution to the genre composed by a Russian. Tchaikovsky recognized its virtues and was significantly influenced by it, particularly in the structure and piano writing of his First Concerto's principal cadenza (examined in more detail on pp. 44–47).

Unfortunately Rubinstein's last concerto, the Fifth, in E-flat, is inferior from every point of view. Its thematic material is of astonishing banality (see Ex. 2-16), and the dull, textbook harmony that accompanies it is hardly

Ex. 2-19. Rubinstein, Piano Concerto No. 4, in D minor, Op. 70: a. first movement, mm. 1-8; third movement: b. mm. 25-32; c. mm. 1-8; d. bridge passage, mm. 57-64; e. first subject, continuation, mm. 73-80; f. bridge passage, mm. 153-54; g. transition, mm. 202-209.

Ex. 2-20. Rubinstein, Piano Concerto No. 5, third movement, mm. 397-401.

an improvement; see, for example, the opening of the second movement (shown in Ex. 2-21). Worse still are the many patches of harmonic careless-ness: ill-conceived modulations (Ex. 2-22), awkward enharmonic shifts (Ex. 2-23), and lengthy passages devoid of any harmonic change whatsoever. Miscalculations in the balance between soloist and orchestra are also characteristic of the Fifth Concerto, though it is not so much the soloist who is overwhelmed—as sometimes happens, even in otherwise fine concertos, such as Tchaikovsky's First and Rachmaninov's Second—as vice versa (see Ex. 2-24).

Ex. 2-21. Rubinstein, Piano Concerto No. 5, second movement, mm. 1-4.

Ex. 2-22. Rubinstein, Piano Concerto No. 3, in G, Op. 45, second movement, mm. 48-52.

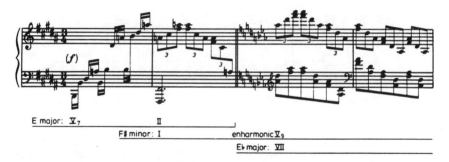

Ex. 2-23.   Rubinstein, Piano Concerto No. 5, first movement, mm. 764-67.

Ex. 2-24.   Rubinstein, Piano Concerto No. 5, third movement, mm. 253-61.

Though Rubinstein's piano writing bristles with many of the virtuosic features popular at that time, when reduced to its fundamentals, it reveals, in its dependence on melodic sequences, unadventurous harmonies, and underlying musical naiveté, an affinity to salon music (see Ex. 2-25). The aggrandizement of basically simple ideas—a consequence of transplanting characteristics of salon music into the concert hall—was also responsible for passages typical of Rubinstein's piano style: hypertrophied chordal writing, encouraged by Rubinstein's enormous span (as in Ex. 2-26); and the "chordal" decoration of otherwise straightforward arpeggio accompaniments (as in Ex. 2-27).

More idiosyncratic of Rubinstein's piano style are the peculiar passages of rapidly repeated chords which occur in the First and Fifth Concertos (see Ex. 2-28) and pyramid-shaped figurations—part chromatic, part arpeggi-

Ex. 2-25. Rubinstein, Piano Concerto No. 5, first movement, mm. 100-105.

Ex. 2-26. Rubinstein, Piano Concerto No. 5, first movement, mm. 785-88.

Ex. 2-27. Rubinstein: a. Piano Concerto No. 4, in D minor, Op. 70, second movement, mm. 69-73; b. Piano Concerto No. 2, in F, Op. 35, second movement, mm. 56-59.

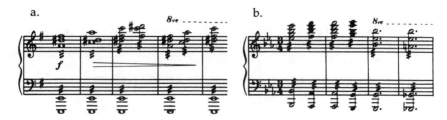

Ex. 2-28. Rubinstein: a. Piano Concerto No. 1, first movement, mm. 699-703; b. Piano Concerto No. 5, first movement, mm. 482-85.

ated—employed extensively in the Third Concerto, the Fifth Concerto (Exx. 2-29a,b), and the *Russian Capriccio* (Ex. 2-29c)—usually as transition and bridge passage material.

The similarity between Rubinstein's piano style, as illustrated by the above examples, and Tchaikovsky's is striking and by no means fortuitous,

Ex. 2-29. Rubinstein, Piano Concerto No. 5: a. first movement, mm. 233-34; b. third movement, mm. 425-26; c. *Russian Capriccio*, mm. 35-36.

as Tchaikovsky was significantly influenced by Rubinstein in matters of piano technique, despite his somewhat ambivalent attitude toward his former teacher's compositions in general. According to his brother Modest,

> While recognizing Rubinstein's great gifts as a composer and valuing some of his works very highly—such as the "Ocean" Symphony, "The Tower of Babel," the pianoforte concertos, "Ivan the Terrible," the violoncello sonatas and many pieces for pianoforte, Tchaikovsky grew angry and impatient over the vast majority of the virtuoso's mediocre and empty creations.[32]

In his correspondence, Tchaikovsky praises *Ivan the Terrible:* "What about Grosny? [Terrible]. A wonderful piece!" he wrote to the composer Ippolitov-Ivanov on 12 June 1889. Tchaikovsky also considered Rubinstein's *Don Quixote* "very interesting and, in places, splendid" and arranged it for piano duet for the publisher Bessel.[33] Only in his diaries did Tchaikovsky candidly air his opinions of Rubinstein's music:

> Played *Nero*[34] after supper. I am still astonished at the impudent liberties taken by its composer: oh you ridiculous clown! By God, I am seized with anger looking at this score. But then I play this abomination because I am conscious of my superiority—at least as to sincerity—and [it] gives support to my energy. You think that you write vilely, but seeing such trash which nevertheless was performed seriously—your soul feels better. I am ashamed that I feel so much anger over this work—but why should I make pretences in my diary?[35]

The final phrase is particularly illuminating. Probably out of self-interest—the lucrative commissions from Bessel, his personal and professional relationship with Rubinstein—Tchaikovsky decided that it would be wiser to conceal his true feelings toward Rubinstein's music.

Considering the degree of his antipathy, one wonders why Tchaikovsky turned to Rubinstein's concertos for ideas while composing his own First Concerto. Possibly it was for the same reason that Balakirev had requested the score of Rubinstein's Second Concerto some fifteen years earlier—as an example of what to avoid.[36] More likely, having embarked on a large-scale form unfamiliar to him (i.e., a piano concerto) and having subsequently encountered difficulties peculiar to the form that he felt ill-equipped to deal with (in particular, the invention of virtuosic passagework in the soloist's part), Tchaikovsky probably needed to consult recently published scores that could offer solutions to these specific problems.

Despite the uneven and often dubious musical qualities of Rubinstein's concertos, from a pianistic point of view they undoubtedly provided Tchaikovsky with a useful and readily accessible source of ideas that could be improved and developed further. It is interesting to speculate to what extent Tchaikovsky and the pianist Alexander Siloti were influenced by a passage in Rubinstein's Fifth Concerto (from the codetta of the first movement's exposition) while they were revising the Introduction of Tchaikovsky's B-flat minor Concerto (see Ex. 2-30) in preparation for its third edition

(1889). The rising diminished-seventh arpeggios that figure prominently in the short cadenza between the two principal statements of Tchaikovsky's introductory theme may also have been inspired by Rubinstein's Fifth Concerto, as a very similar figuration is found in the retransition section of its finale (see Ex. 2-31). Whether Tchaikovsky was directly influenced by this passage is difficult to verify, as Rubinstein's Fifth Concerto was published *after* Tchaikovsky had completed his First Concerto, on 21 February 1875. However, Rubinstein often played compositions still in manuscript for invited audiences, and since this was Rubinstein's first piano concerto in ten years and therefore a relatively important event, it is possible that Tchaikovsky may have heard and even examined it during the autumn of 1874. Tchaikovsky may have been influenced in more than matters of piano technique;[37] he may have actually conceived the idea of composing a piano concerto after hearing Rubinstein's.[38]

Further examples of Rubinstein's influence on Tchaikovsky's piano writing include the chromatic double octaves in the closing bars of the B-flat minor Concerto, which are borrowed from the corresponding bars in Rubinstein's Fifth Concerto (see Ex. 2-32); and the chordal accompaniment to the principal theme of the second movement of Tchaikovsky's Second Concerto, in G major, Op. 44, which are possibly derived from the slow movement of Rubinstein's Fourth Concerto (see Ex. 2-33).

More substantial is Rubinstein's influence on Tchaikovsky's cadenzas. It was, after all, in the cadenzas that Tchaikovsky would have needed most help, as his piano style, being essentially orchestral in concept, was not

Ex. 2-30.   a. Tchaikovsky, Piano Concerto No. 1, in B-flat minor, Op. 23, first movement, mm. 6-8; b. Rubinstein, Piano Concerto No. 5, first movement, mm. 264-67.

Ex. 2-31. a. Tchaikovsky, Piano Concerto No. 1, first movement, mm. 41-42; b. Rubinstein, Piano Concerto No. 5, third movement, mm. 15-16, 20, 24.

Ex. 2-32. a. Rubinstein, Piano Concerto No. 5, third movement, mm. 1035-39; b. Tchaikovsky, Piano Concerto No. 1, third movement, Z(e) , mm. 86-89.

entirely suitable, or so he thought, for the kind of virtuosic display expected of a concerto at that time. The similarity between the principal cadenzas of Tchaikovsky's First Concerto and Rubinstein's Fourth shows that Rubinstein's influence is not confined to piano writing but also involves tempi, tonal schemes, and even overall structure:

a.

b.

Ex. 2-33. a. Rubinstein, Piano Concerto No. 4, in D minor, Op. 70, second movement, mm. 13-16; b. Tchaikovsky, Piano Concerto No. 2, in G, Op. 44, second movement, mm. 66-69.

Rubinstein: Piano Concerto No. 4, in D minor, Op. 70 (1864)

CADENZA (66 bars): Begins on the flattened submediant chord of B-flat major, the key of the preceding second subject.

SECTION I: "Senza tempo." Constructed on a left-hand ostinato arpeggio pattern (see Ex. 2-34a).

TONAL STRUCTURE: G-flat major, C-flat major, B-flat minor.

Tchaikovsky: Piano Concerto No. 1, in B-flat minor, Op. 23 (1875)

CADENZA (75 bars): Begins on the flattened submediant chord of B-flat major, the key of the preceding second subject.

SECTION I: "A tempo rubato." Constructed on a left-hand ostinato arpeggio pattern (see Ex. 2-34b).

TONAL STRUCTURE: G-flat major/F-sharp major (enharmonic shift), B minor, C minor, D-flat major, E-flat major, F major, G major, D minor, C major, C minor, G major, F major, E-flat major, C-flat major.

a.

Ex. 2-34. a. Rubinstein, Piano Concerto No. 4, first movement, mm. 355-57; b. Tchaikovsky, Piano Concerto No. 1, first movement, P , mm. 26-30.

b.

SECTION II: "Tempo I" (*subito accelerando e stringendo sempre quasi Prestissimo*).

SECTION II: (*accel.—a tempo— accel.—a tempo—accel.—a tempo— accel.—*).

TONAL STRUCTURE (rising): B-flat minor, C minor, D minor, E minor, A minor, D minor.

TONAL STRUCTURE (rising): C-flat major/B major (enharmonic shift), E-flat minor/D-sharp minor (enharmonic shift), B major, C minor, D major, E minor, F major, G major, A major, B-flat major, G-flat major.

RITARD.

QUASI ADAGIO.

The most striking similarities can be summarized thus:

(1) Both cadenzas begin on the flattened submediant chord of B-flat major, the key of the preceding second subject.
(2) Both cadenzas are bipartite in construction, with the tempo of the first section "ad libitum" in effect, and the second, characterized by a steady *accelerando*.
(3) The rhythmic character of the melodies of the first sections involve syncopation across bar lines, and the left-hand figurations that accompany them are based on more or less identical musical ideas (see Ex. 2-34).
(4) Both concluding sections are designed to increase tension and excitement, and both achieve it through identical means: sequential treatment of the thematic material rising through a series of keys a major or a minor second apart, fragmentation of this material, and gradual acceleration to a climax.

Rubinstein immediately follows his cadenza with a coda based on the first movement's principal subject accompanied by thunderous double octaves in the soloist's part that encompass the entire range of the keyboard (Ex. 2-35). This passage was later to influence Tchaikovsky's decision, while preparing the third edition (1889) of his concerto, to radically

Ex. 2-35.   Rubinstein, Piano Concerto No. 4, third movement, mm. 436-37.

alter the layout of the last two bars of the bridge passage that immediately precedes the coda to the finale (Ex. 2-36). Furthermore, Tchaikovsky's *fortissimo* double-octave passage, of which Ex. 2-36 shows the concluding four bars, serves the same function as the fourteen bars of double octaves—also characterized by octave leaps—near the end of Rubinstein's D-minor Concerto: both lead into grandiose *tutti* climaxes heralding the beginning of the codas. Tchaikovsky also adopts Rubinstein's tonal scheme: the soloist's octaves begin in the dominant of the principal tonality of the concerto and modulate into the tonic major, which concludes the coda and the work as a whole.

The influence of Rubinstein's Fourth Piano Concerto on Tchaikovsky's more-celebrated Concerto in B-flat minor was acknowledged in Soviet musicological studies. A. A. Nikolaev writes: "Perhaps Russian music would not have acquired the Concerto in B-flat minor by the genius of Tchaikovsky if before that there had not existed the Concertos of Rubinstein and, in particular, the Fourth Concerto in D minor."[39] A. D. Alekseev is of the same opinion: "More than any other work, Rubinstein's Fourth Concerto leads to the B-flat minor Concerto of Tchaikovsky."[40]

Neither writer, however, substantiates his conclusions with concrete evidence or persuasive analysis. On the other hand, the German musicologist Ulrich Niebuhr, who has independently reached several of the conclusions put forward so far in this study, considers that Tchaikovsky may have been influenced by Rubinstein's treatment of thematic material and draws attention to a similarity in approach regarding the construction of

Ex. 2-36. Tchaikovsky, Piano Concerto No. 1, third movement, ⌊Z(e)⌋, mm. 37-40, upper system represents the third edition (1889), lower system the second edition (1879).

subject groups in Rubinstein's Third Concerto and Tchaikovsky's First.[41] In addition, he believes, with perhaps more justification, that there is a connection between the principal theme of the finale of Tchaikovsky's Second Concerto and the jaunty finale theme of Rubinstein's Third Concerto[42] (See Ex. 2-37).

Tchaikovsky was not the only composer to have been impressed by Rubinstein's Fourth Concerto:

> Berlioz—old, stooping, he did not go either to the theatre or to the concert. He went to listen to the D-minor Concerto of Anton Rubinstein, who had performed the day before. A. R. willingly sat down at the piano and began playing. In the shaded room there was also his wife, Heller, Berlioz and myself. Berlioz lay on the couch in his usual posture, head lowered, sad expression and fixed staring eyes. . . . I glanced at him. He lay motionless. Large tears rolled down his emaciated cheeks, and his feverish eyes burned. The playing finished: A. R. stood up and raised his leonine head. Berlioz rested himself on his shoulder and said in a trembling voice "Oh, my friend! It is splendid! It distracts me from my suffering!"[43]

Saint-Saëns was also captivated by Rubinstein at the Russian composer's Paris debut:

> It seemed as if the race of "piano gods" had disappeared when one beautiful day there appeared posters with the name Anton Rubinstein. He made his debut with his Concerto in G major. The next day he was a celebrity, and at the second concert, the hall was crowded to suffocation. I was present at the concert, and I harnessed myself into the chariot of the conqueror.[44]

Ex. 2-37.   a. Tchaikovsky, Piano Concerto No. 2, third movement, mm. 1-6; b. Rubinstein, Piano Concerto No. 3, in G, Op. 45, third movement, mm. 33-36.

Rubinstein's performances of his own compositions were so expressive and brilliant that it was often difficult for contemporary audiences to evaluate his music objectively. This was, of course, to Rubinstein's advantage, and many decidedly inferior compositions were received with rapturous applause, which they hardly merited, particularly during his tours abroad. Rubinstein's Russian contemporaries, on the other hand, were less easily beguiled. Indeed, their criticisms—encouraged by the general atmosphere of intrigue and rivalry between musical factions, particularly the Nationalists and the conservatory trained eclectics—were often little more than thinly disguised personal attacks.[45] Alexander Serov, a composer, critic, and self-confessed Wagnerite, considered Rubinstein a "backward classicist with German training" and refused to recognize his Third Concerto as a Russian composition because "it was not written in the national style created by Glinka and because its composer had been born a Jew."[46] César Cui deplored the many "tedious and commonplace passages" of the Fifth Piano Concerto, particularly those revealing "difficulties not commensurate with their musical objectives and which were written in coarse strokes." Nevertheless, he conceded that there were "some vivacious ideas and interesting passages" and that the concerto revealed "a successful employment of piano and orchestra," concluding, "in any case, this concerto, like all his instrumental music, is better than his operas."[47] Rubinstein's Third Concerto fared even worse: Cui dismissed it as a "weak, tedious and pretentious work of little interest." The Fourth Concerto, on the other hand, he considered "more successful."

Rubinstein's concertos were frequently performed throughout the closing decades of the nineteenth century, not only by the composer himself but by many leading virtuosi, including Anna Esipova (to whom Rubinstein dedicated his *Russian Capriccio*, Op. 102, for piano and orchestra), Rubinstein's brother Nikolai, and the ubiquitous Hans von Bülow, who considered the Fourth Concerto "magnificent."[48] During the early decades of the twentieth century, Rubinstein's Third, Fourth, and Fifth Concertos still maintained a position in the virtuoso's repertoire; the Third was a favorite vehicle of the Polish-American pianist Josef Hofmann (1876–1957), and the Russian pianist Josef Lhevinne (1874–1944) made his American debut in 1919 playing the Fifth Concerto.

In addition to five piano concertos, Rubinstein composed three miscellaneous works for piano and orchestra; the Fantasy in C, Op. 84; the *Russian Capriccio*, in C minor, Op. 102; and the Concertstück in A-flat, Op. 113. The Concertstück, which was composed specifically for Rubinstein's fifty-years jubilee celebration in 1889, is of little significance and can be safely passed over. The other two works are of interest, as they represent Rubinstein's only substantial ventures into monothematicism and multisectional single-movement concerto design. The Fantasy in C, completed in the autumn of 1869 and first performed by Rubinstein in December of that year, follows closely the structural blueprint of Weber's Konzertstück in F minor (1821) and is consequently constructed in four connecting and thematically related sections. Although it exhibits a mildly Russian character in parts, there is too much padding and too little spontaneous melodic invention for the work to maintain a place in the repertoire. Pianistically, the Fantasy is written in the grand manner, as noted by the Russian musicologist Boris Asaf'ev: "The leonine pianism of Anton Rubinstein (as demonstrated in this work) found a clever and ardent continuator in Rachmaninov."[49] A. D. Alekseev believes that Tchaikovsky's piano concertos were influenced by the Fantasy, particularly in the alternation of soloist and orchestra in its exposition.[50]

Rubinstein's finest miscellaneous work for piano and orchestra is the *Russian Capriccio*, in C minor, Op. 102, which dates from his "Russian" period, 1878–82, and was composed around the same time as the opera *The Merchant Kalashnikov.*[51] The *Capriccio* is first mentioned in a letter by Rubinstein to his publisher Senff, dated 12 October 1878. It reveals a curious reappraisal of Rubinstein's former attitude toward Russian nationalism:

> I think it will be effective and that Esipova (to whom the work is dedicated) will be able to perform it—if she won't be put off, that is, by the coldness—or, rather, indifference, that the public and the critics show to everything Russian, be it in art or in science.[52]

In common with the Fantasy, the *Russian Capriccio* is multisectional in design: *Moderato assai—Allegro moderato—Tempo I—Allegro*. The thematic material, three probably spurious folk songs, is cyclically developed to promote unity. Theme A (Ex. 2-38a), on which the *Moderato assai* section is based, reappears in every other section and is even given prominence in the coda (Ex. 2-38f). Theme B is used in the *Tempo I* section and the coda, and Theme C in the *Allegro* section (Ex. 2-38c) and the coda. In the manipulation of these themes Rubinstein exhibits uncharacteristic ingenuity; in the *Allegro moderato* section, for example, theme A is counterpointed by its inversion (Ex. 2-38d), and in the ensuing section, *Tempo I*, theme B, which was initially announced by the soloist, is similarly treated, with the added complexity of being involved in canonic imitation (Ex. 2-38e). In the coda, *Meno mosso*, all three themes are brought together, though in order to make them compatible Rubinstein found it necessary to modify them, either rhythmically or intervallically, or occasionally, both (Ex. 2-38f).

In addition to incorporating folklike thematic material in the *Capriccio* to generate a Russian character, Rubinstein employs a primitive form of *changing background* accompaniment at the beginning of the work, à la Glinka's *Kamarinskaya*. Characteristically, Rubinstein's impatience and inability to "complete" his compositions (to quote Liszt) resulted in the abandonment of this effective treatment after only thirty bars (i.e., the orchestral introduction), and with the entry of the soloist all thoughts of varied and imaginative instrumentation disappear.

Ex. 2-38. Rubinstein, *Russian Capriccio*, Op. 102: a. Theme A, mm. 1-8; b. Theme B, mm. 125-32; c. Theme C, mm. 183-86; d. mm. 88-93 (Theme A appears unchanged in the bass, but inverted in the treble); e. mm. 125-29; f. mm. 591-601.

Despite its shortcomings—the patches of weak orchestration, the over-bearing pomposity of the soloist's part, etc.—the *Russian Capriccio* was generally well received following its first performance. The German pianist Emil von Sauer, who had studied with Nikolai Rubinstein, heard the *Capriccio* on three different occasions (with the Rubinstein brothers and Anna Esipova as soloists) and wrote favorably of it, noting that he found the finale "incomparably brilliant and rhythmically sparkling."[53] Even Tchaikovsky apparently admired it, though "not as piano work but as an orchestral one."[54] Not everyone liked it, however. S. Kruglikov, writing of Rubinstein's music in general, found that:

> Some things are not bad, even in the Caprice Russe—where, incidentally there is a good introduction, but it is very soon replaced by folk thematicism not of root origin, which had already acquired a vulgar shade of pubs and barracks.[55]

The *Russian Capriccio* contains hints of musical developments in Rubin-stein's creativity that, sadly, were never to be realized—glimpses, as it were, of a new path which might have led to achievements of a more substantial nature. It is of little consolation to learn that it may have inspired and influenced a similar work for piano and orchestra that was also banished to obscurity: Arensky's *Fantasia on Themes of I. T. Riabinin* (discussed on pp. 82–84).

3

The Piano Concertos
of the Nationalists
and the Eclectics

Although Rubinstein's first three piano concertos represent the only quantitatively significant Russian contribution to the genre during the 1850s, the more-talented though as yet youthful and undisciplined Mily Balakirev made two attempts at concerto-style composition between 1852 and 1856. The works dating from this period—the *Grande Fantaisie on Russian Folk Songs*, Op. 4, for piano and orchestra, and a projected piano concerto in F-sharp minor—both remained unfinished, testifying not only to Balakirev's impatience and irrepressible urge to move on and explore new musical avenues but also to the enormous, almost insuperable problems facing self-trained composers working in areas where there were few precedents—in Balakirev's case, the composition of a national-style concerto.

Balakirev probably found little of interest or guidance in Villoing's concerto, which was wholly derivative in style. Nor could he turn for support to earlier Russian fantasias or variations on folk songs for piano and orchestra, as almost all of them remained unpublished, and in any case, they were merely weak imitations of their Western European counterparts. Rubinstein's concertos were not readily available to him for perusal, as they did not appear in print until 1858, two years after Balakirev's final youthful attempt, the Piano Concerto in F-sharp minor. Balakirev may have heard Rubinstein play them, but it is doubtful whether the teenage Balakirev would have had the courage to ask the composer if he could examine the scores. Balakirev's early piano compositions show a perceptible influence of Field, Mozart, Schumann, and Hummel (whose A-minor Concerto Balakirev had studied at the age of ten with Field's pupil Dubuque, using Field's fingering). But it was principally in the works of Adolf Henselt, who had been living and working in St. Petersburg since 1838, that Balakirev found ideas that could be developed further and molded into a Russian musical idiom.[1]

Henselt's Piano Concerto in F minor (published in 1846, though the manuscript, according to Clara Schumann, was in existence two years earlier[2]) was especially important in the development of Balakirev's early style, and it may have served as a direct model for a movement of a septet for strings, flute, clarinet, and piano—Balakirev's very first composition (dating from 1852), probably recast three years later as the Octet, Op. 3.[3] It is also possible that in the same year, 1852, Henselt's Variations for piano and orchestra, Op. 11, on "Quand je quittai la Normandie," from Meyerbeer's *Robert le diable*, composed in Russia and published in 1840, may have suggested to the fifteen-year-old Balakirev the idea for a similar work on Russian themes. The result was his "Grand Fantaisie sur airs nationales Russes pour le Pianoforté avec accompagnement d'Orchestre composée et dedicée a son maître Monsieur Charles Eisrich par MILY BALAKIREFF op. 4" (according to the inscription on the manuscript deposited in the Leningrad Public Library).

The composition of this, the earliest of Balakirev's large-scale works, did not come easily, and it is evident from the various inks used on the manuscript and from additional pencil markings, that the piece had been composed at different periods and that passages had been rewritten many times over. Even the initial tempo marking caused Balakirev some anguish; the original *Larghetto-maestoso* in ink was crossed out and *Allegretto* was substituted in pencil; this, in turn, was cancelled and replaced by *Andantino*. That Balakirev could have contemplated such wildly differing tempi for the opening section of the Fantasy is an indication of his musical immaturity and youthful exuberance (though only to be expected from a boy of fifteen). This is further evident from the linguistic hodge-podge inscribed on the final page: "Finis del prima parto Auctor Milius Balakireff." It was clearly his intention to add further sections to the existing score (which was finished on 12 December 1853), but being distracted by more urgent musical projects or, what is more likely, circumstances in his personal life,[4] Balakirev was never able to carry out this plan.

The Fantasy incorporates two Russian folk tunes, "Akh, ne solnyshko zatmilos" (The sun is not eclipsed)[5] and "Sredi doliny rovnye" (Down in the vale); and throughout the remainder of the work Balakirev endeavored to maintain, with varying degrees of success, a national character through the additional use of folklike melodies and rhythms. The folk songs as they appear in the Fantasy are shown in Ex. 3-1.

Balakirev's attachment to folk song, as noted by Vladimir Stasov in his article "25 let russkogo iskusstva" (25 years of Russian art), written in 1882–83,[6] was deeply rooted right from the very outset of his creativity. His treatment of folk songs, particularly during his years of maturity, in works such as the symphonic poem *Russia* (completed in 1884) and the finale of the First Symphony (1897), is unrivaled in nineteenth-century Russian symphonic composition. Balakirev's use of folk song in the early Fantasy is of course considerably less sophisticated than in these masterworks. It is largely based on the principle of variation in which contrast is provided by

Ex. 3-1. a. "Akh, ne solnyshko zatmilos"; b. "Sredi doliny rovnye."

accompaniment figurations employed in a manner similar to Glinka's *changing background* technique. Unsophisticated also, though at times mildly impressive in its somewhat conventional virtuosity, is the writing for the soloist. Most of the thematic material, however, is allocated to the feeble orchestral part.

More successful, though still very much an apprentice work, is the first movement of a projected piano concerto in F-sharp minor premiered by Balakirev at a university concert on 12 February 1856 in St. Petersburg. Both the performance—which represented his debut in the city where he was to live for the remainder of his life—and the concerto itself were highly praised. The composer Alexander Serov, later a fervent opponent of the Nationalists, wrote warmly of the occasion:

> Balakirev's composition (the *Allegro* first movement of his concerto in F-sharp minor) was splendidly performed by the composer and was met with sincere enthusiasm by the public. As expected, the success that followed was unqualified, and the audience's appreciation was ardently expressed by tremendous applause. Indeed, one cannot but be delighted with the concerto, for it is poetically conceived, attractively scored, and rich in charming, graceful melodies. Moreover, it was performed with great mastery, tenderness and yet at the same time, power. . . . Balakirev's talent is a godsend to our country's music.[7]

Judging from the "Op. 1" designation on the title page, this concerto movement may have been a reconstruction of material predating the

Grande Fantaisie (Op. 4) or, more likely, was begun before the Fantasy and was completed some time during 1855–56, with additional revisions in 1857.[8]

The overall style of this early concerto movement strongly reflects two important influences on Balakirev's musical development during his formative years: the many hours spent perusing the scores of the great Classical and early Romantic composers in the fine music library of Alexander Ulybyshev,[9] and the concerts at Ulybyshev's residence, where Balakirev heard these scores brought to life, in particular, the works of Mozart, Field, Mendelssohn, and Hummel. The concerto movement also contains features redolent of Chopin, for it was around this period that Balakirev became acquainted, through Eisrich, with Chopin's Piano Concerto in E minor, Op. 11, a work for which he was to have lifelong admiration.[10]

From a structural point of view, Balakirev's concerto movement closely adheres to Classical sonata form, even to the point of reinstating the opening orchestral *ritornello*. In the development, however, he side-steps the thorny issue of combining piano and orchestra in a working-out of exposition material—and at the same time provides the movement with a substantial solo cadenza—by stating the two forces, i.e., piano and orchestra, separately (thus adumbrating Tchaikovsky's Third Piano Concerto by nearly forty years; see pp. 163–68). Balakirev, however, relies too heavily on sequential repetition for either section to be entirely convincing. Furthermore, the thematic ideas themselves are neither distinctive[11] nor particularly original, being reminiscent of first-subject themes in the concertos of Henselt and Chopin (see Ex. 3-2).

Of greater interest, at least from a historical point of view, is the concerto movement's piano writing, for here and there between passage-work of a

Ex. 3-2.   Opening movement first subjects: a. Balakirev, Piano Concerto in F-sharp minor; b. Henselt, Piano Concerto in F minor, Op. 16; c. Chopin, Piano Concerto in F minor, Op. 21.

more derivative nature are found keyboard figurations in embryonic form that presage the rich mosaics of piano sound which characterize Balakirev's mature works. The rapid alternation of single notes and chords distributed between the hands, as in the concerto's closing sections, are found throughout his later piano works, for example, in the celebrated Oriental fantasy *Islamey* (see Ex. 3-3).

Another feature of Balakirev's mature keyboard style is his use of polyrhythms in the same hand, usually consisting of a triplet eighth- or sixteenth-note countermelody underneath a slower-moving principal thematic line (see Ex. 3-4). Elsewhere however, the spirit of Chopin is never very far from Balakirev's creative thought, and on occasion, the source of his inspiration is scarcely concealed (see Ex. 3-5).

For all its faults—the pseudo-dramatic gestures, the overtly sentimental turns of phrase, and the artificial brilliance of the soloist's part—the Concerto in F-sharp minor is a considerable advance on the Fantasy, Op. 4, particularly in the skillful balance and distribution of thematic material between soloist and orchestra. Why the work remained unfinished is not known. In view of the fact that during the 1850s the speed of Balakirev's musical development far outstripped his rate of composition, it seems likely that by the time the concerto movement had been completed, both his style and his capacity for self-criticism had evolved beyond the concerto's somewhat derivative and anachronistic idiom. Moreover, just a few months before its completion, Balakirev had been introduced to his idol, Glinka. This, and many subsequent meetings were to have a considerable influence on Balakirev's musical aesthetic and to provide a powerful fillip to his own nationalist aspirations. As the concerto movement contains no Russian musical characteristics whatsoever, Balakirev was probably loath

Ex. 3-3.   Balakirev: a. Concerto in F-sharp minor, mm. 330-31; b. Oriental fantasy *Islamey*, mm. 198-200.

Ex. 3-4.   Balakirev: a. Piano Concerto in F-sharp minor, mm. 225-26; b. Mazurka No. 5, in D, mm. 213-16; c. "Spanish Melody," mm. 97-99.

Ex. 3-5.   a. Balakirev, Piano Concerto in F-sharp minor, mm. 236-38; b. Chopin, Etude, Op. 10, No. 1, mm. 1-3.

to continue in the same vein. Better to "wash his hands" of the whole affair and start again.

Balakirev's final and most substantial attempt at concerto form, the Piano Concerto in E-flat, was begun in June 1861 while the composer was on holiday in Nizhny-Novgorod, though it is apparent that the new work had been on his mind for some time: "How goes *Lear*, how goes the concerto?"[12] wrote Vladimir Stasov on 12 June of the previous year. In common with the two earlier works for piano and orchestra and every large-scale composition begun during the following decade, it remained unfinished, and it was left to Balakirev's disciple Lyapunov to complete the concerto nearly fifty years later.[13]

Characteristically, Balakirev needed some kind of external musical stimulus to sustain his inspiration during the composition of the new concerto, and at the same time, he required guidance in matters of orchestration, piano technique, and combining piano with orchestra. He consulted Berlioz's treatise on orchestration, from which, as he informed Stasov in a letter dated 14 July 1861, he gained considerable insight into writing for natural horns and trumpets, which he intended to use in the concerto. For guidance in writing for piano and orchestra he examined Liszt's Piano Concerto in E-flat, informing Stasov, "One can learn much in the use of piano and orchestra from that work";[14] and he expressed the desire to see Liszt's Second Concerto, in A major, which he had been informed had recently been published in full score. Balakirev also asked Stasov to send him Rubinstein's Second Concerto, Op. 35; Chopin's Third Scherzo, Op. 39; and Litolff's Fourth Concerto (Concerto Symphonique), Op. 102. All three, in fact, were to be influential in some way or other. Rubinstein's concerto, as noted, may have encouraged Balakirev to employ fugatos in the opening and closing movements of his new work. Litolff's concerto was specifically requested for its attractive slow movement, *Andante religioso*. Balakirev clearly intended to use it as a model for his *Andante*, which was giving him problems: "I don't remember exactly what kind of *Andante* there is, but I need it very much for my own composition, which is coming together in such a strange manner that I can't attribute it to any form known to me."[15] On 3 August, Balakirev informed Stasov that he intended to base his own *Andante* on a Russian church chant. If Stasov had been exceptionally prompt and had delivered the requested score between 14 July and 3 August, it is just conceivable that the initial idea for a slow movement with definite religious overtones may have come from Balakirev's perusal of Litolff's *Andante religioso*. Balakirev may, in any case, have come across Litolff's concerto (composed c.1852) in earlier years, as he hinted at in the letter quoted above. Certainly from a structural point of view, Balakirev appears to have been influenced by Litolff, as the following points illustrate:

(1) Both movements begin with a short introduction (Litolff 5 bars, Balakirev 6 bars) and then modulate to the tonic key.

(2) Both introductions overlap the principal subject of the movements by
one bar.

(3) Both initial solo statements of the principal subject are in the form of
arpeggiated chords.

(4) Both development sections are entirely based on the principal subject.

(5) Both recapitulations commence with a *tutti* statement of the principal
subject accompanied by similarly scored octave chords in the soloist's
part (see Ex. 3-6).

Litolff's *Andante* also contains a curious anticipation (in the soloist's initial
entry) of the opening theme announced by the piano in the *first* movement
of Balakirev's E-flat Concerto. The similarity is probably fortuitous (see Ex.
3-7). Elsewhere, Litolff's influence is negligible, though the similarity in
keyboard layout shown in Ex. 3-8 may be significant.

The influence of the remaining score requested by Balakirev, Chopin's
Scherzo No. 3, in C-sharp minor, is less substantial and is confined to

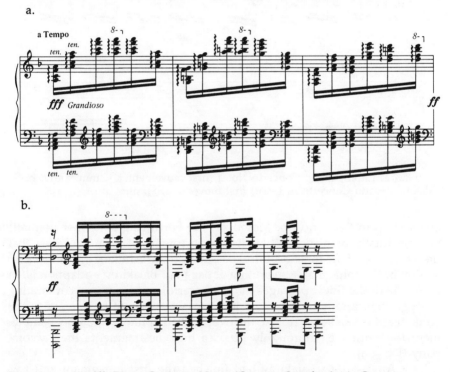

Ex. 3-6.　a. Litolff, Piano Concerto No. 4 (*Concerto Symphonique*), Op. 102,
second movement, mm. 10-12; b. Balakirev, Piano Concerto in E-flat, second
movement, 32, mm. 1-3.

Ex. 3-7.   a. Litolff, Piano Concerto No. 4, second movement, mm. 23-27; b. Balakirev, Piano Concerto in E-flat, first movement, mm. 32-36.

Ex. 3-8.   a. Litolff, Piano Concerto No. 4, first movement, [G], mm. 31-32; b. Balakirev, Piano Concerto in E-flat, first movement, [8], mm. 4-6.

one section in the concerto. Moreover, the borrowing is neither thematic nor essentially pianistic; rather, it is a borrowing of a musical idea that underlies one of the most beautiful passages in the Scherzo (the *Meno mosso* section in the tonic major beginning at bar 155). Balakirev's adaption is, in turn, one of the finest passages in the concerto, and his use of coruscating arpeggio figurations (which, to a less-prosaic ear could be likened to the "tinkling of troika bells," to use the overworked epithet), superbly complement the exquisite, thoroughly Russian melodic fragments they accompany (Ex. 3-9).

By 8 August 1862 Balakirev had finished the first movement and had written at least "a quarter of the second movement" (according to a letter written that same day to Rimsky-Korsakov[16]). Fifty-three pages of sketches exist from this stage in the concerto's genesis, one of which is dated 4

Ex. 3-9. a. Chopin, Scherzo in C-sharp minor, Op. 39, mm. 155-71; b. Balakirev, Piano Concerto in E-flat, third movement, |44|, mm. 4-14.

August; they come to an abrupt halt at the transition to the second theme. Although Balakirev found the work somewhat strenuous and complained that it had a "bad effect on his health," a further quarter was completed after ten days (so he informed César Cui[17]) and ideas for the finale were more or less settled though they were not yet committed to paper. By November, Balakirev had arranged the first movement for piano duet so it could be performed by members of the *Moguchaia Kuchka*.[18] Rimsky-Korsakov apparently thought very highly of the new work, as Balakirev noted in a letter to Stasov dated 11 October 1862: "I played to Korsinka the whole of my concerto, and he declared emphatically, banging his fist on the table, that it was better than Lear."[19]

Rimsky-Korsakov mentions the concerto in his autobiography, though it is probable that the year given (1866) is incorrect, since he was known to have a faulty memory:

> The first movement of his Piano Concerto was ready and orchestrated; there were wonderful intentions for the Adagio and for the finale the following theme [shown in Ex. 3-10]. Then in the middle of the finale the church theme "se zhenikh griadet" [Lo, the bridegroom is coming] was to have appeared, with the piano accompanying it in imitation of the ringing of bells.[20]

Ex. 3-10.

Curiously, the finale known today (orchestrated by Lyapunov in 1910) contains neither of these themes. During the 1860s Balakirev may have completely re-sketched the movement, without informing his friends and colleagues, or, what is more likely, Rimsky-Korsakov had confused the finale with sketches for another work which no longer exists.[21]

Periodically, Balakirev voiced his intention to complete the concerto, but perhaps being aware of the deficiencies of the first movement and consequently reluctant to add to it, he achieved nothing until 1909. In the summer of that year, he produced a revised version of the first movement in response to the continued insistence of his publisher J. H. Zimmermann. The second movement was finished soon after, though he was unable to work on the finale, which he had decided in any case was unsuitable and needed to be recomposed. Four days before Balakirev's death, on 12 May 1910, Lyapunov wrote in the manuscript, on the last page of the second movement: "The composer wishes to strike out the last bar and to pass over without a break into the finale, as indicated in the plan."[22] Lyapunov completed the finale during the summer. The concerto was first performed at a memorial concert he conducted in Berlin on 4 December 1910, with L. Kreutzer as soloist.

The concerto's extraordinarily protracted and fragmented genesis is reflected in its fundamental weakness—the disconcerting difference in quality between the immature and thematically uninspired first movement and the more-complex, richly scored second and third movements (particularly the third, which was somewhat overenthusiastically orchestrated by Lyapunov). As Edward Garden bluntly put it, the concerto was, in effect, "the work of a partially fledged composer realised by a sick old man all but 50 years later. . . . [It] was bound to suffer as a result."[23]

When Balakirev finally resumed work on the concerto in 1909 he may have been aware of the lack of continuity between movements, for there is evidence to suggest that he attempted to remedy the situation by adopting a process of thematic unity. The second subjects of the *Andante* (Ex. 3-11e) and the finale (Ex. 3-11f) resemble both the opening theme of the concerto (Ex. 3-11d) and the motif on which the first movement's fugato is based (derived from the second subject, Ex. 3-11g). Moreover, all appear to be variants of "Sobiraites'-ka, brattsy-rebiatushki,"[24] a folk song that Balakirev suggested to Rimsky-Korsakov as the basis for his Piano Concerto in C-sharp minor (see Ex. 3-11c). Significantly, Balakirev was also to use a variant of this folk song for the opening theme of his fine Piano Sonata, composed in 1905 (Ex. 3-11a).

Apart from thematic transformation, the concerto also contains a neat example of what pundits would describe as "postponed and reversed antecedent and consequent," i.e., a process of thematic unity—almost invariably subconscious—whereby a complete and self-contained melody is created from the reversed juxtaposition of two seemingly disparate, disjunct phrases. In Balakirev's case (shown in Ex. 3-12), it involves the opening movement's two principal subjects (the second of which somewhat disconcertingly resembles the sea shanty "Blow the man down"). Balakirev was not always so successful in the manipulation of his thematic material (that is, assuming that a subconscious process is as valid a part of a composer's creativity as a conscious process). For instance, any advantage gained from using the opening motif of the concerto (Ex. 3-11d) in the bridge passage between the *Adagio* and the finale (following the example of Schumann's Piano Concerto in A minor, Op. 54) and during the course of the finale itself is severely compromised by the blatant artificiality of the procedure.

Balakirev's efforts to draw together the wayward movements of his concerto through thematic means were considerably undermined by structural weaknesses and miscalculations. In the first movement—a fairly large-scale affair by any standards—second-rate ideas are worked to exhaustion; and in one particularly poor spot in the development, a "dry and school-masterly"[25] fugato is introduced, based on an undistinguished motif (Ex. 3-11g) derived from the second subject. The second movement,

Ex. 3-11.   a. Balakirev, Sonata in B-flat minor, opening theme; b. "Sobiraites'-ka, brattsy-rebiatushki"; c. Rimsky-Korsakov, Piano Concerto in C-sharp minor, introductory phrase; Balakirev, Piano Concerto in E-flat: d. first movement, opening theme; e. second movement, second subject; f. third movement, second subject; g. first movement, fugato subject.

built around the beautiful Russian Orthodox chant "so sviatymi upokoi,"[26] is a much finer conception, with imaginative scoring (particularly in the woodwinds), ingenious counterpoint, and a more thoughtfully contrived piano part. However, for its length, the movement lacks contrast; indeed, throughout the course of seven minutes or so, the *Adagio* tempo is maintained without change, apart from the occasional *poco riten, poco allargando,* etc. Nor does the attractive second subject (Ex. 3-11e), derived from the folk song "Sobiraites'-ka, brattsy-rebiatushki," offer anything significant in the way of contrast, also being *Adagio* in tempo.

The finale is the most attractive of the three movements. It contains a wealth of exuberant and effective musical ideas: in particular, the Musorgskian transition section, shown in Ex. 3-13 (reminiscent of the Coronation Scene of *Boris Godunov*[27]), and the splendidly virtuoso second subject,

Ex. 3-12. Balakirev, Piano Concerto in E-flat, first movement: a. second subject, transposed, mm. 37-40; b. first subject, mm. 4-7.

Ex. 3-13. Balakirev, Piano Concerto in E-flat, third movement, 42, mm. 1-4.

shown in Ex. 3-14. Also attractive are the opening theme of the finale, shown in Ex. 3-15 (which resembles the fourth original melody from Balakirev's symphonic poem *Russia*), and the "troika bells" passage quoted in Ex. 3-9b. Again, the movement is too long, for Balakirev (or Lyapunov) could not resist toying with these lovely ideas, which are in themselves perfect and self-contained, not only within the subject groups but also in an extended and decidedly rambling development section.[28]

Ex. 3-14. Balakirev, Piano Concerto in E-flat, third movement, 43, mm. 8-13.

Ex. 3-15.   Balakirev: a. Piano Concerto in E-flat, third movement, [38], mm. 5-9;
b. *Russia*, fourth original melody.

Although Balakirev studied Liszt's E-flat Concerto and noted that "one can learn much in the use of piano and orchestra from that work," Liszt's influence is not readily apparent in either the first movement or the *Adagio*. Certainly the first movement contains several passages redolent of Liszt's piano style and one or two which reveal a direct influence of Liszt's concerto itself (see Ex. 3-16). Nevertheless, the role of the piano is predominantly supportive and suggests an approach closer to Litolff's than to Liszt's. Arnold Schering's description of Litolff's *Concerto Symphonique* No. 1 (1844) could almost apply to the first movement of Balakirev's concerto:

> The orchestra is conceded an exceptional position; it has become the chief bearer of the ideas and it reserves for itself the last and most important word, while upon the piano devolves the role of an obbligato orchestral instrument, similar to the Beethoven Choral Fantasia, although to be sure, with a strong virtuoso tendency. The composer no longer works with solo and tutti in a one-sided fashion, but seeks to effect externally . . . as well as internally, a complete parallel to the symphony.[29]

Balakirev's *Adagio* fared even worse in regard to the distribution of thematic material between piano and orchestra. Out of a total of 154 bars, the soloist is allocated a mere ten and a half: six and a half of the chant "so sviatymi upokoi" expressed through solemn, widely spaced *arpeggiando*

Ex. 3-16.   Balakirev, Piano Concerto in E-flat, first movement, [19], mm. 14-17.

chords and four bars of the second theme in unison octaves. In the remaining 144 bars the soloist is assigned the "role as commentator on the proceedings rather than as a participant."[30] But despite the grandeur of the piano writing—the passages of double octaves, sweeping arpeggios, and sonorous chords exploiting the extremes of the keyboard (see Ex. 3-6a)— the piano reveals itself as a commentator with little of significance to say, and in one passage (Ex. 3-17) is so noisy it distracts from the proceedings themselves.

The finale is altogether more successful in its use of piano and orchestra, though how much this can be attributed to the talents of Lyapunov remains unknown. From the outset, the two forces are exploited on equal terms; the soloist takes on the angular first phrase of the opening theme (Ex. 3-15a), and when the strings enter with the more-lyrical second phrase, beautifully complements it with a delicate filigree of sixteenth notes. After sixteen bars the roles are reversed, but so skillfully is this managed that there is not the slightest hint of artifice. The transition is similarly well wrought, though Lyapunov's orchestration is at times heavy-handed. The second subject group is better, particularly the "troika bells" passage (Ex. 3-9b). The remainder of the finale is likewise considerably more enterprising in its contrasts of texture and instrumentation than the previous two movements, though, as already noted, it shares with them a tendency to overestimate the potential of the material.

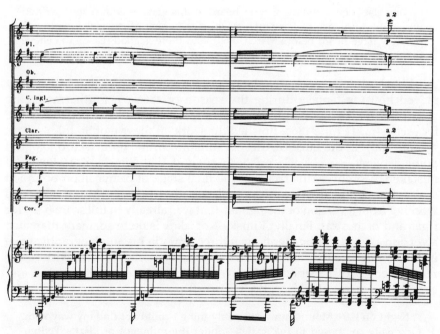

Ex. 3-17.   Balakirev, Piano Concerto in E-flat, second movement, [33], mm. 1-2.

Musorgsky

Apart from Rubinstein's Piano Concerto in D minor, Op. 70, composed in 1864, Balakirev's unfinished concerto represents the only significant work for piano and orchestra composed in Russia during the 1860s. Rimsky-Korsakov believed, however, that Musorgsky may also have attempted a concerto-style work:

> During the season of 1866–7 I became more intimate with Moussorgsky . . . he played me many excerpts from his opera *Salammbo* which greatly delighted me. Then also, I think, he played me his fantasy *St. John's Eve* for piano and orchestra, conceived under the influence of the Todtentanz [of Liszt]. Subsequently the music of this fantasy, having undergone many metamorphoses, was utilized as material for *A Night on Bald Mountain*.[31]

Musorgsky's biographer M. D. Calvocoressi suggests, however, that Rimsky-Korsakov was mistaken in his belief that the fantasy was initially conceived for piano and orchestra and accuses him of "thickening the fog" which has enveloped the early genesis of the work. But a great deal of the fog can be attributed to Calvocoressi himself, for he misquotes Rimsky-Korsakov as saying that the work was composed "at the beginning of the sixties"[32] and subsequently draws the conclusion that

> no one else seems to have seen or heard of this version with piano "written under the influence of Liszt's *Danse macabre* (which Mussorgsky could not possibly have heard before March 1866), and there is good reason to believe that it never existed outside Rimsky-Korsakov's notoriously faulty memory.[33]

But Rimsky-Korsakov clearly states in his autobiography that Musorgsky played him the fantasy during the season of 1866–67. Furthermore, the inscription on the autograph score reads "Planned in 1866.[34] Began to write for orchestra, 12 June 1867, finished the work on the eve of St. John's Day, 23 June 1867, in the Luga District on Minkino Farm." From a chronological point of view, no obstacle exists to suggest that Rimsky-Korsakov was mistaken. Moreover, the fact that the final stage of composition occupied so brief a period (eleven days) indicates that perhaps Musorgsky was working from a version of the fantasy that was already in full score (i.e., for *piano* and orchestra). Finally, Rimsky-Korsakov is quite adamant that such a version existed, for he mentions it three times in his autobiography; once in his recollections of the years 1866–67 (quoted above) and twice in his reminiscences of a period (1882–83) during which he was revising and completing many of Musorgsky's works:[35]

> A Night on Bare Mountain was the only thing I could not find my way with. Originally composed in the sixties—under the influence of Liszt's Todtentanz—for the piano with accompaniment of orchestra, this piece (then called

St John's Eve and both severely and justly criticised by Balakirev) had long
been utterly neglected by its author, gathering dust among his unfinished
works. [p. 261]

In working on Moussorgsky's piece I made use of the last version for the
purpose of closing the composition. Now then, the first form of the piece was
for piano solo with orchestra: the second form and the third, vocal compositions and for the stage, into the bargain (unorchestrated!). [p. 262][36]

Could Rimsky-Korsakov's "notoriously faulty memory" have deceived
him on four separate occasions (in addition to his reference to the work in
the Preface to the score of *Night on Bare Mountain*)? If not, there existed for
almost a year, an unusual, powerful, and, judging from the subsequent
versions, musically significant work for piano and orchestra by one of the
greatest of Russian composers. Edward R. Reilly is understandably non-
committal, in view of the lack of conclusive evidence that such a version
existed:

The surviving manuscript incorporates changes made after the work was first
composed. Thus the possibility that these alterations were even more substantial than is currently known cannot be entirely ruled out. It is also
possible that Musorgsky originally sketched the work with piano and orchestra in mind, but subsequently orchestrated it without piano, because of the
similarity to Liszt's *Todtentanz*.

Reilly concludes his investigation by siding with Calvocoressi: "In my
opinion it is most likely that Rimsky-Korsakov simply made a mistake."[37]

Taneyev

Another recollection chronicled in Rimsky-Korsakov's autobiography[38]
was of a very young Sergei Taneyev. He had recently graduated from the
Moscow Conservatory and came to St. Peterburg in 1876 to show Rimsky-
Korsakov his unfinished Piano Concerto in E-flat[39] and other compositions. First, however, Taneyev took the new work, on Tchaikovsky's
recommendation, to Anton Rubinstein for his opinion. As Taneyev wrote
to Tchaikovsky on 2 December 1876:

I spent an entire evening at his house. He listened to both movements[40] of the
concerto, examined them in great detail and made many remarks for which I
am very grateful and which I will undoubtedly put to use. The following
points contain the essence of these remarks regarding the first movement:

(1) Too long.
(2) Rhythmically monotonous. The first two subjects are both in 4/4—which
is very wearisome.

(3) Lack of interesting ideas in the piano part. There is not a single place where the pianist can "show off."

(4) The piano hardly ever plays in the higher registers—mainly in the lower. The first theme is too often stated "ff" after a crescendo on the dominant.

The majority of these remarks suggest alterations which can be made to the piano part, and in accordance with this I am prepared to rewrite it. As far as the second movement is concerned, he really did not like it, in fact, he said that he could say nothing about it, as he could find no music in the piece whatsoever. . . . On the basis of these observations Anton Grigorevitch advised me to completely rewrite both movements and what has already been composed could be useful as an outline only . . .[41]

On the following day Taneyev played the concerto at the home of P. L. Peterson,[42] accompanied by Gustav Kross on second piano. Among those present were Lev Vasilevich Davidov (Tchaikovsky's brother-in-law), Cui, and Rimsky-Korsakov.[43] Although Taneyev had not discussed Rubinstein's comments with them, their observations were along very similar lines. Characteristically, Cui had further criticisms to make. In particular, he noted that many of Taneyev's melodies began with the repetition of their opening bar or bars and that these bars were often introduced into the middle of the phrases as well. He pointed out in no uncertain terms the monotonous effect this created, which he found throughout the movement. He singled out as examples the two phrases shown in Ex. 3-18.

Taneyev's letter continues:

Nothing definite was said about the second movement, but everyone agreed that it was worse than the first. However, Cui advised me not to rewrite the concerto, but to finish it and even have it published. Then, making use of all that is lacking in this work, try to improve future compositions. It seems to

Ex. 3-18. Taneyev, Piano Concerto in E-flat (unfinished), first movement: a. [10], mm. 1-4; b. [28], mm. 1-13.

me that I should try and find a compromise between his opinion and that of A. G. [Rubinstein].

Unless I compose new melodies there is no way I can avoid the rhythmic monotony and repetitiveness of the themes. I think I will leave the themes as they are, reduce everything as much as possible and then completely rewrite the piano part. I would very much like to hear your opinion of this. . . .[44]

In his reply, dated 16 December, Tchaikovsky was more tactful than Rubinstein and Cui. Characteristically, Tchaikovsky endeavored to raise Taneyev's spirits by referring to the Concerto as "charming" and expressing his belief that "despite its formal drawbacks, not a single musician can deny its strong and appealing qualities."[45] He did acknowledge, however, that there was something lacking and suggested to Taneyev that he should not only utilize the knowledge gained from composing the Concerto in future works, but also use it immediately to improve the Concerto itself, "otherwise [it] will never be finished. . . . Try to add a more virtuoso element to the first movement, without completely reducing or changing your original material." Tchaikovsky also suggested that Taneyev write a brilliant finale, "in which the pianist can express some freedom and which makes up for the lack of virtuoso effects in the preceding two movements. . . . But be determined . . . for God's sake, write the finale as soon as possible!"[46]

Taneyev was clearly discouraged by the broadside of friendly but severe criticisms from Rubinstein, Cui, and Tchaikovsky, for he left the slow movement in its arrangement for two pianos and made no attempt to start the finale (though he informed Tchaikovsky in a letter dated 24 March 1877, from Paris, that he intended to compose it during the summer).[47]

According to B. Yagolim, in the Preface to the score of Taneyev's concerto (published in Moscow in 1957), Tchaikovsky had pointed out a number of flaws in the instrumentation, which he (Tchaikovsky) considered "not quite equal to the first-rate beautiful passages in which the composition abounds." In fact, Tchaikovsky had scribbled nearly a hundred corrections, comments, and revisions in the margin of the score; evidently his composer's sense compelled him to point out weaknesses wherever they existed. He did not mince words either; comments such as "I don't like the instrumentation of these two bars, nor the previous two; it is feeble, inconsistent and illogical" are characteristic and are in sharp contrast to the paternal magnanimity of his letters.[48] In the subsequent checking-through, every nook and cranny of Taneyev's orchestration was perused, every musical stone turned over.

In view of the extent to which Taneyev's concerto needed revising, Tchaikovsky must have realized that it was not destined for publication. Nevertheless, it must have peeved him that his efforts were to have served so little purpose, for Taneyev, not surprisingly, dropped the work like a hot potato soon after. He was probably right to do so, for its weaknesses are so fundamental and extensive that no amount of rewriting could render it acceptable. Rubinstein's advice, that Taneyev should completely recompose both movements "and use what has already been written as an outline only," was harsh, but just, as were his comments enumerated in Taneyev's letter. Rubinstein's first criticism, that the work was too long, is certainly valid, for although the two movements are fairly conventional in size, the thematic material is so poor and spun out to such an extent that an impression of length is created by the monotony that results. Medtner's views on the subject, expressed in a letter dated 13 September 1926, to Rachmaninov, who at the time was seriously worried about the length of his Fourth Piano Concerto (in G minor, Op. 40), sums up the intrinsic problem of Taneyev's early work:

> Naturally there are limitations to the lengths of musical works, just as there are dimensions for canvases. But within these human limitations, it is *not the length* of musical compositions that creates an impression of boredom, but is rather the *boredom* that creates the impression of length. . . .[49]

It is not clear how this was supposed to reassure Rachmaninov, for Medtner does not account for the presence of boredom in the first place!

Taneyev's melodies are not only dull and repetitive (for example, the two cited by Cui and quoted in Taneyev's letter to Tchaikovsky, see Ex. 3-18); several are also hideously unmusical. The theme shown in Ex. 3-19 must surely be one of the ugliest, most ungainly opening subjects in concerto literature. Moreover, its unusual intervallic spacings suggest that it was perfunctorily conceived at the keyboard and was not the product of genuine musical inspiration. Neither is the principal theme of the *Andante funebre* second movement, shown in Ex. 3-20, particularly attractive. Both themes are subjected to considerable repetition. The passage in Ex. 3-21, based on Ex. 3-20, is a fairly typical example, which displays a harmonic awkwardness characteristic of much of the concerto.

Ex. 3-19. Taneyev, Piano Concerto in E-flat, first movement, mm. 1-8.

Ex. 3-20. Taneyev, Piano Concerto in E-flat, second movement, [2], mm. 2-6.

Ex. 3-21.   Taneyev, Piano Concerto in E-flat, second movement, ③, mm. 1-4.

Rubinstein's strictures concerning the soloist's part—that it "lacks virtuosity" and that it occupies far too great a period of time in the lower registers of the instrument—are also valid, though to be fair to Taneyev, he was probably aiming for a more symphonic approach to his concerto writing (in the manner of Tchaikovsky) and was thus less concerned than Rubinstein with external glitter. Much of the piano writing, in fact, leans substantially on Tchaikovsky's First Concerto, which had been composed two years earlier, though, needless to say, the ideas are not so convincingly realized. Taneyev was intimately involved in the genesis of Tchaikovsky's famous concerto[50] and was also one of its leading exponents, so it is hardly surprising to find similarities in material and design. The passage shown in Ex. 3-22, for instance, is a pallid imitation of Tchaikovsky's "orchestrally conceived" piano writing; compare it with the second subject of the first movement of Tchaikovsky's First Concerto, Ex.

Ex. 3-22.   Taneyev, Piano Concerto in E-flat, first movement, ③1, mm. 1-8.

4-26, a characteristic of which is the distribution of thematic material between the hands in the form of a dialogue. More blatantly imitated is the celebrated passage of double octaves that introduces the first cadenza in Tchaikovsky's concerto (first movement, development, bars 348–58). In his own concerto (Ex. 3-23), Taneyev varies the piano's initial few bars but the borrowing is obvious. One wonders why Tchaikovsky did not comment on this clear act of plagiarism.

Taneyev's work suggests that the composer was also acquainted with Rubinstein's piano concertos, in particular No. 5, in E-flat, Op. 94, composed in 1874 and published the following year. In addition to the Rubinsteinian rhythmic diminution of the soloist's opening statement (see Ex. 3-24), Taneyev also indulges in a somewhat brash effect created by the rapid repetition of chords—a rare and unusual figuration employed in Rubinstein's First and Fifth concertos (compare this passage with Ex. 2-28). The presence of Liszt is evident, particularly in the scales of chromatic thirds (borrowed from the latter's Concerto in E-flat) leading into the coda to the first movement and in the use of contrary-motion chromatic octaves, as in the Hungarian Rhapsody No. 6. Even Brahms makes a brief appear-

Ex. 3-23.   a. Taneyev, Piano Concerto in E-flat, first movement, [55], mm. 1-5; b. Tchaikovsky, Piano Concerto in B-flat minor, Op. 23, first movement, mm. 352-55.

a.

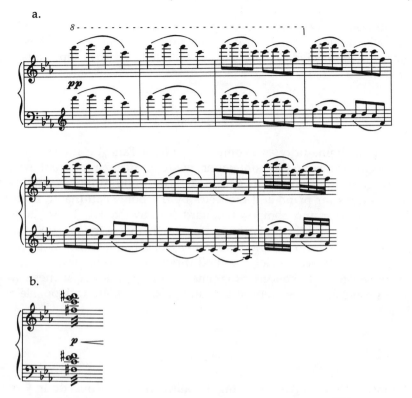

b.

Ex. 3-24. Taneyev, Piano Concerto in E-flat, first movement: a. [17], mm. 1-7; b. [24], m. 4.

ance in the employment of octave trills, an important feature of his First Concerto, in D minor, Op. 15.[51]

To summarize, Taneyev's musical style, as displayed in his early Concerto in E-flat, is derivative, unsettled, and, above all, immature. The piano writing possesses neither the fluency of Rubinstein's nor the gripping "orchestral" quality of Tchaikovsky's, though elements of both, in the form of weak imitation, are found throughout. Taneyev's writing did mature, though as David Brown points out, it did not blossom into anything particularly distinctive or distinguished: "Taneyev's style was to develop a more broadly based eclecticism which ultimately achieved an illusion of individuality through its constant capacity to avoid commitment to the style of any one composer."[52] Nevertheless, it is to be regretted that Taneyev never attempted to write a piano concerto later on in life, for he was undoubtedly more talented, both as a composer and a pianist, than many of his contemporaries. Like Balakirev, however, his creative gifts were more often than not dissipated in the guidance of others. Taneyev also became increasingly involved in the science of musical theory and counterpoint.[53] Only on one occasion did he revisit the concerto genre, ironically enough, to orchestrate another work for piano and orchestra that remained unfinished: Tchaikovsky's *Andante and Finale*, Op. 79 (see pp. 168–70).

Napravnik

Despite his immaturity as a composer, at least Taneyev attempted to cast his abortive concerto in a contemporary idiom, turning to recent examples of the genre for inspiration and ideas. The same cannot be said of the compositions for piano and orchestra by the Bohemian (naturalized Russian) conductor and composer Eduard Napravnik. His Piano Concerto, Op. 27 (1877), and the fantasias on Russian themes, Op. 30 (1878) and Op. 39 (1881), date from a period (1876–81) when Napravnik was director of the Russian Musical Society, and all three works were clearly composed for inclusion in its concert programs.[54] Little is known of these works; in all probability they were of the "pot-pourri" variety fashionable at the time.

Arensky

Of more interest is Arensky's highly polished Piano Concerto in F minor, Op. 2, composed during his final year of study at the St. Petersburg Conservatory (1881–82). Perhaps highly "Polish" is a more suitable epithet, for Arensky's work leans very heavily on the concertos of Chopin, in particular No. 2, Op. 21 (also significantly in F minor). Indeed, so extensive is this influence, that it prompted the Russian critic R. Genika, writing in *Russian Musical Gazette* in 1906, to conclude: "[In this concerto] there is more that is borrowed and derivative than original."[55] Two examples should suffice to illustrate the extent to which Arensky's somewhat weak musical individuality was subordinated by Chopin's. The first—the soloist's initial entry (see Ex. 3-25)—cannot be attributed to any one passage in Chopin's music; however, it pursues Chopin's style to such an extent that it could easily be mistaken for parody or for a passage from one of Chopin's juvenile sketchbooks. The second is the soloist's entry in the second movement, *Andante con moto*. Its similarity to passages in the first movement of Chopin's F-minor concerto is striking (see Ex. 3-26). In his working-out of Ex. 3-26b Arensky employs tremolo strings as an accompaniment, also an important feature of Chopin's concerto.

Whereas Chopin's influence reigns supreme in the lyrical sections, Arensky turned to Liszt's Concerto in E-flat for ideas in the more dramatic episodes.[56] The opening motif of Arensky's concerto and much of the soloist's virtuoso writing is derived from the majestic introduction (i.e., the

Ex. 3-25. Arensky, Piano Concerto in F minor, Op. 2, first movement, mm. 169-73.

Ex. 3-26. a. Chopin, Piano Concerto No. 2, in F minor, Op. 25, first movement, mm. 206-208; b. Arensky, Piano Concerto in F minor, second movement, mm. 6-8.

piano's opening passage of double octaves and the cadenza) of Liszt's concerto, Arensky also makes use of a harmonic progression from Liszt's Transcendental Etude No. 1, *Preludio*, in the coda of the finale (see Ex. 3-27). The two passages are identical apart from Arensky's modifications to the left-hand chords and the transposition down a whole step. The most

Ex. 3-27.   Arensky, Piano Concerto in F minor: a. opening motif; b. third movement, mm. 208-209; c. Liszt, *Preludio*, mm. 10-11.

intriguing "borrowing" of all, however, is not from Chopin or Liszt but from Balakirev.

For some obscure reason, Arensky used, for his second subject, the corresponding theme from Balakirev's unfinished Piano Concerto in F-sharp minor. Perhaps Arensky's teacher Rimsky-Korsakov suggested the theme as an example of a second subject to be studied, and Arensky went a stage further and incorporated a variant of it in his concerto (see Ex. 3-28). It is to be regretted that he did, for the theme is the weakest in the concerto, being a sugary-sweet affair more redolent of the Russian salon than of the concert hall. Arensky was apparently oblivious to its short-comings, for he subsequently apotheosed the theme—with an off-beat *ff* chordal accompaniment—in a passage of unbelievable banality in the closing section of the exposition. Without a doubt, it rivals, in sheer awfulness, the final pages of Rubinstein's First Concerto, and the orchestral state-

a.

Ex. 3-28. a. Balakirev, Piano Concerto in F-sharp minor, mm. 50-54; b. Arensky, Piano Concerto in F minor, first movement, mm. 70-74.

ments of the first episodic theme in Tchaikovsky's finale from the *Andante and Finale*, Op. 79, which was zealously orchestrated by Taneyev after Tchaikovsky's death.

The concerto's saving grace is its last movement, a rondo cast in the somewhat unusual time signature of 5/4. Arensky retained a lifelong fascination for unorthodox rhythms and time signatures[57] and was particularly interested in quintuple time. Tchaikovsky was not impressed by these experiments and pleaded with Arensky to give them up. In connection with Arensky's piano piece *Basso Ostinato*, for example, he wrote:

Dear Anton Stepanovich,
    Pardon me if I force my advice upon you. . . . It seems to me that the mania for 5/4 time threatens to become a habit with you. . . . I made the discovery yesterday that in this instance 5/4 time was not at all necessary. You must own that a series of three bars of 5/4 is mathematically equal to a similar series of 3/4 [presumably Tchaikovsky meant five bars of 3/4 time]; in music, on the contrary, the difference between them is quite as sharp as between 3/4 and 6/8. . . . In my opinion your *Basso Ostinato* should be written in 3/4 or 6/4 but not in 5/4. I cannot imagine a more distinct five-bar rhythm in 3/4 time. What do you think?[58]

Arensky was not convinced, for he preserved the *Basso Ostinato* in its original 5/4 format. Ironically, Tchaikovsky changed his mind concerning the musical merits of quintuple time, for he cast the entire second movement of his Sixth Symphony, Op. 74 (*Pathétique*), in 5/4.

The finale of Arensky's Concerto begins with a motif inspired by the opening of Grieg's Piano Concerto in A minor (see Ex. 3-29). Curiously, Grieg was later to use this same phrase in the second of his Symphonic Dances, Op. 64, composed in 1898, some sixteen years after Arensky had written his finale. The connection, however, is probably fortuitous. The second theme is an attractive imitation of folk song and bears a superficial resemblance to other folk themes, spurious or otherwise, found in the Russian symphonic repertoire[59] (see Ex. 3-30). In common with the second subject of the finale of Chopin's Concerto in F minor, Arensky introduces

Ex. 3-29. Arensky, Piano Concerto in F minor, third movement, m. 1.

Ex. 3-30. Arensky, Piano Concerto in F minor, third movement, mm. 54-57.

this theme in unison octaves on the piano accompanied by pizzicato strings. In this instance, however, the influence of Chopin is negligible, and Arensky succeeds in creating some measure of national coloring (hence the nickname "Russian" occasionally attached to the work).

Although Arensky's teacher Rimsky-Korsakov regarded the concerto as "an ideal student work"[60] (probably in reference to the undeniable skill with which the twenty-year-old student constructed and orchestrated it), the piece did not impress Taneyev, who considered it Arensky's most feeble composition up to that time. Neither was the Russian critic and musicologist Boris Asaf'ev particularly enamored with the new work: "The salon-lyrical themes are insipid and lacking in contrast. . . . In parts, there is an overindulgence in decorative passage-work which hinders the degree of symphonic development."[61] Nevertheless, for a brief period, Arensky's concerto was taken up by pianists Pabst (who gave its first performance), Goldenweizer, and Ginsburg and was included in the repertoire of teaching material at Russian conservatories.

Ten years later, Arensky composed his second and last work for piano and orchestra: *Fantasia on Themes of I. T. Riabinin*, Op. 48, which was published by Jurgenson in 1899. Ivan Trofimovich Riabinin (1844–?) came from Seryodki, a village on the coast of the White Sea in the former Olonyetsk Government (now part of Karelskaia), and like his equally celebrated father, Trofim Grigorevich, was a *starinshchik* (reciter) of *bylini* (epic tales and legends).[62] In 1892 Ivan Trofimovich was invited to Moscow to give a recital of *bylini* in the small hall of the Conservatory. During this performance Arensky found the thematic material for his projected work for piano and orchestra. As Alexander Goldenweizer explained:

I sat next to Arensky, and while we were listening I noticed that he was writing down Riabinin's tunes in a notebook. He actually wrote only a couple which were later to form the basis of a fantasy or something—it's not a work I know.[63]

The first theme Arensky chose is a slow-moving *Andante sostenuto* melody entitled "Iz togo li goroda iz Muromlia," which comes from an ancient Russian folk tale about the boyar Skopin-Shuisk. The second is a contrasting, more lively tune called "Zhil Sviatoslav debianosto let," from a well-known folk bylina based on the legend of the Russian heroes Vol'g and Mikul.[64]

The *Fantasia* is constructed in three contrasting sections. The first two each comprise half a dozen or so variants (as opposed to variations) on Riabinin's themes; the third is a kind of résumé containing a section in which the two themes are combined (see Ex. 3-34) and a coda in which they alternate. Sandwiched between the first two sections is a brief cadenza and a fugato. Arensky's treatment of the bylini material is characteristically highly polished and effective, though in all probability, his harmonic vocabulary and orchestration are not sufficiently imaginative to convey fully the powerful images evoked during Riabinin's recitations (Arensky's teacher Rimsky-Korsakov would have been more successful from this point of view). The writing for the soloist takes us little further than Rubinstein and Tchaikovsky in its somewhat conventional virtuosity, though Arensky's predilection for widely spread left-hand arpeggiando figurations was to have a profound influence on the piano styles of his pupils Rachmaninov and Scriabin (see Ex. 3-31).

Elsewhere, Arensky occasionally employs heavy-handed chordal writing in the accompaniment to the Riabinin themes, for example, in the second variant on "Iz togo li goroda iz Muromlia," shown in Ex. 3-32. (This treatment was probably inspired by the *Allegro deciso* section of Liszt's Second Piano Concerto—see Ex. 2-6a.) The second bylini theme, "Zhil Sviatoslav debianosto let," fares little better as far as imaginative treatment is concerned, though it does represent, in its rhythmic assertiveness (Ex. 3-33), an ideal countermelody to the more languid first theme. Following Rubinstein's example (in the *Russian Capriccio*, Op. 102, dating from 1878), Arensky combines the two bylini themes in a piano solo (Ex. 3-34) accompanied by lower strings. It is reminiscent in its chordal textures of some of Tchaikovsky's more awkward keyboard writing (in his Sonata in G, Op. 37, for example).

According to Tsuipin, Arensky's *Fantasia* was an immediate and sensational success, second only in popularity to his D-minor Trio.[65] The fact that Goldenweizer, a renowned pianist very active on the Russian musical scene, did not know of the work, seems to suggest otherwise.[66] In any case, the *Fantasia* sank rapidly into oblivion soon after, despite the attempts of the Soviet pianist M. Grinberg to revive it, and the work has probably never been performed publicly in the West.

Ex. 3-31.   Arensky, *Fantasia on Themes of I. T. Riabinin*, mm. 13-15.

Ex. 3-32.   Arensky, *Fantasia*, mm. 22-23.

Rimsky-Korsakov

The neglect afforded Arensky's early compositions for piano and orchestra in concert halls today is understandable in view of its feeble musical ideas and heavy stylistic dependence on others. The same cannot be said of Rimsky-Korsakov's fine Piano Concerto in C-sharp minor, Op. 30. It is immensely appealing, both in the beauty of its themes and in the virtuosity with which these splendid ideas are presented. Its absence on concerto programs, as Edward Garden has pointed out,[67] can only be attributed to the fact that small-scale concertos and concerto-style works are no longer fashionable.[68]

Though Rimsky-Korsakov, in his autobiography, could not recall exactly when he first conceived the idea of composing a piano concerto, or when the work was completed, it is apparent from a letter dated 14 January 1883,

Ex. 3-33. Arensky, *Fantasia*, mm. 60-65.

Tempo I (Andante sostenuto)

Ex. 3-34. Arensky, *Fantasia*, mm. 120-24.

to S. N. Kruglikov, that he had been busy finishing and orchestrating the work during the Christmas/New Year holidays 1882/83. Furthermore, "Jan 3, 1883, N. Rimskii-Korsakov, Pyter" is inscribed on the final page of the score. What prompted him to embark on a piano concerto is not known. Certainly, piano concertos and concerto-style works figured prominently in his musical activities during the year 1882.[69] Moreover, if his repeated references to the existence of a version of Musorgsky's fantasy *St. John's Eve*, for piano and orchestra are to be believed (see pp. 70–71), it is possible that the initial idea of composing a piano concerto was inspired by his study of Musorgsky's score (Rimsky-Korsakov was then deeply engrossed in completing and revising, among other works, Musorgsky's *Khovanshchina*). Apparently, the new concerto surprised and delighted Balakirev, who never previously credited Rimsky-Korsakov with the skill for either playing the piano or composing for the instrument:

> It must be said that it sounded beautiful and proved entirely satisfactory in the sense of piano technique and style; this greatly astonished Balakirev, who found my concerto to his liking. He had by no means expected that I, who was not a pianist, should know how to compose anything pianistic.[70]

Rimsky-Korsakov was, in fact, a finer pianist than Balakirev or any of the other members of the *Moguchaia Kuchka* realized, for as early as 1866 he had surreptitiously set out to acquire a firm foundation in piano technique:

> I diligently conned Czerny's *Tägliche Studien*, played scales in thirds and octaves, studied even Chopin's etudes. These studies were carried on with-

out the knowledge of Balakirev, who never suggested to me work at the piano—though how necessary that was! Balakirev had long given me up as a pianist; usually he played my compositions himself. If occasionally he sat down to play four-hands with me, he would quit playing at my first embarrassment, saying he would rather play it afterwards with Moussorgsky. In general, he made me feel uncomfortable, and in his presence I usually played worse than I really knew how. I shall not thank him for that. I felt that I was making progress in my playing, after all—working rather hard at home. But I was afraid to play before Balakirev, and he was utterly unaware of my progress; moreover, I was rated "without capacity for playing" by others, especially by Cui. Oh, those were wretched times! The circle often made fun of Borodin and me for our pianistic achievements, and therefore we, too, lost faith in ourselves.[71]

Rimsky-Korsakov's clandestine studies certainly bore fruit in the concerto, for it is rich in imaginative, if not wholly original, piano writing. Some figurations are clearly derived from Liszt (to whom the work is dedicated), and Rimsky-Korsakov quite openly admitted that he was influenced by the Hungarian composer: "in all ways the concerto proved a chip from Liszt's concertos."[72] To a certain extent this is true, particularly in regard to its multisectional single-movement design and extensive employment of thematic transformation. However, whereas Liszt went to extraordinary lengths, particularly in the Second Concerto, in A Major, to unify his structure still further by superimposing sonata form principles onto the existing framework, Rimsky-Korsakov maintained a distinct four-section design with the soloist providing connecting links in the form of short cadenzas. No further unifying element was deemed necessary, for Rimsky-Korsakov rightly considered the monothematic scheme of the work (see Fig. II) more than sufficient for this purpose.

Rimsky-Korsakov's compositional methods *within* this structure also contrast sharply with Liszt's, for in place of a traditional development or "working-out" of thematic material, Rimsky-Korsakov adopted a mosaic-like approach to the many and varied transformations of the theme using a procedure not dissimilar to Glinka's *changing background* technique. The resulting kaleidoscopic range of textures, harmonies, and tone color is often breathtakingly beautiful, and nowhere does the underlying mono-thematicism pall.

M. F. Gnessin's description of Rimsky-Korsakov's creative procedures in general applies particularly well to his Concerto:

> [He] starts with the careful choice of a rich and expressive central idea . . . which is the first and essentially vivid link in a series of vivid links, from which the artistic whole is gradually built up. Thematic repetitions, constant reminders of the idea, ensure against the introduction of elements which have no direct relation to the plan. . . . Melodic-rhythmic variations on the theme in different sections of the work, by enriching it with important and sometimes unexpected details, make the chief features and idea of the theme all the more strongly felt. The surrounding of the theme by constantly changing harmonies illumines it on all sides. The variation of exposition plays

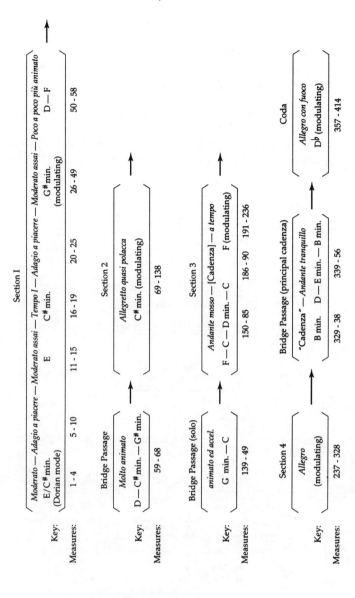

Fig. II.   Rimsky-Korsakov, Piano Concerto in C-sharp minor

its part in the interpretation of the theme. The moments when the theme is transposed into different tonalities intensify its apprehension and make it felt as it were in different surroundings, while at the same time they *quantitatively* intensify the impression created by the theme. These are all ways of *analysing* the theme which is being impressed on the listener. . . .[73]

The thematic idea on which the concerto is based, the folk song "Sobiraites'-ka, brattsy-rebiatushki," was chosen "not without Balakirev's advice";[74] as mentioned earlier, it comes from Balakirev's collection of forty folk songs published in 1866 (see Ex. 3-35). The folk song was fairly widely

Ex. 3-35. "Sobiraites'-ka, brattsy-rebiatushki," in Balakirev, 40 *Russian Folk Songs.*

known in Russia during the nineteenth century and was subsequently published in several other collections. It was apparently a military recruitment song of the type known as "heavy," because of the difficulties of performance, and it was greatly valued. Rimsky-Korsakov was not the only composer to make use of its beautiful, mournful Dorian-mode characteristics. Eduard Napravnik incorporated the song in his *Folk Dance* for orchestra (1875–76), M. Slavinsky arranged it for voice and piano, and most significant of all, Balakirev used variants of it in the first movement of his Piano Sonata (see Ex. 3-11a) and throughout the Piano Concerto in E-flat, most notably, in the opening theme and the subsidiary subject of the second movement (Exx. 3-11d and e). A variant of the folk song—almost identical to the opening of Rimsky-Korsakov's concerto—also appears in Rachmaninov's beautiful *Etude-tableau* in D minor, Op. 33, No. 5[75] (see Ex. 3-36). Although Rimsky-Korsakov's treatment of the song is ingenious and exhaustive, employing all manner of compositional device, such as fragmentation, inversion, retrograde (see Ex. 3-37), and canon (Ex. 3-38a),[76] this artifice never detracts from the inherent beauty of the folk song. Nor is it readily apparent. The tabulation in Ex. 3-37 clarifies the more important derivations.

Perhaps the most striking feature of Rimsky-Korsakov's process of metamorphosis is that each fragment—usually derived from the first or the second phrase of the theme (see Ex. 3-37b, a b)—is melodically as attractive as the original folk song. This quality, which is rare among works based on thematic transformation, is probably the most potent factor in the success of the concerto and is even more remarkable since all the fragments

Ex. 3-36. a. Rimsky-Korsakov, Piano Concerto in C-sharp minor, Op. 30, mm. 1-4 (transposed); b. Rachmaninov, *Etude-tableau*, Op. 33, No. 5 (Op. posth.), mm. 53-55.

Ex. 3-37. Rimsky-Korsakov, Piano Concerto in C-sharp minor: a. mm. 1-3; b. mm. 5-10; c. C, mm. 7-9; d. C, mm. 16-17; e. C, mm. 28-31; f. E, mm. 3-7; g. E, mm. 19-21; h. F, mm. 1-2; i. F, mm. 3-5; j. F, mm. 9-10; k. G, mm. 15-16; l. K, mm. 7-11; m. M, mm. 7-10; n. Cadenza, M, mm. 20-21; o. Coda, M, mm. 38-39.

Ex. 3-38. Rimsky-Korsakov, Piano Concerto in C-sharp minor: a. m. 10; b. F,
mm. 19-22; c. M , mm. 12-14.

are derived from one source. Also remarkable is the variety of moods
encompassed, ranging from the somewhat pensive folk song itself through
the wistfully lyrical *Andante mosso* themes (Exx. 3-37i, j, and k) and ending
with the fiery coda (Ex. 3-37), which bears no resemblance to the folk song,
though its origin becomes clear if one retraces one's steps through Exx.
3-37k–h–e.

In addition to basing the Concerto's thematic material on the folk song,
Rimsky-Korsakov constructed all the cadenzas and many of the accompaniment figurations, in both the orchestra and the soloist's parts, on fragments of "Sobiraites'-ka" (see Ex. 3-38). As Exx. 3-38b and c clearly illustrate, he was fully capable of writing idiomatically for the piano. Balakirev
was not only astonished by this discovery but may even have considered
some of Rimsky-Korsakov's pianistic figurations fine enough to use in his
own piano works. Ex. 3-39 shows instances of this in Balakirev's Mazurka
in D (which forms the second movement of his Piano Sonata, the first
movement of which, as noted on p. 65, is based on the same folk song as
Rimsky-Korsakov's Concerto).

Borodin may also have been influenced pianistically by Rimsky-Korsakov, as there is a similarity in layout between an accompaniment figuration
from his Scherzo in A-flat (1885) and a left-hand pattern from the first
section of Rimsky-Korsakov's Concerto (see Ex. 3-40). In the coda of the
Concerto, however, Rimsky-Korsakov borrowed a left-hand figuration

Ex. 3-39.   a. Rimsky-Korsakov, Piano Concerto in C-sharp minor, [F], mm. 9-10; b. Balakirev, Mazurka No. 5, in D, mm. 147-50; c. Rimsky-Korsakov, Concerto, [M], mm. 23-26; d. Balakirev, Mazurka, mm. 225-28.

from "Limoges," the seventh number in Musorgsky's *Pictures from an Exhibition* (see Ex. 3-41).

Not all of Rimsky-Korsakov's compatriots considered the piano writing in his Concerto idiomatic. In an interview published in *The Etude* in 1923, Rachmaninov stated:

> I believe in what might be called indigenous music for the piano; that is, music which the Germans would describe as "klaviermässig." So much has been written for the instrument that is really alien. Brahms is a notable

Ex. 3-40. a. Borodin, Scherzo in A-flat, mm. 14-15; b. Rimsky-Korsakov, Piano Concerto in C-sharp minor, E, mm. 31-32.

Ex. 3-41. a. Musorgsky, "Limoges," mm. 3–4; b. Rimsky-Korsakov, Piano Concerto in C-sharp minor, P, mm. 18-19.

> example. Rimsky-Korsakov is possibly the greatest of Russian composers; yet no one ever plays his concerto in these days, because it is not klaviermässig. On the other hand the concertos of Tchaikovsky are frequently heard because they lie well under the fingers![77]

It is curious that Rachmaninov should have cited Tchaikovsky's concertos as being *klaviermässig,* for the piano writing of the Concerto No. 1, in B-flat minor, the only one he actually performed, is now widely recognized as being "orchestral" in concept and not idiomatically written for the instrument. Admittedly, several passages in Rimsky-Korsakov's Concerto are awkward, particularly when the soloist is in contention with the orchestra. However, these difficulties, which are mainly related to stretch, are infrequent and are easily negotiated by pianists with a large span. Rachmaninov would not have had any problem with the passage in Ex. 3-42.

Rimsky-Korsakov's Concerto, which was published in Leipzig in 1886, was first performed in St. Petersburg by N. S. Lavrov at a Free School Concert on 27 February 1884. It was favorably reviewed by Cui, who praised its "thematic and harmonic details, its modulations and unusual delicacy and irresistible splendor."[78] However, Cui considered the ending "too compact" and that, as a whole, the Concerto was "more of an orchestral piece with piano obbligato." His first criticism is perhaps justified, for the coda is just a little too frenetic in its modulations and too heavily scored

Ex. 3-42. Rimsky-Korsakov, Piano Concerto in C-sharp minor, C̄, mm. 6-7.

to complement the more transparent, leisurely paced preceding sections. His second criticism, however, is without foundation, for in addition to the solo cadenzas, the impressive passages of double octaves, the sweeping glissandi (inspired by Liszt's Second Concerto), and other virtuosic artifacts, the piano part contains a fair proportion of thematic material, which it presents simply, yet effectively. Indeed, the role of the soloist is beautifully calculated, either being in contest with the orchestra or complementing it with arabesque-like figurations derived from the folk song. Only in the first half of the coda is there a tendency for soloist and orchestra to vie for attention at the same time—this is often a weak moment in concerto writing.

Lyapunov

The Piano Concerto in E-flat minor, Op. 4, by Sergei Lyapunov, composed between 1888 and 1890, is also cast in one movement and also reveals similar cyclical resemblances to Liszt's concertos, to which it is indebted. According to Lyapunov's correspondence with Balakirev, his close friend and mentor, during June and July 1888, the composition of the new concerto did not come easily, though Lyapunov was pleased with the soloist's part. The main stumbling block, so he informed Balakirev, was the *Andante* movement—a problem which he also encountered in his First Symphony. Balakirev suggested that he study the concertos of Chopin, the *Larghetto* of Henselt's Piano Concerto, and the *Andante* movement of Arensky's Concerto. But Lyapunov found it impossible to reconcile the cyclical elements in his concerto with the introduction of a separate, self-contained slow movement. Instead, he compromised and incorporated an *Adagio non tanto* episode, in the unrelated key of D, a favorite key of Balakirev's, into a multisectional single-movement design: "As your concerto is in E-flat minor," wrote Balakirev, "then for the *Andante* the best key would be B major or D major as a perfect contrast in its color or brightness with the gloomy E-flat minor."[79]

Lyapunov's difficulties with his First Piano Concerto chiefly stem from his inability to handle large-scale structures. Unlike Balakirev, who possessed an uncanny talent for producing convincing broadly canvased works through often very unconventional means, Lyapunov lacked architectural foresight, and his large works are sometimes fragmentary in effect.

c.

Ex. 3-43. Lyapunov, Piano Concerto No. 1, in E-flat minor, p. 4: a. first section, mm. 1-21; b. second section, mm. 14-19; c. third section, mm. 93-106.

The E-flat minor Concerto is constructed in sonata allegro form and is unusual in that its thematic material is stated in reverse order in the recapitulation (suggesting that Lyapunov was acquainted with Rubinstein's Third and Fifth Piano Concertos, which both employ this rare procedure). Lyapunov's thematic material, though not particularly striking, is pleasantly evocative in its national characteristics; in both its underlying harmonies and pianistic treatment, it is very close to Balakirev's style (see Ex. 3-43). Indeed, Lyapunov's Concerto was greatly influenced by Balakirev, who may have recomposed parts of it.[80] Even during the final stages of the composition, Balakirev could not refrain from meddling: "Your concerto has been copied out. It was necessary to alter one or two passages where the harmonies did not agree at the end."[81] However, as Calvocoressi pointed out,

> despite all the spiritual affinities between the two, Liapunov, as a composer, remained very different from Balakirev. His music is more purely lyrical, less vehement, fundamentally contemplative. He was endowed with a keen sense of colour and poetry, but not with the burning energy (and attendant restlessness of imagination) that characterizes Balakirev. . . .[82]

Many would dispute these somewhat sweeping generalizations, particularly in regard to Lyapunov's later Piano Concerto (in E, Op. 38) and the resplendent *Transcendental Studies*. However, with respect to the early Concerto in E-flat minor, there is perhaps a grain of truth in Calvocoressi's remarks, for the work's more robust episodes sound contrived, and the soloist's virtuoso passage-work is forced and lacking in spontaneity. Nevertheless, Lyapunov's First Concerto enjoyed some success after its première on 8 April 1891,[83] and it was taken up by many eminent pianists, including Hofmann, Igumnov, and V. I. Scriabin (the wife of the composer Alexander Scriabin).

Rachmaninov

In the late 1880s the young Rachmaninov was making his first tentative steps in the direction of concerto writing. Fourteen pages of sketches for a piano concerto in C minor, dating from November 1889, are deposited in the Rachmaninov Room in the State Central Museum of Musical Culture in Moscow. The composition did not come easily to the sixteen-year-old boy, as indicated by the many changes and deletions (including the crossing-out of seven pages of a cadenza). Though the work is clearly that of an apprentice,[84] characteristics of his more mature style, such as syncopation and rising and falling sequential melodic patterns, are found from the outset in the short sketches of the opening orchestral tutti (see Ex. 3-44). The sketch of the soloist's entry is also stylistically interesting, being a hodgepodge of other, more-celebrated concerto openings (in particular the concertos of Grieg and Schumann). It is more likely, however, that Rachmaninov was imitating the pianistic style of Tchaikovsky's First Concerto (and, indirectly, the source of Tchaikovsky's inspiration, Rubinstein's Octet in D minor; compare Ex. 3-45 with Exx. 2-1a and 2-2). Certainly, Tchaikovsky's Second Piano Concerto provided the inspiration for the opening passage of double octaves of the revised version (1917) of Rach-

Ex. 3-44. Rachmaninov, projected piano concerto in C minor, first movement (unfinished), mm. 1-8.

Ex. 3-45. Rachmaninov, projected piano concerto in C minor, first movement. mm. 245-46.

maninov's first published piano concerto, in F-sharp minor, Op. 1 (see Ex. 3-46).

Rachmaninov first mentioned this concerto in a letter to his cousin Natalya Skalon, dated 26 March 1891:

> In your letter you asked me what I am now composing. A piano concerto. Two movements have already been written down,[85] the last movement is composed but not yet written; I will probably finish the whole concerto by late spring, and then during the summer orchestrate it.[86]

The last two movements were composed and written down in great haste, as Rachmaninov informed his close friend Mikhail Slonov in a letter dated 20 July:

> On 6 July I finished composing and scoring my piano concerto. I could have completed it much sooner, but after the first movement I idled for a long time

Ex. 3-46. a. Tchaikovsky, Piano Concerto No. 2, in G, Op. 44, first movement, mm. 195-97; b. Rachmaninov, Piano Concerto No. 1, in F-sharp minor, Op. 1 (revised version, 1917), first movement, mm. 1-5.

and began to write the remaining movements on 3 July. I composed and
scored the last two movements in two and a half days. You can imagine what
a job that was. I wrote from five in the morning till eight in the evening, so
after finishing the work I was terribly tired. Afterwards I rested for a few
days. While working I never feel fatigue (on the contrary—pleasure). With
me, fatigue appears only when I realise a big labour is finished. I am pleased
with the concerto. . . .[87]

The first performance of the new work took place on 17 March 1892 at a
students concert at the Moscow Conservatory, conducted by the Director,
V. I. Safonov, with Rachmaninov as soloist. The concert was on a grand
scale, consisting in the main of concertos, concerto movements, and arias
by eleven composers, including Saint-Saëns, Rubinstein, Mendelssohn,
and Gluck. It ended with Scriabin playing Liszt's Piano Concerto in E-flat.
Rachmaninov's Concerto was ninth on the program and apparently made
"an agreeable impression" on the critic A. H. C., who pointed out in
particular the "unquestionable skill already at his [Rachmaninov's] disposi-
tion," though he noted that due to nerves, the performance as a whole was
not completely "self-assured."[88] Rachmaninov's nervousness may in part
be attributed to the importance of the occasion, and his agitation was
probably exacerbated by his disagreements with Safonov during rehearsals
over tempi and Safonov's repeated suggestions on how to improve the
work. Rachmaninov's relationship with the Director was not, in any case,
particularly amiable at the best of times.

The initial idea of composing the Concerto in F-sharp minor probably
occurred while Rachmaninov was spending his summer holidays on the
Satins'[89] country estate, Ivanovka, in 1890. There he heard, on an almost
daily basis, Grieg's Piano Concerto in A minor, as his cousin Alexander
Siloti was practicing it in preparation for forthcoming concerts. The influence of Grieg's Concerto imprints itself not only on Rachmaninov's
piano style but also substantially on the principal musical ideas of the new
concerto (see Exx. 3-47, 3-48, 3-49). Grieg's Concerto may also have suggested to Rachmaninov the interpolation of a slower interlude (in D major,
Andante expressivo) in the finale.

Though Rachmaninov never performed Grieg's Piano Concerto,[90] he
greatly admired it, particularly from a pianistic point of view. In his 1923
interview in *The Etude*, he stated that "although he [Grieg] could not be
classed as a great master pianist, [he] had the gift of writing beautifully for
the piano and in pure 'klaviermässig' style."

Rachmaninov's Piano Concerto in F-sharp minor was published in 1893.
Though at first the new work was favorably received, Rachmaninov soon
became aware of its deficiencies—the unimaginative scoring, densely
chordal piano writing, and episodic passages of little structural or thematic
significance. The borrowings from Grieg's Concerto may also have embarrassed him, for in the revised version of 1917, they were either excised

Ex. 3-47.   a. Rachmaninov, Piano Concerto No. I (original version, 1891), first movement, mm. 1-4; b. Grieg, Piano Concerto in A minor, Op. 16, first movement, mm. 1-4.

altogether or refined to such an extent that the influence of Grieg was no longer immediately apparent (compare Ex. 3-50 with Ex. 3-49b).

Rachmaninov clearly regretted the premature publication of his First Concerto.[91] In 1897 he even toyed with the idea of composing a new and finer work to erase the memory of it, though these plans came to nothing. About ten years later he returned to his Op. I and voiced his intention, in a letter to Nikita Morozov, dated 30 March 1908, to revise it completely:

> Tomorrow I plan to take my first concerto in hand, look it over, and then decide how much time and work will be required for its new version, and whether it's worth doing anyway. There are so many requests for this concerto, but it's so awful in its present state. . . . Of course, it will have to be completely rewritten, for its orchestration is worse than its music. So tomor-

Ex. 3-48. a. Grieg, Piano Concerto in A minor, first movement, mm. 26-27; b. Rachmaninov, Piano Concerto No. 1 (1891 version), mm. 1-6; c. Grieg, Piano Concerto in A minor, third movement, H , mm. 25-26.

row I'll come to a decision concerning this matter and I'd like to decide in the affirmative.

I have three pieces that frighten me: the first concerto, the Capriccio, and the first Symphony. How I should like to see all of these in a corrected, decent form![92]

It was nine years before Rachmaninov achieved his objective. The revised Concerto was completed on 10 November 1917 and handed to the publisher Koussevitzky just weeks before Rachmaninov left Russia in self-imposed exile.[93]

Though it was a unique and masterly reworking of youthful ideas undertaken at the height of Rachmaninov's creative powers, this "Cinderella" of a concerto has always remained in the formidable shadows of its two

Ex. 3-49. a. Rachmaninov, Piano Concerto No. 1 (1891 version), third movement, mm. 1-3; b. Grieg, Piano Concerto in A minor, third movement, mm. 1-6.

elder (though far from ugly) sister works, the piano concertos in C minor and D minor (Op. 18 and Op. 30 respectively), and unless fashions change, it is likely to remain so despite its undeniable merits and freshness of appeal.

Scriabin

Fashions certainly do change, however, as exemplified by the varying fortunes of Scriabin's Piano Concerto in F-sharp minor (1896–97), one of

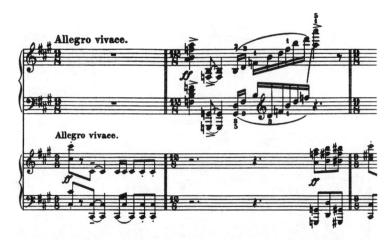

Ex. 3-50.   Rachmaninov, Piano Concerto No. 1 (1891 version), third movement, mm. 1-5.

the finest nineteenth-century Russian piano concertos. Today, this work is fairly regularly performed and is appreciated for its lyrical beauties and delicate, transparent scoring. Several decades ago, however, it was all but forgotten. Abraham Veinus's otherwise excellent volume *The Concerto* (1944, revised 1964) makes no mention of the work or its composer, although attention is paid to inferior concertos which are now hardly ever performed, such as those of Moscheles and Paderewski.

The idea for Scriabin's first published work outside of an exclusively piano-solo idiom[94] came to the composer some time in the autumn of 1896; it is first mentioned on 12 October in a letter to his publisher Beliaev. The following month Scriabin informed him that the concerto was finished and that he had begun to orchestrate it. The final stages of composition took longer than anticipated and were laced with uncertainty: "I can say nothing about the Concerto for the present—innate doubt prevents me."[95] Early the following year, Scriabin was still working at the orchestration, adding the finishing touches to the variations in the second movement and supervising the arrangement for two pianos made by his fiancée, Vera Isaakovich.[96] When Beliaev finally received the manuscript in April 1897, he immediately sent it to Rimsky-Korsakov and Lyapunov, who had agreed to examine any new work Beliaev intended to publish. Rimsky-Korsakov was so furious at the shoddy workmanship, inaccuracies, and general untidiness of the score that he felt compelled to reprimand Scriabin, who was subsequently deeply embarrassed and hurried to make amends:

> I have just received your letter, which plunged me into depression. There is nothing I can say to vindicate myself apart from one or two small things which prevent me from concentrating in general and writing the score in

particular. This is neuralgia, and I've been suffering from it for several days now. I am so ashamed!! I will do *everything that I can* to sort out the rest of the concerto now. . . .[97]

By the middle of May, Beliaev was, understandably, beginning to lose his patience, as Scriabin was still toying with the orchestration of the second and third movements: "You promised not to keep the rest of the Concerto and now you feed me 'tomorrows.' You are wrecking my stomach. . . ."[98] When Beliaev finally received the completed score, he again forwarded it to Rimsky-Korsakov, whose remarks were again highly critical, this time in connection with the orchestration. Having lost Rimsky-Korsakov's address, Scriabin was unable to reply. However, in a letter to Lyadov dated 14 May, he poured out his indignation at Rimsky-Korsakov's strictures and at the same time gave a rare, lucid account of his creative processes:

> Yesterday I received a letter from Nikolai Andreevich [Rimsky Korsakov] which grieved me. I am very grateful to him for his kind help, but has he wasted all this time on the Concerto only to say the orchestration is weak? Since he is so kind couldn't he have noted those places which seem to him most weak and explain why?
>
> To orchestrate a concerto, you don't have to have written several symphonies or preliminary exercises. Nikolai Andreevich says that a concerto is very difficult to orchestrate and that it is easier to write for orchestra alone.
>
> Let us suppose that all this is true. But that is for an *ideal* orchestration. What *I* want for my first try is a *decent* orchestration. This goal can be reached through advice and a little help from people who know. It is easy to say "study orchestration," but there is only one way, and that is to hear one's own composition *performed*. Trial and error is the best teacher.
>
> Now, if I don't hear my music, and nobody tells me anything, then how can I learn? I have read scores, am reading, and will of course continue to read them, but I always come up against the same thing . . . the need for wisdom's experience.
>
> I am working every day, but it leads nowhere. I can make as many inventions and combinations as I like. I can create patterns Nikolai Andreevich himself never dreamed of. But *without practice*, this adds up to naught.
>
> Forgive me for prattling on. But all this is rather painful for me. I had counted Nikolai Andreevich as good, good, and now I see he is only kind. At any rate, I am *ashamed* to have bothered him and I will not repeat that mistake *in the future*. I will manage on my own. Advise me, please, what should I do? In any case send me the score (you have it). I will reorchestrate it and answer for it myself.
>
> Sergei Ivanovich [Taneyev] is so generous, he wants to do everything to make the orchestration a success. He is working with me. . . .[99]

Despite Scriabin's intention to reorchestrate the concerto in collaboration with Taneyev, a comparison of the original manuscript with the score as published by Beliaev in 1898 reveals no significant alterations, despite the many comments scribbled by Rimsky-Korsakov on the score: "How sloppy to put rests *here!*" "To hell with this!" "Why *this* suddenly?!" When he handed over the score to Lyadov, Rimsky-Korsakov enclosed a covering note of undisguised rancor:

> Look at this filth, *I* have! There is much I don't understand. It is beyond my powers. I am in no condition to cope with such a mush-headed genius. Best to let the composer publish it for two pianos and have someone else orchestrate it. . . . As for me, I have cleaner work to do, I have no time to scrub Scriabin.[100]

However, the Soviet philosopher and musicologist Valentin Asmus points out in his introduction to Scriabin's letters that when Rimsky-Korsakov passed judgment on the demerits and imperfections in Scriabin, they were the demerits and imperfections of a genius. And, indeed, in his autobiography, Rimsky-Korsakov referred to Scriabin rather ambiguously as "that star of first magnitude, newly risen in Moscow, the somewhat warped, posing, and self-opinionated A. N. Scriabin."[101] So underneath the vitriol, the sarcasm, and the apparent animosity, there lay admiration and, as Rimsky-Korsakov admitted to his friend and secretary Vasily Yastrebtsev in a moment of self-confession, professional jealousy: "I found in myself clear indications of Salieri. To a degree, I am irritated by the success of Chaliapin, Scriabin, Nikisch, d'Alheim, and others. I behave more kindheartedly with a talented mediocrity."[102]

The first performance of Scriabin's Piano Concerto took place on 11 October in Odessa, conducted by Safonov with the composer as soloist. All went well, according to a letter from Scriabin to Beliaev written the day after.[103] Safonov confirmed this in a letter to Cui: "Yesterday the Odessa programme went brilliantly. Scriabin had enormous success with his remarkable concerto. . . ."[104] By 10 December 1898, when the Concerto was first heard in St. Petersburg, Rimsky-Korsakov had apparently changed his opinion of the new work and even made it known that he was willing to conduct the Concerto if there was the possibility of another performance in the capital. His strictures must have still rankled, for Scriabin was to have none of it. Instead, he and Safonov took the Concerto to Moscow, where it was given its première performance in that city on 30 March 1899. Ironically, the critic Yuri Engel singled out Scriabin's orchestration for particular praise.

It is difficult to comprehend Rimsky-Korsakov's objections to the Concerto. Clearly his critical faculties were momentarily obscured by emotions which he was unable to suppress, for as Bowers states, "No more inoffensive or domesticated music exists."[105] Indeed, this very quality could be considered the Concerto's principal weakness, for the work treads so lightly that no new ground is broken, and stylistically it stays well within the comfortable Chopinesque idiom typical of Scriabin's early style. The soloist's part, though technically exacting, eschews conventional virtuosity and rarely takes center stage. There is not even a cadenza for the soloist to come to grips with. The Concerto is a beautifully crafted musical *collaboration* between piano and orchestra, as opposed to the more traditional *confrontation* found in the concertos of Scriabin's contemporaries, and from this point of view it is almost unique in Russian concerto literature. Perhaps this in itself could be considered innovative.

The most immediately striking quality of Scriabin's Concerto is the constantly changing flow of the thematic ideas, themselves often diffuse or fragmentary, reflecting perhaps the quicksilver, vacillating mental processes of the composer himself. There is, in fact, a parallel between the overall character of the Concerto and a description of its composer by the Russian musicologist Leonid Sabaneev:

> This fearfully restless, minute man lacked the power which inner psychic muscles give, which Wagner, for instance, that no less active and expansive man, had.
>
> Of course, the matter does not rest in their nervousness or their small stature. It is something else, something that shines through their work. Scriabin lacked *power*, but he had a burning, blinding unearthly joy. . . . His exterior and his psyche were in strange harmony with his half-childish caprices which showed up in his quick changes of mood, his sudden drop in spirits. . . . His delicacy and refinement were the product of his early pampering and advantages.[106]

Sabaneev's epithets—"restless," "joyful," "capricious," "delicate," and "refined"—summarize to perfection the varied moods of this elegant concerto. So too does the suggestion that Scriabin lacked power, for the work is sketched in pastel shades rather than the strong primary colors of, say, the concertos of Tchaikovsky or Rachmaninov, and it is dwarfed by them in terms of emotional range and depth.

Structurally, Scriabin's Concerto adheres closely to traditional concerto form with the exception of the slow movement, which is in the form of theme and variations. The seemingly spontaneous, improvisatory nature of the music conceals a very closely wrought structure, as do almost all Scriabin's larger-scale compositions. The Concerto also contains a hint of the intensively organized harmonic-melodic system on which almost all his mature works were to be based, for its opening subject is constructed on a descending sequence of three-note figures, indicated in the score by accents (see Ex. 3-51).

Faubion Bowers quotes an important discussion between Sabaneev and the mature Scriabin concerning the composer's creative processes and their application in the early piano concerto:

> For this strange man of fantasy, how doubly odd that so much came "from his head." His creativity in music was half-intuitive, a half if not more,

Ex. 3-51.   Scriabin, Piano Concerto in F-sharp minor, Op. 20, first movement,
mm. 8-14.

constructed as logically as geometry. He himself told me that he rarely
"improvised" themes, that rather he formalized them. He loved to show
these "rational constructions" in his compositions, after they were written.

"Thought must always be present in composition and in the creation of
themes. It is expressed by means of *principle*. Principle guides creation. I
create my themes mainly by principle, so they will have concordant proportion.

"Take for example my Concerto. The bedrock of its design is the descending sequence of notes. Against this background the whole theme grows and
unfurls." He played me the theme of the Concerto and accented these
descending steps richly, and the melody took on quite a different meaning
and sense.[107]

These three-note "nuclei" (see Ex. 3-51) were subsequently to play an
important role in the development of the first movement, particularly in
the bridge passage leading to the recapitulation (and thus back to the first
subject, from which the pattern is derived). The charming second movement, *Tema con Variazioni*, is supposedly based on a theme composed
during Scriabin's childhood. The theme itself is unremarkable, being wholly diatonic and sequentially repetitive. Its treatment, however, is imaginative. Of particular interest is the second variation, which transforms the
Andante theme into a rousing *Allegro scherzando* cameo characterized by
sprightly syncopated staccato chords and octaves. The third variation is a
lugubrious *Adagio* exploiting the lower range of the piano (Ex. 3-52).

The most immediately appealing of the three movements is the rondo
finale, for its leading thematic ideas, though not as profound as in the first
movement or as scintillatingly decorated as in the second, are more virile in
concept. The principal theme (shown in Ex. 3-53) is a splendid example.
The episodic theme shown in Ex. 3-54, which appears later in the movement, is typical of Scriabin's soaring melodies during his so-called early
period. Pianistically, though, its layout anticipates the many melodic-
chordal figurations found in his "transitional" works—the *prestissimo* finale
of the Fourth Sonata, Op. 30, and the first subject of the Fifth Sonata, Op.
53. The left-hand accompaniment, however, is based on a figuration first
extensively employed in Scriabin's most famous piano work: the Etude in

Ex. 3-52.   Scriabin, Piano Concerto in F-sharp minor, second movement, Variation 3, mm. 1-4.

D-sharp minor, Op. 8, No. 12, the influence of which saturates much of the piano writing in the rondo's episodes. The second episode also contains an unashamed borrowing from the lovely Prelude in C minor, Op. 11, No. 20, composed in 1895. One can hardly blame Scriabin—it is a phrase of exceptional beauty (see Ex. 3-55). Rather than conclude his Concerto with an aggrandized version of the second theme (Ex. 3-54), in the manner of Tchaikovsky or Rachmaninov, Scriabin based his coda on a tiny fragment of melody extracted from the first movement—the four-bar corollary to the first subject. Understandably enough, the tonalities are different, as Scriabin's intention in the coda was to bring the Concerto to a close in a blaze of F-sharp major. From all other aspects—orchestration, piano writing, etc.—the two passages are more or less synonymous (see Ex. 3-56). So efficiently does this thematic interloper fulfil its function and so naturally does it grow from the main body of the rondo that its presence usually passes by unnoticed, even by experts in the field.[108]

Ex. 3-53. Scriabin, Piano Concerto in F-sharp minor, third movement, mm. 1-4.

Ex. 3-54. Scriabin, Piano Concerto in F-sharp minor, third movement, ③, mm. 1-6.

Scriabin was to make much use of thematic recall in later compositions, and as he endeavored more and more to translate his creative dictum "From the greatest delicacy (refinement) via active efficacy (flight) to the greatest grandiosity" into musical terms, so these "recalls" became increasingly important.[109]

a.

b.

Ex. 3-55.   a, Scriabin, Prelude in C minor, Op. 11, No. 20, mm. 4-6; b. Scriabin, Piano Concerto in F-sharp minor, third movement, 14, mm. 15-16.

a.

Ex. 3-56. Scriabin, Piano Concerto in F-sharp minor: a. first movement, ⓘ, mm. 19-22; b. third movement, ⒘, mm. 12-16.

b.

Ex. 3-56. (continued)

4
The Piano Concertos
of Peter Tchaikovsky

Concerto No. 1

There is no tonal blend, indeed the piano cannot blend with the rest, having an elasticity of tone that separates from any other body of sound, but there are two forces possessed of equal rights, i.e., the powerful, inexhaustibly richly coloured orchestra, with which there struggles and over which there triumphs (given a talented performer) a small, insignificant but strong-minded rival. In this struggle there is much poetry and a whole mass of enticing combinations of sound for the composer. . . . To my mind, the piano can be effective in only three situations: (1) alone, (2) in a contest with the orchestra, (3) as accompaniment, i.e., the background of a picture.

Thus Peter Tchaikovsky wrote to Nadezhda von Meck, on 24 October 1880.[1] In the autumn of 1874, he had began work on what was to become, despite an unpromising start, one of the most popular and frequently performed piano concertos in the repertoire: the Piano Concerto in B-flat minor, Op. 23. Tchaikovsky's decision to embark on a piano concerto as his next major work after the opera *Vakula the Smith* is curious, considering his antipathy toward the genre during his student days[2] and his dislike, in particular, of the combination of piano and strings. During the years following his graduation from the St. Petersburg Conservatory in 1865, however, it appears that his tastes in matters of structure and, more important, instrumental timbres (to which he was especially sensitive), underwent a dramatic reappraisal. It is difficult to imagine how Tchaikovsky could have tolerated, let alone conceived, the Introduction to the First Piano Concerto (scored almost exclusively for piano and strings), not to mention the quasi–triple concerto for violin, cello, and piano (the *Andante non troppo* movement of the Second Piano Concerto in G, Op. 44), unless he had discovered some way of reconciling these two seemingly disparate elements. Perhaps Tchaikovsky's initial antipathy toward the piano concerto stemmed not so much from an instinctive dislike of the tonal juxtaposition of piano and orchestra but from a realization of the immense difficulty of combining the two forces and a growing awareness of his inexperience at dealing with them.

Whatever the reasons behind this antipathy, Tchaikovsky nevertheless appreciated other composers' concertos (an ambivalence referred to by his brother Modest as a "platonic hatred"). He considered Litolff's *Concerto Symphonique* in D minor, for instance, as "one of the most brilliant works in piano literature." He also admired Liszt's *Todtentanz*, and, while listening to a performance of Liszt's Concerto in E-flat, he scribbled the word "brilliant" on his concert program.

Most nineteenth-century piano concertos were created by composer-virtuosi as vehicles for their own use, but this was clearly not the case with Tchaikovsky. Though he was technically capable of playing his own piano works, as testified by his private performance of the First Concerto just three days after it had been completed (see p. 116),[3] temperamentally he was unsuited to the rigors of the concert platform and was more than willing to step back and allow others the attendant glory.

So the question still remains: what factor or factors encouraged Tchaikovsky to undertake a large-scale musical form unfamiliar to him? It is possible that the Piano Concerto in B-flat minor may have been composed specifically for his friend and colleague Nikolai Rubinstein. This is hinted at in a letter Tchaikovsky wrote to his brother Anatoli, dated 21 November 1874: "I am now totally immersed in the composition of the piano concerto. I am particularly anxious that [Nikolai] Rubinstein should perform it at his concert. . . ."[4]

On the other hand, the concerto may have been written for the German pianist and conductor Hans von Bülow, to whom it was eventually dedicated. Tchaikovsky greatly admired his playing (he first heard Bülow in St. Petersburg in 1864). When Bülow gave a recital at the Bolshoi Theatre in Moscow in March 1874, the year the First Concerto was composed, Tchaikovsky wrote a very flattering review, praising, above all, the "passionate intellectuality" of his playing. Bülow quickly reciprocated, writing to a friend that he intended to play Tchaikovsky's Variations, Op. 19, in a forthcoming concert. Furthermore, some two months later, while reviewing the Milan première of Glinka's *A Life for the Tsar* for the *Allgemeine deutsche Musik-Zeitung*, Bülow mentioned in glowing terms Tchaikovsky's First Quartet, his first two symphonies, and, in particular, the Overture *Romeo and Juliet*. Tchaikovsky was very grateful for this commendation—which doubtless boosted his reputation in Europe—and in May 1875, as a token of gratitude, sent him the score of the First Concerto by way of the publisher Karl Klindworth, entrusting Bülow with its first performance. Bülow replied to Tchaikovsky on 1 June: "I am proud of the honor bestowed on me to première this work, which is delightful from every point of view."[5] The première took place in Town Hall, Boston, on 25 October 1875, conducted by Benjamin Johnson Lang.

Whatever the inspiration behind the First Piano Concerto, its composition was an ordeal for Tchaikovsky, as his correspondence reveals. On 26 November 1874 he wrote to his brother Modest: "I'm submerged with all my soul in the composition of the piano concerto; the thing is advancing, but very badly."[6] The difficulties encountered probably concerned the piano part, for the rest of the Concerto is comparatively free of the kind of flaws so often indicative of a troublesome incipience, and only minor alterations in the orchestral part were deemed necessary in the subsequent preparation of the Concerto's second and third editions (1879 and 1889 respectively). In the same letter of 21 November 1874 to his brother Anatoli that expressed the wish that Rubinstein perform the new concerto, Tchaikovsky mentions the difficulties he had in writing the soloist's part: "The work progresses very slowly and doesn't come at all easily. I push myself on principle and force my brain to think out piano passages; the result is nervous irritability."[7]

It was for this reason that he sought advice from Nikolai Rubinstein. On 21 January 1878, Tchaikovsky wrote to von Meck:

> As I am not a pianist, it was necessary to consult some virtuoso as to what might be ineffective, impracticable and ungrateful in my technique. I needed a severe, but at the same time, friendly critic, to point out in my work these extreme blemishes only.

Apparently, he already had reservations about playing for Rubinstein, for the letter continues:

> Without going into details, I must mention the fact that some inward voice warned me against the choice of Nikolai Rubinstein as a judge of the technical side of my composition. However, as he was not only the best pianist in Moscow, but also a first-rate all-round musician, and knowing that he would be deeply offended if he heard I had taken my concerto to anyone else, I decided to ask him to hear the work and give me his opinion of the solo part.[8]

Tchaikovsky subsequently played his First Concerto for Rubinstein on Christmas Eve, 1874 (5 January 1875 according to the new-style calendar). Also present were Tchaikovsky's former fellow student Nikolai Hubert and Nikolai Kashkin, a music critic and professor at the Conservatory. Instead of complying with Tchaikovsky's wishes and limiting his comments to the piano part, Rubinstein set out, with what appears to be near maniacal fury, to condemn the concerto as whole. As Tchaikovsky continued in his letter:

> [Rubinstein considered] my concerto was worthless, absolutely unplayable; the passages so broken, so disconnected, so unskillfully written, that they could not even be improved; the work itself was bad, trivial, common; here and there I had stolen from other people; only one or two pages were worth anything; all the rest had better been destroyed, or entirely rewritten. . . .[9]

Tchaikovsky's emotionally heightened account of what happened (written some three years after the event) was probably induced by a fit of pique over Rubinstein's meddling in his private affairs.[10] Nevertheless, as will become clear later on, a few of Rubinstein's comments are not without justification, particularly, his observation that passages were unskillfully written and that Tchaikovsky had "stolen" from other people.

Despite Tchaikovsky's initial apprehension about composing a work for piano and orchestra and his shortcomings in matters of piano style, what eventually emerged was a truly magnificent concerto. In fact, the soloist's part is very fine (disregarding for a moment, the comparatively superficial blemishes noted by Rubinstein, which were amended in the second edition [1879]; see below) and was very efficiently integrated into the texture of the concerto. One surmises that perhaps the difficulties Tchaikovsky mentioned in his letter of 21 November 1874 to Anatoli were not so much connected with the piano writing *per se* as with the problems of combining the soloist's part with the orchestra. Indeed, except for an occasional passage where the piano tends to be overwhelmed, a fault common to many otherwise excellent concertos, the balance and integration are superbly achieved. In this respect the success of the First Concerto is mainly due to the "orchestral" conception of Tchaikovsky's piano style. Many key passages in the soloist's part (for example, the statement of the opening movement's second subject [Ex. 4-1b] and the *Andantino semplice* second theme [Ex. 4-1d]) are little more than transcriptions of the orchestral score—a procedure that is perhaps pianistically unimaginative but supremely effective musically, as it creates a strong sense of thematic homogeneity and continuity. Furthermore, the orchestral quality of the piano writing in the First Concerto discouraged Tchaikovsky from indulging in the inconsequential note-spinning so prevalent at the time. Though the soloist's part is rich in complex virtuosic passages, these passages are invariably conceived in accordance with the underlying musical ideas.

Tchaikovsky ignored Rubinstein's probably sound advice on how to improve the piano part: "I shall not alter a single note," he declared, "I shall publish the work precisely as it stands."[11] The Concerto was brought out, without amendment, by Jurgenson in 1875, though he published only the orchestral parts and an arrangement for two pianos; the full score of the first edition was not published until 1955, in Volume 28 of the Soviet Complete Edition.

Immediately after the Moscow première,[12] in December 1875, Tchaikovsky apparently experienced a change of heart, for he decided to undertake some revisions after all. He wrote to Hans von Bülow of his intentions— presumably because Bülow was the only person to have shown genuine interest in the new work—and received the following reply:

You write to me that you want to make some changes in your Concerto? I shall, of course, receive them with great interest—but I should like to express my opinion that they are not at all necessary—except some enrichment of the piano part in certain tuttis, which I took it upon myself to make, as I also did

Ex. 4-1. Tchaikovsky, Piano Concerto No. 1, in B-flat minor, Op. 23, first movement: a. E mm. 1-4; b. E, mm. 9-12; second movement: c. mm. 24-26; d. mm. 28-30.

in Raff's concerto. And allow me one other observation: the great effect of the finale loses something if the triumphant 2nd motive, before the last stretta, is played "molto meno mosso."[13]

The Strasbourg-born pianist Edward Dannreuther, who gave the English première of the concerto at the Crystal Palace on 23 March 1876, sent Tchaikovsky further and more extensive suggestions. As James Friskin points out, "His approach must have been considerably more tactful then Rubinstein's,"[14] as Dannreuther received a most cordial reply from the composer. The letter, which was first published in the *Musical Times* of November 1907, thanked Dannreuther for his "very sensible and practical suggestions" and assured him these amendments would be incorporated into the Concerto "as soon as the question of a second edition arises." Tchaikovsky was true to his word, for Dannreuther's suggestions (which are almost entirely confined to the piano part of the first movement and involve some 140 bars) were incorporated into the second edition, published by Jurgenson in August 1879, both as a full score "revised and corrected by the composer," and as an arrangement for two pianos.[15]

A closer examination of the first and second editions reveals not only how efficiently Dannreuther revised the "unskillfully written" piano part but also, in the light of these amendments, how justified Nikolai Rubinstein was in his criticisms.[16] The first major revision involves the redistribution of notes forming the piano's opening chords[17] (see Ex. 4-2). Dannreuther then proceeded to facilitate other awkward chordal passages by rearranging the left-hand part into more manageable close-position chords (see Ex. 4-3). The left hand is also modified in an important solo passage (bars 144–47) found between the two principal statements of the first

Ex. 4-2. Tchaikovsky, Piano Concerto No. 1, first movement, mm. 1-3: a. second edition; b. first edition.

a.

Ex. 4-3. Tchaikovsky, Piano Concerto No. 1, first movement, Ⓐ, mm. 11-12:
a. second edition; b. first edition.

subject (shown in Ex. 4-4). More-drastic revisions occur in mm. 252, 430–
43, and 635–40 (see Ex. 4-5).

Whereas the revisions shown in Exx. 4-2, 4-3, and 4-4 are mainly concerned with facilitating unnecessarily awkward passages stemming from
Tchaikovsky's inexperience in writing virtuoso piano music, Exx. 4-5a, c,
and e go a stage further in that they alter his initial conception by bringing
the soloist's part more to the fore. Dannreuther achieved this by exploiting
more fully the piano's percussive capabilities, either by welding together

a.

Ex. 4-4. Tchaikovsky, Piano Concerto No. 1, first movement, Ⓒ, mm. 13-14:
a. second edition; b. first edition.

Ex. 4-5. Tchaikovsky, Piano Concerto No. 1, first movement, G , m. 7: a. second edition; b. first edition; M , mm. 19-20: c. second edition; d. first edition; P , mm. 124-26: e. second edition; f. first edition.

the sixteenth notes in Tchaikovsky's original part into octaves and octave chords (as in Ex. 4-5c) or (as in Ex. 4-5e) by eliminating the arpeggios altogether and substituting a chordal accompaniment (the lowest notes of which venture into a register unexploited by the orchestra). Being an experienced pianist, Dannreuther was aware, of course, that octaves and octave chords produce considerably more volume than do arpeggios, as they can normally be struck from a height.

Even with Dannreuther's improvements Tchaikovsky was not entirely satisfied with his Concerto. During the winter of 1888–89, while preparing a third edition of it for Jurgenson, he consulted the pianist Alexander Siloti, a former pupil of Liszt, who had become one of the Concerto's leading exponents.[18]

Tchaikovsky revised several tempo markings, including modifying the *Andante non troppo* in the Introduction to *Allegro non troppo e molto maestoso* (see Ex. 4-6b) and changing the middle section of the second movement from *Allegro vivace assai* to *Prestissimo*.[19] He replaced seventeen bars in the finale (a passage he whimsically referred to as "die verfluchte Stelle") with five bars of more suitable material and made extensive changes to the layout of the soloist's introductory chords (see Ex. 4-6b). It is a matter of some conjecture as to whether Tchaikovsky was, in fact, responsible for this last drastic revision; as Friskin argues:

> It is hard to believe that Tchaikovsky, admittedly not an expert pianist, would have so far departed from his original conception as to rewrite it in a manner

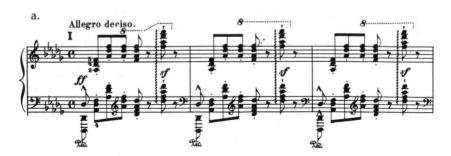

Ex. 4-6. a. Liszt, Piano Concerto No. 2, in A, [I], mm. 1-3; b. Tchaikovsky, Piano Concerto No. 1, first movement, mm. 6-8.

that tempts the soloist, as it almost invariably does, to overpower the main theme, marked merely mezzo forte in the orchestra.[20]

Friskin surmises, therefore, that the "influence of some keyboard virtuoso would seem more probable."[21] He cites Siloti as a possible contender, adding that such a treatment was, according to many who knew him, "characteristic of his pianism." A devoted admirer of Liszt, Siloti may have suggested to Tchaikovsky a pianistic reappraisal of the Introduction similar to the *Allegro deciso* section of Liszt's Second Concerto (see Ex. 4-6).

The initial source of inspiration, however, had more humble origins: the incomplete and unpublished Nocturne in C minor by Siloti's fourteen-year-old cousin, Sergei Rachmaninov (Ex. 4-7). The Nocturne, the last of a set of three, was composed on 12 January 1888, the same year that Tchaikovsky and Siloti embarked on the revisions of Tchaikovsky's First Concerto. In the spring, Rachmaninov was promoted to the senior department of the Moscow Conservatory where he entered Siloti's piano class. As the Nocturnes were his first serious attempt at piano composition, it can be assumed that Rachmaninov played them for Siloti, particularly as Siloti was "family" and had already shown a keen interest in his young cousin's musical development. Later that year, with the majestic chordal writing of the final Nocturne still fresh in his memory, Siloti may have sketched the version of the introductory chords of Tchaikovsky's Concerto that we know today. Siloti's daughter Kyriena, herself a pianist, has repudiated so direct an involvement by her father, so it is more likely that Siloti suggested

Ex. 4-7. Rachmaninov, Nocturne in C minor (unpublished), middle section, mm. 1-12.

to Tchaikovsky a revision of the soloist's part based on Rachmaninov's
C-minor Nocturne and that Tchaikovsky himself penned the final version.

Another keyboard virtuoso who might also have influenced Tchaikovsky's decision to rethink the soloist's part was Dannreuther, whose role in
the development of Tchaikovsky's First Concerto is generally considered to
have ended with the second edition of 1879. Dannreuther, however, continued his correspondence with Tchaikovsky after 1879—or at least resumed it a few years later—as he played host to the Russian composer at
his home in London in the late 1880s. According to Dannreuther's son
Hubert, their meeting, which was conducted in French, was most cordial.
As Dannreuther was intimately involved in the Concerto's development
and was in part responsible for its enormous success—for which
Tchaikovsky must have been very grateful—it seems reasonable to assume
that the First Concerto was a major topic of conversation. Certainly
Tchaikovsky would have been receptive to any further ideas Dannreuther
might have had concerning the piano part and may even have pressed him
for them. Indeed, this might have been the reason for Tchaikovsky's visit
in the first place.[22]

The influence of Anton Rubinstein's Fifth Piano Concerto on Tchaikovsky's Introduction (see above, pp. 43–44) is also a possibility that merits
consideration; certainly from a purely pianistic point of view, Rubinstein's
codetta material from the first movement of his Concerto bears a striking
resemblance to Tchaikovsky's chordal writing (compare Exx. 4-8 and 4-6b).

The question of Anton Rubinstein's influence on Tchaikovsky's First
Concerto, which, as has already been demonstrated, was decidedly more
widespread than hitherto acknowledged, leads one conveniently to another criticism by Nikolai Rubinstein: that Tchaikovsky had "stolen from
other people." Although Tchaikovsky did not specify in his letter to
Nadezhda von Meck the composers he had been accused of "stealing"
from, one could hazard a guess that Nikolai Rubinstein's brother Anton

Ex. 4-8. Rubinstein, Piano Concerto No. 5, in E-flat, Op. 94, first movement,
mm. 264-67.

figured prominently among them, considering the extensive and incontrovertible evidence to that effect[23] (see pp. 43–49). It is difficult, however, to imagine who else Nikolai Rubinstein had in mind. Certainly the pianistic layout of several passages superficially resemble sections of Balakirev's essay in transcendental virtuosity, the Oriental fantasy *Islamey*, composed in 1869. Both Rubinstein and Tchaikovsky knew the work well. In fact, Tchaikovsky was present during much of the composition of *Islamey* and it was through his friendship with Jurgenson that the piece was subsequently published in 1870. As Tchaikovsky was to all intents and purposes a nationalist during the period he conceived his First Concerto, it would seem only natural that he would have had some interest in what was, until Musorgsky composed *Pictures from an Exhibition* in 1874, the only significant large-scale Russian piano composition to date. However, although *Islamey* could have provided Tchaikovsky with a wealth of useful Lisztian pianistic features spiced with rhythmic and melodic idiosyncrasies of Russian folk song, its influence on Tchaikovsky's First Piano Concerto is negligible, being confined to passage-work of little structural or thematic significance (Ex. 4-9).

As for Nikolai Rubinstein's remaining strictures—that passages in the First Concerto were "broken, disconnected" and that the work as a whole was "worthless, absolutely unplayable; bad, trivial and common"—history has proved otherwise. It must be remembered, however, that Rubinstein heard the Concerto only once, which was hardly sufficient to assess a

Ex. 4-9.   a. Balakirev, *Islamey*, m. 264; b. Tchaikovsky, Piano Concerto No. 1, first movement, P, m. 68; Balakirev, *Islamey*: c. m. 154; d. m. 244; e. Tchaikovsky, Piano Concerto No. 1, second movement, S, m. 28.

difficult and complex work, and the performance itself was presumably in a form which did little justice to its musical merits. Nevertheless, one performance was apparently enough for his musical perceptiveness, heightened perhaps by a tinge of jealousy, to have rooted out the Concerto's principal weaknesses. It is surprising therefore that Rubinstein did not comment on what has generally been considered the concerto's most glaring defect—the Introduction.

Much has been written about this famous passage, particularly concerning its apparent extraneousness. Eric Blom, for example, wrote:

> The great tune's strutting upon the stage at the rise of the curtain, like an actor-manager in a leading part, and then vanishing suddenly and completely, leaves the hearer disconcerted and dissatisfied. He feels as though he were witnessing a performance of Hamlet in which the Prince of Denmark is killed by Polonius at the end of the first scene. It is this even more than its appearing in the wrong dress of D flat major which makes Tchaikovsky's introduction, for all its magnificence, or at least magniloquence, one of the most baffling solecisms in the music of any great composer.[24]

So disconcerted was Blom by the theme's isolated occurrence at the beginning of the concerto that, in an attempt to justify its existence, he put forward the theory that Tchaikovsky may have intended to reintroduce the theme later on in the Concerto.[25] Blom even sketched a combination of the introductory theme and the second subject of the finale—a somewhat pointless undertaking as Tchaikovsky would never have contemplated such a procedure[26] (Ex. 4-10).

In fairness to Blom, however, just as he considered that Tchaikovsky

Ex. 4-10.   Eric Blom, sketch for a combination of the introductory theme and the second subject of the finale of Tchaikovsky's Piano Concerto No. 1.

was perhaps "groping towards"[27] the reintroduction of his opening theme into the finale, so Blom himself was groping intuitively toward the explanation of the Introduction's function which is generally accepted today:

> Is it too fantastic to suggest that Tchaikovsky had some sort of return of his initial theme up his sleeve and really did intend it to assume the function of a "motto" but that somehow in the heat of composition he failed to let this part of his plan take shape? One cannot do more than formulate some such theory, but it is quite possible to make it appear credible if one takes the trouble to think it out.[28]

As recent analytical studies have revealed, Tchaikovsky did indeed reintroduce the opening theme, not in the form of a direct statement, but broken up into fragments and scattered among the principal thematic material of the rest of the Concerto. To be more precise, the introductory theme—the contours of which were possibly derived from the Ukrainian folk song "Oi, kriache, kriache, chernyi voron" (Oh, caw, caw, black raven),[29] which serves as the first subject of the ensuing exposition—represents a rich source of melodic fragments on which the majority of the Concerto's themes are based (see Exx. 4-11 and 4-12). The initial discovery of the thematic interconnections in the First Concerto, though still unacknowledged in the West, was made by the Soviet musicologist Alexander Alekseev who wrote, in 1969, "The themes of the concerto have a lot in common, and they grow out of the Introduction."[30]

Alekseev also offers a novel explanation of the discrepancy between the initial statement of the slow movement's principal theme (see Ex. 4-11e, b')[31] and the movement's remaining statements (Ex. 4-11f, b") by suggesting that the melody itself is derived from bars 6 and 7 of the Introduction's theme (Ex. 4-11a, b' and b"). Less convincing, however, is his conjecture that the first subject of the finale (Ex. 4-11g, c') is derived from the first subject of the first movement (Ex. 4-11b) or vice versa. Both themes, as is well known, are Ukrainian folk songs, so any resemblance is purely incidental and is, in any case, irrelevant to the issue of Tchaikovsky's thematic procedures.

Alekseev's belief that the Introduction to Tchaikovsky's First Piano Concerto represents a "prologue to the work" and that its "grandiose melody contains germs of forthcoming themes"[32] has been recently substantiated in the West by Edward Garden and David Brown.[33] Brown's tabulation of the thematic interrelationships (which also incorporate Garden's discoveries) is so comprehensive and well structured that it merits being quoted in its entirety. The interconnections shown in Ex. 4-12 speak for themselves.

Brown also toys with the idea that Tchaikovsky may have consciously introduced ciphers into his thematic material—hence the pEtEr tsCHAikowsky and DESirée Artôt in Exx. 4-12a and b, on which the opening theme and the second subject are supposedly constructed.[34] If this

Ex. 4-11. Tchaikovsky, Piano Concerto No. 1, analysis according to Alekseev: a. first movement, introductory theme; b. first movement, first subject; c. first movement, second subject, opening theme; d. first movement, second subject "muted-strings" theme; e. second movement, principal theme, first statement; f. second movement, principal theme, later statement; g. third movement, first subject.

is true, Tchaikovsky was probably influenced by Schumann, who employed a similar system of ciphers in his Piano Concerto in A minor, Op. 54, composed some thirty years earlier. Schumann derived almost all of its thematic material from letters taken from his own name, sCHumAnn (curiously, the same notes and in the same order as those found in Tchaikovsky's name when transliterated), and that of his wife, Clara, using the diminutive form CHiArinA. Regarding Tchaikovsky's thematic interconnections as a whole, however, Brown is quick to point out that they were probably "casual" and not deliberately thought out:

> It is, in fact, difficult to believe that Tchaikovsky invented his own melodies with such cold-blooded calculation as [Ex. 4-12] might suggest; rather these thematic relationships seem to have sprung from a particularly intensive application of those natural habits of mind that had produced the families of themes we have already noted in certain earlier compositions, including the recent "Vakula." The opening theme of the concerto is as heavily involved in these relationships as any.[35]

Ex. 4-12.   David Brown, *Tchaikovsky*, vol. 2, *The Crisis Years*, Ex. 97, p.23.

The opening theme and the harmonies underlying the first two bars of the Concerto (Exx. 4-12h, i) are not the only thematic and harmonic features exploited later in the Concerto, though they are the most important, particularly the former. For example, the last five notes of the opening thematic statement of the Concerto (preceding the principal theme; Ex. 4-13a) have considerable significance in the development section commencing at the *Alla breve* (Ex. 4-13b). Furthermore, the descending triplet sixteenths in the Cadenza between the first and second statements of the introductory theme (Ex. 4-14a, which may have been derived from the last three notes of Ex. 4-13a) were probably the idea behind the stunning fortissimo double octaves which occur between the second statement of the two themes and which constitute the second subject (Ex. 4-14b).

Ex. 4-13. Tchaikovsky, Piano Concerto No. 1, first movement: a. mm. 1-6; b. Ⓚ, mm. 15-18.

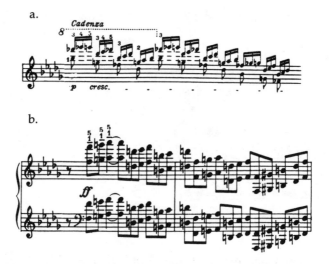

Ex. 4-14. Tchaikovsky, Piano Concerto No. 1, first movement: a. m. 48; b. Ⓖ, mm. 8-9.

The development section of the first movement also employs, fairly extensively, the pianissimo trumpet fanfare (from the closing section of the Introduction)[36] which heralds the first statement of the first subject (Ex. 4-15). Initially, this fanfare motif appears in the same instruments (trumpets in F). After four bars it is reinforced by horns and announced fortissimo. On the other hand, the similarity between the piano's *accelerando* double octaves leading into the Introduction's cadenza and the French chansonette "Il faut s'amuser, danser et rire," the principal theme of the

Ex. 4-15. Tchaikovsky, Piano Concerto No. 1, first movement, B, mm. 16- 19, trumpets in F.

slow movement's middle section, is perhaps fortuitous. As an example of Tchaikovsky's thematic unity on a subliminal level, it is most illuminating (see Ex. 4-16).

A further connection between the Introduction and the remainder of the Concerto involves the tail-end of the opening theme's antecedent phrase (shown in Ex. 4-17). This rhythmic pattern, either in its original form or in a variant which omits the quarter note tied to the triplet eighth, reappears several times in the Introduction. This is not in itself unusual (see Ex. 4-18), but the pattern assumes an important role in the rest of the movement, most notably in the soloist's double octaves (see Ex. 4-14b) and in the accompaniment to the second part of the second subject group (see Ex. 4-19). (This style of accompaniment, according to Edward Garden, was first introduced by Glinka in the Persian Chorus of his opera *Ruslan and Lyudmila.*[37]) The pattern is also used extensively, in both original and variant forms, in the principal cadenza (Ex. 4-20; see also Ex. 4-9b).

a.

Ex. 4-16. Tchaikovsky, Piano Concerto No. 1,: a. second movement ["Il faut s'amuser"], T, mm. 1-4 (transposed); b. first movement, mm. 32-34.

Ex. 4-17. Tchaikovsky, Piano Concerto No. 1, first movement, mm. 15-16.

Ex. 4-18. Tchaikovsky, Piano Concerto No. 1, first movement: a. mm. 31-32; b. mm. 36-37; c. B, mm. 1-2.

Ex. 4-19. Tchaikovsky, Piano Concerto No. 1, first movement, H, mm. 1-4.

Ex. 4-20. Tchaikovsky, Piano Concerto No. 1, first movement, P, mm. 83-84.

In addition to the superb original melodies in the First Piano Concerto, in particular, the dual themes of the first movement's second subject and the principal theme of the slow movement, Tchaikovsky incorporated three borrowed melodies—the French chansonette "Il faut s'amuser, danser et rire" and two Ukrainian folk songs—and may also have used a variant of another folk song, "Podoydu, podoydu vo Tsar-Gorod," in the finale.

The first borrowed melody to be employed was noted down by Tchaikovsky while staying with his sister and brother-in-law at Kamen-ka,[38] in the Ukraine. It was identified by G. A. Tumenev as "Oi, kriache, kriache, chernyi voron" (Oh, caw, caw, black raven; see above, Note 29). It assumes the important role of the opening movement's first subject (Ex. 4-11b). Although some consider the song lacking in thematic appeal ("pal-try in the extreme," according to Blom[39]), in the context of the concerto as a whole, i.e., sandwiched between the almost excessive lyricism of the opening theme and the sweet melodiousness of the second subject, its rhythmic bite and quirky melodic contours provide welcome and necessary contrast.[40]

The second borrowed melody, "Il faut s'amuser, danser et rire," which was popular in Russia around the time the First Concerto was composed,[41] is incorporated in the prestissimo section of the second movement (Ex. 4-12d). The chansonette has a motivic significance, insofar as its rocking character has much in common with the first movement's second subject (compare Exx. 4-12d and e), the consequent phrase of the opening melody, and the theme of the first movement's coda (mm. 2 and 3 in Ex. 4-12j). In addition, it provides the main thematic interest in a section which, accord-ing to Alekseev, represents the equivalent of a scherzo in a four-movement concerto.

The third borrowed theme is a Ukrainian round dance entitled "Viidi, viidi, Ivanku" (Come, come, Ivanka), which Tchaikovsky took from A. V. Rubets's collection of 216 Ukrainian folk songs published by Jurgenson in 1872. It is employed as the first subject of the finale. Although it is rhythmically and melodically repetitive almost to the point of monotony (a feature of Ukrainian dance tunes), the folk song is preserved in its original form (Ex. 4-21). Tchaikovsky even retains its two-voice character by scoring the soloist's part in thirds—yet another example of his habit of creating piano passage-work by directly transcribing the original material (Ex. 4-22).

Until recently, these three melodies have been considered the only borrowed thematic material incorporated in the Concerto. However, Hen-ry Zajaczkowski suggests that another folk song may have been employed:

> The Introduction theme is similar to an actual folk theme, "Podoydu, podoydu vo Tsar-Gorod" (which incidentially is almost certainly the direct model for the D flat subject of the finale)—No. 30 in Tchaikovsky's collection of 50 Russian folk songs. . . .[42]

It is difficult to see how Zajaczkowski finds similarities between this folk song and the opening theme of the First Piano Concerto. However, his

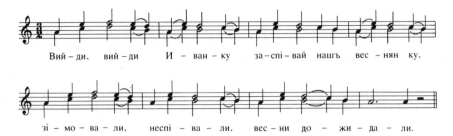

Ex. 4-21.   "Viidi, viidi, Ivanku," a Ukrainian round dance.

Ex. 4-22.   Tchaikovsky, Piano Concerto No. 1, third movement, mm. 5-12.

Ex. 4-23.   a. Tchaikovsky, Piano Concerto No. 1, third movement, second subject; b. the folk song "Podoydu podoydu vo Tsar-Gorod."

theory that it may have been a model for the finale's second subject is quite convincing (see Ex. 4-23).[43]

Tchaikovsky was not unaccustomed to using folk song in such a manner. As David Brown points out in connection with Tchaikovsky's treatment of folk song in the incidental music to Ostrovsky's play *The Snow Maiden* (composed a year before the First Piano Concerto):

Nothing reveals more clearly Tchaikovsky's attitude towards folksong than his treatment of these borrowed melodies. . . . For him the people's musical artifacts were not sacred, even if they were precious. If folksongs needed modification or supplementation to suit their broader function in his work, then modified or supplemented they would be, for he had faith enough in their capacity to retain a recognisable character of their own, even when so changed.[44]

Tchaikovsky also incorporated four folk songs in his opera *Vakula the Smith*—the last large-scale work he undertook before composing the First Piano Concerto—and his treatment of them is very similar to that in *The Snow Maiden*. It comes as no surprise, therefore, to discover that, in addition to direct quotations of folk material (i.e., Ukrainian dance tunes), his First Piano Concerto should also contain a melody, hitherto regarded as original, which uses a folk song as a prototype.

The close thematic relationships inherent in the Concerto's melodies significantly influenced his overall structural considerations and encouraged Tchaikovsky to adopt a strategy of symphonic development which he had previously eschewed (a notable exception being the original version of the Second Symphony, Op. 17). Indeed, in the majority of works composed before the First Piano Concerto, the self-contained nature of the thematic material tended to demand an episodic rather than a developmental approach. As John Warrack observed:

[Tchaikovsky was] too successful a melodist. [His] basic act of invention was not structural and hence symphonic, but melodic. The melody that is of itself complete will obviously not be susceptible of development: as Taneyev pointed out, it can do little more than be repeated. . . .[45]

But even episodic construction tends to expose any structural deficiencies a composer might have, particularly in the welding together of thematic chunks. Tchaikovsky was well aware of his own weaknesses in this matter:

I cannot complain of poverty of imagination, or lack of inventive power; but, on the other hand, I have always suffered from my lack of skill in the management of form. Only after strenuous labor have I at last succeeded in making the form of my compositions correspond, more or less, with their contents. Formerly I was careless and did not give sufficient attention to the critical overhauling of my sketches. Consequently my seams showed, and there was no organic union between my individual episodes. This was a very serious defect, and I only improved gradually as time went on; but the form of my works will never be exemplary, because, although I can modify, I cannot radically alter the essential qualities of my musical temperament.[46]

With the exception of the First Piano Concerto, all of Tchaikovsky's works for piano and orchestra suffer in varying degrees from this structural defect. The worst is the Second Concerto; whether because of boredom, apathy, or a growing dislike for the musical ideas he was working with, Tchaikovsky made little attempt to forge "organic unions" between the blocks of thematic material.

In the First Concerto, on the other hand, the "seams," which are stitched in a variety of styles, are neatly concealed and are, in any case, interesting in themselves. A fine example is the dovetailing between the first and second subjects of the opening movement. Tchaikovsky eliminates the transition altogether (as in the original version of the Second Symphony's first movement) and inserts two bars from the second subject into the concluding bars of the first. Eric Blom muses over this compositional procedure:

> This occurs so naturally that one could not possibly say whether Tchaikov-sky had first invented the second subject independently and then devised this premonition of it or whether the snatch quoted in the second bar of [Ex. 4-24] first came to him as an indefinite glimmer and gradually developed into a theme; and it is precisely this impossibility of detecting his procedure which proves that we have here an example of spontaneous ingenuity, not of mere mechanical contrivance.[47]

The procedure adopted by Tchaikovsky is not really so difficult to detect; the "indefinite glimmer" referred to by Blom is, in fact, derived from the contours of the first subject (Ex. 4-25). What we have, therefore, is

Ex. 4-24.   Tchaikovsky, Piano Concerto No. 1, first movement, D, mm. 33-40.

Ex. 4-25.   Tchaikovsky, Piano Concerto No. 1, first movement, ☐, m. 35-36.

not merely an adroit overlapping of two important and distinctive themes but an organic development of one theme from another, cemented together through a process of dovetailing.

Tchaikovsky refrains from using a similar procedure to forge a connection between the constituent themes of the dual second subject. Instead (as shown in Ex. 4-26), he extends the final phrase of the first theme with reminders of the opening of the Concerto,[48] x, in dialogue with a fragment from the first subject, y. He then overlaps the concluding bars of the second subject's second (muted-strings) theme with the return of the first, exploiting the rocking figure of descending fifths and fourths which concludes the former in order to establish some form of thematic link (Ex. 4-27).

Having found a solution to his "eternal transition problem," to quote David Brown, Tchaikovsky was then confronted with the formidable task of providing the opening movement with a development section of matching ingenuity. Thematic transformation again assumes a primary role, and Tchaikovsky makes this objective clear at the very outset in an orchestral ritornello based initially on the "muted-strings" theme of the second subject interspersed with fragments of the first subject (Ex. 4-28).

Deprived of its legato slurs, the second subject immediately reveals a more aggressive side to its character and subsequently undergoes an even

Ex. 4-26.   Tchaikovsky, Piano Concerto No. 1, first movement, ☐, mm. 13-18.

Ex. 4-27.   Tchaikovsky, Piano Concerto No. 1, first movement, Ⓔ, mm. 25-31.

Ex. 4-28.   Tchaikovsky, Piano Concerto No. 1, first movement, Ⓘ, mm. 1-4.

more dramatic transformation. In order to create a flowing eighth-note figuration to counterbalance its symmetrical, martial character and, at the same time, generate a useful accompaniment pattern, Tchaikovsky doubles the original tempo and obsessively exploits the theme's first four notes (Ex. 4-29). The transformation first appears some four bars earlier in the bassoons, accompanying a motif unmistakably derived from mm. 2 and 3 of the Introduction's principal subject (Ex. 4-30). Ex. 4-29a is then inverted to accompany its former self, now stated *forte* and *poco accelerando*, while the trumpet fanfare motif from the Introduction (see Ex. 4-15) contributes more weight to the texture. The last five notes of the Concerto's opening

a.

b.

Ex. 4-29.   Tchaikovsky, Piano Concerto No. 1, first movement: a. Ⓘ, mm. 12-13; b. "muted-strings" theme (transposed).

Ex. 4-30.   Tchaikovsky, Piano Concerto No. 1, first movement, ☐, mm. 9-10.

theme (Ex. 4-11a) are then powerfully invoked in the form of triplet quarter notes, which then disintegrate into a descending eighth-note pattern based on the inversion of Ex. 4-30, which was initially derived from the second subject, "muted-strings" theme (Ex. 4-29b).

The brief cadenza that follows, like the cadenza in Tchaikovsky's Third Piano Concerto (see p. 166), is skillfully integrated into the development and is predominantly based on an ingenious transformation of the wood-wind theme of the second subject (Ex. 4-31). After a short bridge passage, an apparently new motif appears in an impassioned dialogue with itself over some forty bars, first on the piano alone and then joined by the orchestra (Ex. 4-32). Since almost every thematic fragment to appear so far in this movement is derived from earlier material, it seems unlikely that Tchaikovsky would have introduced a new idea into such an important section of the development. In fact, on closer examination, this "thematic interloper"[49] reveals itself to be a further example of Tchaikovsky's thematic transformation—on this occasion a fragment of the first subject previously employed in a quasi-developmental capacity in the exposition (Ex. 4-33).

The final section of the development (which superficially resembles the opening section) gradually resumes thematic normality, with fragments of the first and second subjects resourcefully distributed among the orchestra, accompanied by arabesquelike passage-work in the soloist's part. Its function is very much one of preparation for the return of the first subject proper, which immediately follows.

In the recapitulation, Tchaikovsky's principal intention was, first, to reduce or eliminate thematic material that has been extensively used in the

a.

Ex. 4-31.   Tchaikovsky, Piano Concerto No. 1, first movement: a. ☐, mm. 9-10; b. ☐, mm. 38-39.

Ex. 4-32.   Tchaikovsky, Piano Concerto No. 1, first movement, ⌷L⌷ mm. 1-5.

Ex. 4-33.   Tchaikovsky, Piano Concerto No. 1, first movement: a. ⌷K⌷, mm. 52-53; b. ⌷B⌷ m. 47 (transposed).

development—hence the isolated statement of the first subject and the omission of the second subject's "strings" theme—and, second, to generate a feeling of excitement, movement, and impending resolution by excluding material of a more quiescent nature. Much to his credit, little compromise seems to have been necessary to achieve both objectives, and the flow from one thematic idea to another is efficiently accomplished without resort to structural artifice.

The principal cadenza of the first movement, which replaces the recapitulation's closing section, forms an organic link between the recapitulation and the coda, and is itself developmental in character. Following closely the scheme of the cadenza of Rubinstein's Fourth Piano Concerto (see pp. 44–47), it is bipartite in construction (with a recitative-style link to the coda) and contains thematic references to all the principal subjects.

The first section of the Cadenza begins with a dialogue between the first three notes of the second subject's "wind" theme, x, and a four-note motif from the link passage between this theme and its "muted-strings" counterpart, y, which was itself initially derived from the first subject (see Ex. 4-34). The accompaniment, which closely resembles Rubinstein's Cadenza opening (see Ex. 2-34a), grows organically out of the piano's arpeggiated chords of the conclusion of the preceding section.

The "muted-strings" theme of the second subject makes its first appearance since the development in a form similar in character to its initial statement in the exposition. It adopts the same broken-chord accompaniment as in Ex. 4-34, with the additional complexity of a trill figuration executed by the same hand. The following section of the Cadenza is devoted to reflective statements of the second subject "strings" theme interspersed with aggressive octaves based on the triplet eighth-note rhythm of the introductory theme's tail-end (Ex. 4-11a), followed by the sequential treatment of the second subject's "strings" theme. After a build-up in tension modeled on the closing section of Rubinstein's Cadenza, the first subject makes a veiled appearance (in the original key of B-flat minor; Ex. 4-35).

The *Quasi Adagio* section, which brings the Cadenza to a close and which also functions as a link to the coda, is devoted to further contemplation of the so-called Artôt motif. The coda is ushered in by the same rhythmically

Ex. 4-34. Tchaikovsky, Piano Concerto No. 1, first movement, P, mm. 25-33.

Ex. 4-35. Tchaikovsky, Piano Concerto No. 1, first movement, P, m. 65.

augmented version of the second subject's "strings" theme that was extensively exploited in the development. After a complete and more or less exact statement, a hybrid melody appears (see Ex. 4-12j) and dominates the remainder of the coda. Motivically, this closing theme represents a counterpart to the Introduction's principal subject (Ex. 4-11a), for it not only contains references to the Concerto's opening theme but also inherits the rocking pattern from the second subject group.

Tchaikovsky was never again able to compose a concerto movement of comparable precision, structural ingenuity, and lyrical invention. It was as if the mold had been broken immediately after its completion. Nevertheless, the remaining movements of the First Piano Concerto, though less complex thematically and also perhaps emotionally, beautifully complement the intricate and impulsive drama of the first movement by their sustained melodic appeal and structural clarity.

The *Andantino semplice* second movement, as already noted, incorporates the French chansonette "Il faut s'amuser, danser et rire" in its *prestissimo* middle section.[50] It "neatly combines two structural blueprints," according to David Brown, "ternary in respect of speed scheme, simple rondo with regard to thematic recurrence and key."[51] (see Fig. III).

Tchaikovsky appears to abandon his former preoccupation with thematic interrelationships, as none of the themes is motivically connected to any other.[52] Nevertheless, he considered structural unity sufficiently important to have inserted fragments of the principal melody into the link passage between sections B and A (i.e., ABA'CA"), and, more significantly, he reintroduced the introduction to B into the *prestissimo* middle section. The somewhat gauche character and the structural incongruity of Ex. 4-36a suggest that Tchaikovsky may have originally conceived it at a faster tempo, the *prestissimo* of Ex. 4-36b, and inserted it earlier in the movement as an afterthought. Apart from some melodic imitation based on fragments of "Il faut s'amuser, danser et rire" in the *prestissimo* section, no substantial thematic development takes place in this movement. Instead, Tchaikovsky adopts a *changing background* technique, à la Glinka, to vary each successive statement of the subject material. Particularly attractive is the statement by two solo cellos of the principal theme (in section A²), accompanied by sixteenth-note chords in the piano part, which are rhythmically derived from the preceding B section (Ex. 4-37).

Schubert's "Trout" Quintet, in A major, may have been the model for the second half of this section,[53] for the piano's syncopated chordal accompaniment is reminiscent of the fifth variation of the quintet's fourth movement. The unison trills which immediately precede this section (a feature of both the fifth variation of the fourth movement and the slow movement of the "Trout" Quintet) also suggest Schubert's influence, as does the more extensive use of trills in Tchaikovsky's coda. The central *prestissimo* section, on the other hand, reflects the influence of Chopin. In

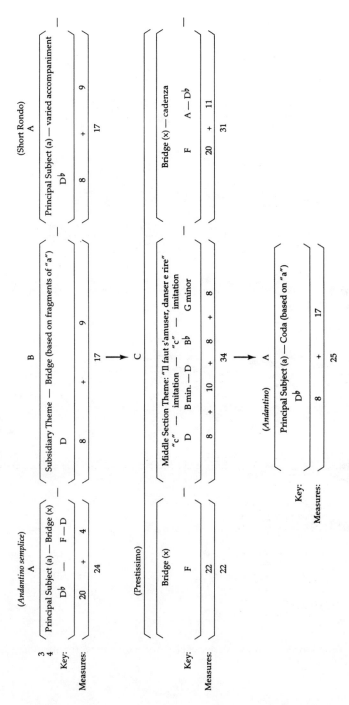

Fig. III. Tchaikovsky, Piano Concerto No. 1, second movement

Ex. 4-36. Tchaikovsky, Piano Concerto No. 1, second movement: a. mm. 22-25; b. ⑤, mm. 19-22.

Ex. 4-37. Tchaikovsky, Piano Concerto No. 1, second movement, mm. 1-4.

particular, the vertiginous octave sixteenth-note passage-work recalls the finale of the Sonata in B-flat minor, Op. 35, and the outbursts of chromaticism are reminiscent of the Etude in E major, Op. 10, No. 3 (see Ex. 4-38). Less convincing perhaps, and fanciful to boot, is the possibility that Tchaikovsky's cello counter-melody in the "Schubertian" section, mentioned above, may have given Rachmaninov the thematic basis for one of his most famous melodies—the second-subject theme of the first movement of his Concerto in C minor (Ex. 4-39).

Much has been written about the thematic inconsistency of the principal theme's opening bar. It has led to a wide variety of hypotheses, from Alekseev's plausible idea that it was influenced by the contours of the Concerto's introductory theme to the belief of performers, conductors, and even publishers[54] that it is a mistake on either Tchaikovsky's or the printer's part that warrants correction. Eric Blom's more moderate viewpoint is generally considered acceptable:

> It is quite possible that Tchaikovsky, having first hit on the less striking form of the phrase and then introduced the more telling one in the piano part, decided to let the discrepancy stand in order to give the solo an added importance by making it heighten the significance of his theme.[55]

Perhaps the contemplative *Quasi Andante* section of the first movement's principal cadenza provides an answer, for contained within its first five

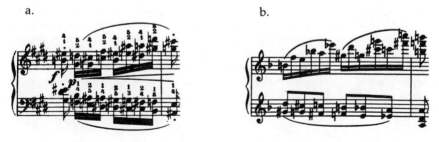

Ex. 4-38. a. Chopin, Etude in E, Op. 10, No. 3, mm. 38-39; b. Tchaikovsky, Piano Concerto No. 1, second movement, ⑤, mm. 29-30.

Ex. 4-39. a. Rachmaninov, Piano Concerto No. 2, in C minor, Op. 18, first movement, ④, mm. 9-10 (transposed); b. Tchaikovsky, Piano Concerto No. 1, second movement, ⑤, mm. 10-11.

notes, the contours of which are unmistakably those of the *Andantino*'s principal theme, are both versions of its opening bar (see Ex. 4-40). This poignant little phrase also contains the so-called Artôt motif from the second subject of the first movement. Could it have been Tchaikovsky's intention, therefore, to begin the second movement with a variant of the Artôt motif as a further tribute to his ex-fiancée?

The finale of the B-flat minor Piano Concerto, though essentially sonata-rondo in structure and character (insofar as its highly contrasted thematic material is juxtaposed in seemingly unrelated blocks rather than developed and dovetailed), exhibits enough features of first-movement or sonata form to make a clear-cut structural designation impractical. Opinions differ, however: John Warrack, for example, states emphatically that "the finale is again in sonata form,"[56] whereas the Soviet musicologist Yuri Tyulin considers the movement to be a rondo with an ABAB¹ARB²K structural framework ("R" indicating *Razrabotka* [development] and "K" coda).[57]

David Brown's sonata-rondo designation is perhaps closest to the mark, and his summary of the finale's structure is particularly trenchant:

> While in the "aria situation" of the "Andantino semplice" it had been natural to think in enclosed musical sections, the sonata rondo scheme that was usual for the concerto finale required rather more than Tchaikovsky supplied in his alternation of two thematic blocks supplemented by brief self-contained chunks of transition containing only the lightest hint of quasi-development intent. Tchaikovsky's marshalling of these neatly processed lumps of material is tidy, and he offers some token of developmental activity by contrapuntally engaging some of his thematic materials above the extended dominant preparation that leads to the final titanic delivery of the broad second theme. The movement makes a simple and effective finale, but it largely avoids those questions of organic growth that Tchaikovsky had so boldly confronted in the first movement.[58]

Ex. 4-40. Tchaikovsky, Piano Concerto No. 1, second movement, U̅, mm. 26-27.

It could be argued, of course, that had Tchaikovsky employed the kind of organic growth displayed in the first movement, the finale would not have been so clear-cut and effective as the version we know today.[59] However, Tchaikovsky compensates for its lack of thematic development by basing almost all its subsidiary melodies on the rhythmic cell ♪♪ ♩ ♪♪, extracted from the Ukrainian folk song "Come, come, Ivanka," on which the movement is based. The cell is also employed in the bridge passage linking sections A^1 and A^2 with B^1 and B^2 respectively—again based on the Ukrainian folk song first subject (x, in Ex. 4-41).

Echoes of the first movement are also present in this bridge passage, though they are probably fortuitous. The first and third measures of Ex. 4-41 (marked y) are reminiscent of the "thematic interloper" (initially derived from the first subject) employed in the development's passionate dialogue between piano and orchestra (see Ex. 4-32). Furthermore, the whirling sixteenth-note patterns are very similar to the eighth-note passage-work found near the beginning of the first movement's development (Ex. 4-29).

More significant, however, is the "fresco," or *changing background*, technique, which Tchaikovsky adopts as a means of varying the accompaniment of the Ukrainian folk song. Among the procedures used are pizzicato strings,[60] which, according to Edward Garden, suggest "the influence of Glinka (for example, *Kamarinskaya on Two Russian Folksongs*) and Balakirev (*Overture on Three Russian Folksongs*)";[61] quasi-canonic imitation (in the woodwinds); an effective employment of hemiola (with the strings in compound duple time against the piano's simple triple); and "off-beat chirps and skirls on the flute and clarinet."[62]

Although in the brief working-out section of the finale Tchaikovsky adopts a more conventional process of thematic development, because of its innate transitional nature it cannot really be considered a bona fide development. It begins, depending on one's viewpoint, either at m. 183, *Molto più mosso*, a section devoted to alternating fragments of the first and

Ex. 4-41. Tchaikovsky, Piano Concerto No. 1, third movement, W, mm. 1-3.

second subjects accompanied by vertiginous octave passage-work in the soloist's part (reflecting, perhaps, the influence of the finale of Rubinstein's Third Piano Concerto, Op. 35, a popular and frequently performed work at that time), or at the *Tempo I ma tranquillo* section that follows, which is closer to a conventional development section in that its treatment of the finale's thematic material is more tightly organized. The *Tempo I ma tranquillo* section is predominantly constructed around a neat combination of second subject fragments and the Ukrainian folk song's skipping figure. These elements in themselves could have provided Tchaikovsky with the foundations of a satisfying and self-contained central ritornello. Instead, he incorporated them in an imposing 29-bar buildup over a dominant pedal in the lower horns, timpani, and double basses, leading—through nine bars of *fortissimo* double octaves from the soloist (see Ex. 4-43)—to the final statement of the second subject, *Molto meno mosso*.

Even more so than the previous two movements, the piano writing in the finale is skillfully tailored to the underlying musical ideas, and despite a pronounced virtuosic character, it displays little of the superfluous note-spinning present in Tchaikovsky's remaining works for piano and orchestra. Edward Dannreuther had little to suggest in the way of improvements to the piano writing in the finale (his proposed amendments were almost entirely confined to the pianistically more expansive and ambitious first movement). Nor had Siloti, whom Tchaikovsky had consulted in regard to the third edition (1889) of the Concerto; though two small changes which were subsequently incorporated may have resulted from their collaboration: the replacement of part of the skipping figure with more forceful and rhythmically impetuous octave sixteenth notes (Ex. 4-42) and the simple

Ex. 4-42. Tchaikovsky, Piano Concerto No. 1, third movement, Ⓩ, mm. 12- 14: a. second edition; b. third edition.

yet extremely effective redistribution, à la Rubinstein, of the double octaves immediately preceding the second subject's final statement (Ex. 4-43).

With the completion of the Concerto in B-flat minor (which the eighteen-year-old Sergei Taneyev intuitively dubbed "the first Russian piano concerto" some four days before it had been finished[63]), Tchaikovsky's contribution to the development of the genre effectively came to an end. Although his remaining works for piano and orchestra (the Concertos in G, Op. 44, and E-flat, Op. 75; the *Concert Fantasia*, Op. 56; and the unfinished *Andante and Finale*, Op. 79) display some novelties of formal construction, they offer nothing radically new in terms of musical thought, piano technique, or treatment of soloist and orchestra. On the contrary, all exhibit a marked decline in practically every aspect of musical composition, particularly the opening movement of the Second Concerto and the *Andante and Finale* (which Tchaikovsky's overzealous disciple Sergei Taneyev orchestrated and introduced to the public after the composer's death).

Clearly Nikolai Rubinstein's criticisms concerning the First Concerto went very deep indeed and cast a shadow over all Tchaikovsky's future attempts at composing for piano and orchestra. It is also apparent from contemporary diary entries and correspondence during the period of "emotional relaxation and creative torpor" (to quote Edward Garden[64]) following the crisis of his marriage in 1877, that the quality of Tchaikovsky's music depended to a significant extent on his mood at the time and his attitude toward the *process* of musical composition, which was often

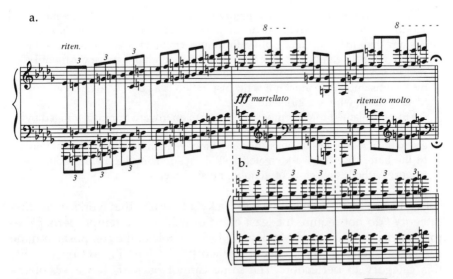

Ex. 4-43. Tchaikovsky, Piano Concerto No. 1, third movement, Z(e), mm. 37-40: a. third edition; b. second edition.

governed by these moods. In an illuminating letter to Nadezhda von Meck, dated 24 June 1878, Tchaikovsky gives a detailed account of these processes:

> You want to know my methods of composing? Do you know, dear friend, that it is very difficult to give a satisfactory answer to your question, because the circumstances under which a new work comes into the world vary considerably in each case.
>
> First I must divide my works into two categories, for this is important in trying to explain my methods.
>
> (1) Works which I compose on my own initiative—that is to say, from an invincible inward impulse.
>
> (2) Works which are inspired by external circumstances: the wish of a friend, or a publisher, and commissioned works.
>
> Works belonging to the first category do not require the least effort of will. It is only necessary to obey our inward promptings, and if our material life does not crush our artistic life under its weight of depressing circumstances, the work progresses with inconceivable rapidity. Everything else is forgotten, the soul throbs with an incomprehensible and indescribable excitement, so that, almost before we can follow this swift flight of inspiration, time passes literally unreckoned and unobserved. There is something somnambulistic about this condition. On s'entend pas vivre. It is impossible to describe such moments. Everything that flows from one's pen, or merely passes through one's brain (for such moments often come at a time when writing is an impossibility) under these circumstances is invariably good, and if no external obstacle comes to hinder the creative glow, the result will be the artist's best and most perfect work. . . .
>
> For the works in my second category it is necessary to get into the mood. To do so we are often obliged to fight with indolence and disinclination. Besides this, there are many other fortuitous circumstances. Sometimes the victory is easily gained. At other times inspiration eludes us, and cannot be recaptured. I consider it, however, the duty of an artist not to be conquered by circumstances. He must not wait. Inspiration is a guest who does not care to visit those who are indolent. . . .
>
> I have explained that I compose either from an inward impulse, winged by a lofty and undefinable inspiration, or I simply work, invoking all my powers, which sometimes answer and sometimes remain deaf to my invocation. In the latter case the work created will always remain the mere product of labour, without any glow of genuine musical feeling.[65]

Dismissing, for a moment, Tchaikovsky's assertion that works in the first category "do not require the least effort of will"—an attempt, perhaps, to romanticize in the eyes of Mme. von Meck the role of the composer and the composer's relationship to his or her work—the First Piano Concerto fits this category to perfection. The same cannot be said, however, of the Second Piano Concerto or, indeed, of any of the remaining works for piano and orchestra, for unfortunately they belong to the second category and were composed merely to fill lacunae which appeared sporadically in Tchaikovsky's creativity. Moreover, all (except the Second Concerto) utilize and develop material initially intended for other works but rejected on grounds of unsuitability or poverty of invention, and all were subject to delays and interruptions of various kinds.

Concerto No. 2

The historical background of the Second Piano Concerto, as documented in Tchaikovsky's correspondence—in particular, to Mme. von Meck, the pianists Taneyev and Siloti, and the publisher Jurgenson—succinctly illustrates Tchaikovsky's attitude toward the process of composition at that time. In a letter to Mme. von Meck, dated 12 October 1879, just two days after Tchaikovsky had begun composing the concerto, he wrote

> I am now convinced more than ever before that I cannot live long without working. A few days ago I began to sense in my innermost heart a kind of indefinable dissatisfaction with myself which was gradually beginning to turn into boredom. . . . I realised that what I lacked was work, and began to apply myself a little. Immediately the boredom went and I felt altogether lighter in spirit. I have begun to compose a piano concerto. I will work without hurrying, straining or tiring myself in any way.[66]

Three days later, again to Mme. von Meck, Tchaikovsky continued in the same vein and also indulged in a little self-delusion to justify his newly adopted sobriety:

> My new musical child is beginning to grow, and little by little its structural character is taking shape. I am composing with great inspiration, but am trying to avoid the usual feverish hurrying which is always badly reflected in my music.[67]

One wonders what became of the "great inspiration" Tchaikovsky was referring to. Certainly, from a thematic point of view—an invariably accurate barometer of musical inspiration—the Second Concerto is poorly provided for and contains nothing comparable to the material in the First Concerto. The Second Concerto lacks a central, pervading melodic idea or prototype, for whereas almost all the principal original melodies of the First Concerto sprang from folk sources, the themes of the Second, apart from a few negligible similarities, are eclectic and entirely autonomous. Moreover, they are undistinguished and leave no lasting impression on the listener. As Eric Blom picturesquely put it: "The G major contains little we are tempted to hum on leaving the concert-room, much less while occupying the bathroom."[68]

The Schumannesque first subject, for example, is not only unprepossessingly symmetrical in construction but also rhythmically clumsy and harmonically unimaginative (see Ex. 4-44). Tchaikovsky's melodic writing rallies slightly in the second subject, which begins with an impassioned dialogue between clarinet and horn constructed on a tonic pedal (Ex. 4-45). However, Tchaikovsky inadvisedly continues the pseudocanonic treatment for an additional fourteen bars in the soloist's part—maintaining the tonic pedal throughout—and subsequently subjects fragments of this flimsy thematic idea to extensive repetition. Both on paper and in performance, this section of the Concerto, as indeed, do many in the first movement, resembles more the efforts of a gifted student than of a mature and highly respected composer.

Thematically, the *Andante non troppo,* the last movement to be composed, is more successful, though again its leading ideas are subjected to excessive

Ex. 4-44.   Tchaikovsky, Piano Concerto No. 2, in G, Op. 44, first movement, mm. 8-16.

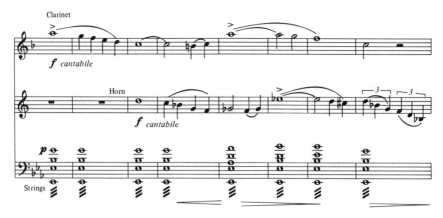

Ex. 4-45.   Tchaikovsky, Piano Concerto No. 2, first movement, mm. 80-87.

repetition, particularly in the inordinately long central episode. Tchaikovsky was justly proud of the closing section of the movement, perhaps the only portion of the Concerto with genuine Tchaikovskian lyricism (see Ex. 4-46).

More difficult to assess are the lively, bustling melodies employed in the finale. They are undoubtedly effective, if not sufficiently contrasted, though again, the impression is more of clever artifice than of genuine inspiration.

Despite the colorless quality of the Second Concerto's thematic material, Tchaikovsky distributed it liberally over a huge canvas and framed the result in a structure distended by his pursuit for grandiloquent effects. "There is a sense of grandeur being consciously sought rather than resulting from a genuine musical impetus," wrote John Warrack.[69] In the first and second movements, the somewhat prosaic deployment of the thematic material—based primarily on fragmentation and repetition—fails to sustain this "sense of grandeur" convincingly. As a consequence, the Concerto, in particular the structurally more ambitious first movement, tends toward discursiveness and contains an inordinate amount of padding. Had

Ex. 4-46.   Tchaikovsky, Piano Concerto No. 2, second movement, mm. 221-24.

Tchaikovsky adopted the kind of thematic transformation and motivic development employed in his First Concerto, he might have been able to compensate for the Second's inferior melodic writing by drawing upon untapped motivic potential. One suspects, however, that given his peculiarly relaxed approach to composition at the time, he was probably trying to avoid the kind of complexities displayed in his First Concerto.[70] As was so often the case with Tchaikovsky's creativity, the more problematic and arduous the composition of a new work, the finer the music that resulted. Tchaikovsky never quite grasped the significance of this connection. Perhaps if he had understood the implications of the ease with which he composed the Second Concerto, for example, he might have been more self-critical.

Tchaikovsky's reluctance to confront even fairly conventional problems of a symphonic nature is evident not only in the Second Concerto's impoverishment of thematic development but also in his lackadaisical approach to the construction of its bridge-passage and transition material. Nowhere, in fact, in the Second Concerto does one find the brilliant solutions to his "eternal transition problem" displayed in the First Concerto, such as the dovetailing between first and second subjects in the opening movement (Ex. 4-24) and the link passage between the principal themes of the finale motivically generated from surrounding material (Ex. 4-41).

In the Second Concerto, Tchaikovsky's approach is generally more straightforward and invariably less effective, involving bridge passages based on thematic fragmentation (in the finale, the link between the second and third themes), the elimination of bridge-passage material altogether (between the first and second themes of the finale), and, reflecting the influence of Anton Rubinstein, the replacement of conventional transitions with short virtuosic piano cadenzas of little or no thematic interest (links between all the principal subjects in the first movement).

The link between the first and second subjects of the opening movement is particularly unsatisfactory. Apart from the disconcerting tonal shift from G major to E-flat major, separated by a tacit bar—a gesture of dubious taste revealing Tchaikovsky's predilection for Meyerbeerian melodrama—the link is devoid of any melodic interest whatsoever. Furthermore, it is brutally written, particularly for the soloist (see Ex. 4-47).

The interminably long and episodic development of the first movement also reflects the crisis in Tchaikovsky's creativity at the time. Although it begins with a fine orchestral ritornello, parading a richly harmonized variant of the second subject, the poverty of Tchaikovsky's inventiveness soon becomes devastatingly evident as the music passes through a link to the next section (as shown in Ex. 4-48). It is hard to believe that the composer of this insipid and instrumentally threadbare passage had previously penned some of the most lusciously orchestrated music in the repertoire of the nineteenth-century piano concerto, Russian or otherwise.

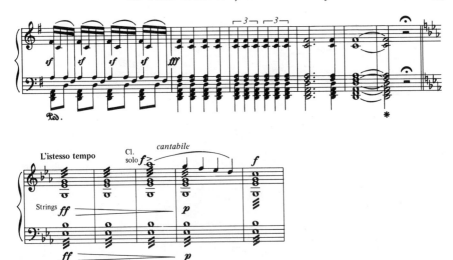

Ex. 4-47.   Tchaikovsky, Piano Concerto No. 2, first movement, mm. 72-82.

Ex. 4-48.   Tchaikovsky, Piano Concerto No. 2, first movement, mm. 236-44.

But passages such as these are by no means uncommon in the Second Concerto. Ex. 4-49 reveals a further example, the contrived sequential treatment of the second subject's consequent phrase.

From a harmonic point of view, Tchaikovsky furnished his Second Concerto with structures entirely appropriate for the thematic material in that they, too, are bland and unimaginative, as all the musical excerpts quoted so far clearly illustrate. Anton Rubinstein's influence on the Second Concerto is apparent in this respect, particularly in the extraordinarily

Ex. 4-49.   Tchaikovsky, Piano Concerto No. 2, first movement, mm. 249-58.

protracted tonic and dominant pedals (Exx. 4-45, 4-47, and 4-48) and
passages of little or no harmonic variety whatsoever (Exx. 4-47 and 4-48).
Tchaikovsky's reappraisal of the relationship between soloist and orchestra
also suggests Rubinstein's influence. Whereas in the First Concerto, soloist
and orchestra co-exist in a continual state of confrontation and interaction,
in the Second, the peace treaty has been signed, as it were, with the two
forces either alternately taking the center stage with large-scale ritornelli
(orchestra) and cadenzas (soloist) or cooperating, with the piano assuming
a more subordinate role as accompanist. In all situations, Tchaikovsky's
piano writing is both more idiomatic than in the First Concerto and considerably less convincing musically. Clearly still smarting from Nikolai
Rubinstein's criticisms regarding his First Concerto, Tchaikovsky was anxious to "improve" his piano style. His efforts were destined to fail from the
outset, for, as Edward Garden points out:

[Tchaikovsky] was incapable of being inspired by the piano as an instrument.
. . . The success of the First Piano Concerto can be attributed to the fact that
he was not thinking in terms of the piano at all, but of the orchestra. All the
themes are conceived in their orchestral form (Tchaikovsky told Mme. Von
Meck that he always composed with instrumental colouring in mind), and
the piano, even if it introduces a theme, is merely having an arrangement,
however good, of an orchestral conception. . . . It is clear that, after Rubinstein's severe strictures about the piano part in the First Concerto, Tchaikovsky in the Second was sincerely trying to compose in terms of the piano

rather than the orchestra, and it may be that this was partially responsible for the manifest inferiority of the later work.[71]

In his attempts to formulate a more idiomatic piano style, Tchaikovsky borrowed ideas from Liszt, significantly from the same Transcendental Etude (*Mazeppa*) that which served as a principal source of inspiration for that other great white elephant of the Russian concerto repertoire, Anton Rubinstein's Fifth Concerto in E-flat (see Ex. 4-50). Tchaikovsky also turned to Rubinstein's concertos themselves for ideas, as he had during the composition of the First Concerto. Again, it is in the solo cadenzas that this influence is most evident, though Tchaikovsky surpasses Rubinstein in virtuosity and technical demands. Even the intrepid Taneyev had difficulty in negotiating some of the thornier passages in the Second Concerto, as he mentioned in a letter to the composer dated 9 April 1882:

> I find really awkward four pages in the cadenza where the hands have alternating chords [Ex. 4-51]. They are very difficult to play though this is not readily apparent in performance. I think the audience will get slightly bored by the end of the second page, and by the end of the fourth, will begin to lose its patience. . . .[72]

In the *Andante non troppo* the piano is much less assertive; indeed, a major criticism of this movement is that the soloist is too often assigned the role of accompanist supporting the solo violin and cello. Nevertheless, Tchaikovsky was apparently satisfied with the piano writing in this "triple concerto" movement—despite continuing reservations concerning the combination of piano and strings—for the following year he composed the

Ex. 4-50.   a. Tchaikovsky, Piano Concerto No. 2, first movement, mm. 289-90; b. Liszt, *Mazeppa*, m. 6.

Ex. 4-51.   Tchaikovsky, Piano Concerto No. 2, first movement, mm. 427-30.

Piano Trio, Op. 50, and based some of its piano figurations on passage-work from the *Andante* (see Ex. 4-52).

Only in the finale of the Second Concerto does Tchaikovsky succeed in creating a piano style both idiomatic and appropriate for the underlying musical ideas. At times, the virtuosic writing—in particular, the sparkling octave sixteenth notes accompanying the second subject (reminiscent of the finale of Rubinstein's Third Concerto)—anticipate the bold, percussive concerto writing of Prokofiev and Shostakovich. The soloist's part is also more satisfactory, for in addition to assiduously underpinning the orchestra with brilliant passage-work it also announces all three principal themes and actively participates in the remaining sections.

Structurally, also, the finale is a considerable improvement on the ram-

Ex. 4-52.   Tchaikovsky: a. Piano Concerto No. 2, second movement, mm. 298-300; b. Piano Trio in A minor, Op. 50, second movement, Variation 9, mm. 1-2.

bling discursiveness of its companion movements, and neither Tchaikovsky nor Siloti considered cuts necessary when the Concerto as a whole underwent revisions in later years (see p. 162). Nevertheless, in his pursuit of clarity, Tchaikovsky veers somewhat too enthusiastically on the side of compactness and brevity, and consequently the finale is not altogether satisfactory as the concluding movement of a large-scale piano concerto.

Although various attempts have been made to categorize the structural design of the finale—ranging from Yuri Tyulin's *Svabodnaia forma* (free form)[73] to Roger Fiske's "very bald Sonata form"[74]—the movement is best described as an adroit fusion of rondo and sonata form, i.e., the superimposition of rondo characteristics (clear-cut sectional divisions, recurring tonic statements of principal thematic material, etc.) on a modified sonata-form structure (see Fig. IV).

In this respect, the finale could be considered more innovative structurally than the corresponding movement in the First Concerto. Innovation, however, does not necessarily imply superior musical thought. Neither should the apparent originality of the finale's structure be attributed to a conscious effort on Tchaikovsky's part to tread new paths, for like Rubinstein, Tchaikovsky often inadvertently created new forms or implemented seemingly innovative modifications while attempting to find alternative solutions to troublesome structural complexities.

On the completion of the Second Piano Concerto, early in 1880, Tchaikovsky again sought the advice of Nikolai Rubinstein on how to improve the work. On this occasion, however, he considered it more expedient to send Rubinstein the score rather than risk another unpleasant confrontation. Tchaikovsky's decision to consult his volatile colleague was not taken without some trepidation, as his letter to his publisher Jurgenson, dated 20 February 1880, reveals:

> I tremble at the thought of the criticisms I may again hear from Nikolay Grigorevich [Rubinstein] to whom the concerto is dedicated. Still, even if once more he does criticise yet nevertheless goes on to perform it brilliantly as with the First Concerto, I won't mind. It would be nice, though, if on this occasion the period between the criticism and the performance were shorter.[75]

On 13 May Tchaikovsky wrote to Rubinstein, "if in editing the piano part you find it necessary to alter anything entrust these corrections to Taneyev."[76] Apparently, Rubinstein did consult Taneyev on the matter, for the latter wrote to Tchaikovsky that "there was absolutely nothing to be changed."[77]

The following month, after perusing the score for a second time, Rubinstein was tactful enough to confine his comments to matters concerning

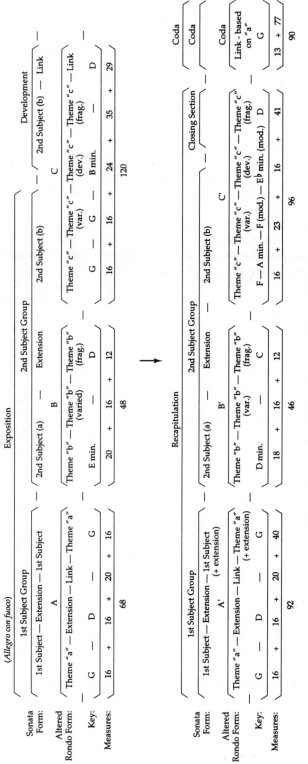

Fig. IV. Tchaikovsky, Piano Concerto No. 2, third movement

the piano part and cautious enough to admit that, in any case, his conclusions might perhaps, be wrong owing to "having scarcely played the
concerto once through."[78] In a somewhat petulant letter to Mme. von
Meck, dated 28 September, Tchaikovsky not only rejected outright Rubinstein's quite justifiable comments concerning the new concerto but also
pounced on, and twisted to his own advantage, Rubinstein's diplomatic
peroration:

> Nikolai Grigorevich has given me his opinion of my concerto that it seems the
> piano part is too episodic and not sufficiently separated from the orchestra. I
> think he is wrong. However, he only knows it from a superficial run-through
> and I hope that on closer acquaintance with it his opinion will alter. In
> general, Rubinstein tends too often to be unjust in his assessment of a new
> piece which he has not yet learnt. I can think of many cases when he has hurt
> me deeply with his hostile attitude to some new work or other and then, after
> a year or two, has radically altered his judgement.[79] I hope that such is the
> case this time, for if he is right I shall feel very annoyed as I took particular
> care to make the solo instrument stand out in as much relief as possible from
> the orchestral background.[80]

Because of the sudden death of Nikolai Rubinstein in Paris on 11 March
1881, the Russian première of the Second Concerto was postponed until 18
May 1882, when it was performed by Taneyev (with Anton Rubinstein
conducting) at the opening concert of the Industrial and Cultural Exhibition in Moscow. However, the first public performance of the new concerto
had taken place on 12 November 1881 in New York, with the young
English pianist Madeleine Schiller, a pupil of Sir Charles Hallé, and Theodore Thomas conducting.

On 18 June, a month after the Russian première, Taneyev wrote to
Tchaikovsky about the concerto's reception:

> Opinions of this work vary quite a lot, but they all come down to this: that the
> first and second movements are too long. One hears opinions that it is one of
> the most beautiful concertos and very brilliant in performance, that some
> prefer it to the first concerto etc.—few approve of the solo violin and cello in
> the second movement, they say that nothing much is going on in the piano,
> in which perhaps, it is impossible not to agree, and that there is too great an
> emphasis on the part of the other two instruments.[81]

In an "amusing mixture of sarcasm and humour,"[82] to quote David Lloyd-
Jones, Tchaikovsky expressed his annoyance on receiving this thinly disguised condemnation of his new work:

> Most grateful for your performance of the concerto. I will freely admit that it
> uffers from being too long and regret that those people to whom critical
> amination of the work was entrusted two years ago did not point to this
> ficiency at the time. In doing so they would have rendered me a great

service, greater even, perhaps, than performing this concerto so magnificently in its present imperfect state. All the same, merci, merci, merci, merci.[83]

Tchaikovsky heeded Taneyev's comments and undertook three small cuts for the St. Petersburg première, on 5 November 1888, given by Vasily Sapellnikov, with Tchaikovsky himself conducting.[84] Jurgenson had offered to bring out a new edition of the Concerto, so one month before this performance, Tchaikovsky decided to consult Siloti about possible improvements. Siloti's suggestions must have been fairly drastic, for Tchaikovsky responded, on 8 January 1889:

> I really can't agree to your abridgments, especially the alterations in the first movement . . . my composer's sense is greatly outraged by your rearrangements and changes and I can't bring myself to permit them. The version of the Second Concerto that I want is the one I had Sapelnikov play. . . . With my modifications the consistency and logical sequence of the sections are not destroyed. My . . . hair stood on end at your idea of transferring the cadenza to the end.[85]

Nevertheless, the work's inordinate length continued to prey on the composer's mind. In a letter dated 30 March 1891, Tchaikovsky admitted to Jurgenson that he found the Second Concerto intolerable "in its present form."[86] Jurgenson, sensing that Tchaikovsky was perhaps prepared to compromise over the matter of cuts, assigned Siloti the task of editing the third edition. After several letters of protest, in which Tchaikovsky objected to Siloti's attempt to do away with both the central section of the *Andante* and the recapitulation in the first movement (letter dated 26 July 1893) and to implementing radical changes to the first movement's principal cadenza (letter dated 8 August), he finally capitulated, at least to some of the lesser amendments. On 20 August he wrote to Jurgenson:

> I have agreed to certain of Siloti's changes, others I quite definitely cannot accept. He is overdoing it in his desire to make this concerto easy, and wants me literally to *mutilate* it for the sake of simplicity. The concessions I have already made and the cuts which both he and I have introduced are quite sufficient. I am exceedingly grateful to you for your readiness to republish this concerto. There will be no great changes—it will be a matter of cuts only.[87]

However, the edition, which Jurgenson eventually brought out (in 1897, four years after Tchaikovsky's death), contained all the changes, alterations, and cuts to which Tchaikovsky so strongly objected. It bears the ignominious title "Nouvelle Edition, revue e diminuée d'après les indications de l'auteur par A. Ziloti."

Concerto No. 3

Tchaikovsky's grudging acknowledgment of the Second Concerto's principal weakness, i.e., its excessive length, may explain why his third and last piano concerto, in E-flat, Op. 75, remained unfinished. It was composed more or less contemporaneously with his haggling with Siloti over cuts in the Second Concerto. The *Andante* and the finale of the Third Concerto were left in short score and were orchestrated by Taneyev after the composer's death (see pp. ooo–oo). As Tchaikovsky explained to Siloti in a letter dated 25 September 1893: "Since it is inordinately long, I have decided to leave it as one movement which I'll call 'Allegro de concert,' or perhaps 'Konzertstück.' "[88] Tchaikovsky expressed the same intention in a letter to S. Stoyovsky:

> I am working now on the instrumentation of the concerto for our kind Diémer.[89] Tell him, when you see him, that when I began orchestrating I was uneasy and disturbed about the length of this concerto. Then I decided to retain just one movement, the first, and that will become the whole concerto. The work can only gain from this, since the last two movements contain nothing in particular.[90]

This letter was, until recently, in the possession of Vladimir Horowitz (a photostat copy is preserved at the Tchaikovsky House-Museum in Klin). It settles once and for all the issue as to whether the *Andante* and Finale movements—published in Taneyev's arrangements by Beliaev in 1897 as Op. 79—should seriously be considered part of a three-movement concerto commencing with the *Allegro brillante* first movement, which was brought out by Jurgenson in 1894. Tchaikovsky's intentions on this matter are clear and unequivocal: "I decided to retain just one movement, the first, *and that will become the whole concerto* [italics added]."

The idea for a third piano concerto probably arose as early as 1888, when Diémer asked Tchaikovsky to compose something for him. Four years later, while on his fourth and longest visit to London, Tchaikovsky again met Diémer, and it is reasonable to assume that the issue of the new concerto was raised. Always loath to waste material, Tchaikovsky decided to return to the discarded sketches of a projected symphony in E-flat (composed in May and October 1892) and reconstruct them in the form of a piano concerto. By any standard this was an inauspicious and unpromising start for a new composition, and the possibility of something enduring and profound resulting from such a procedure would seem even more unlikely in view of Tchaikovsky's earlier assessment of the defunct symphony:

> Have gone over attentively and, so to speak, looked with an impartial eye at my new symphony, which fortunately, I have not had the time to orchestrate

and release for performance. The impression it produces is far from flattering, in a word, the symphony was written just for the sake of writing something, and contains nothing interesting or appealing. I have decided to scrap it and forget about it. This decision is irrevocable, and it is a good thing I have taken it.[91]

Thus not only did Tchaikovsky intend to utilize material originally planned for another work soon to be abandoned, but the material itself—which he freely admitted contained "nothing interesting or appealing"—had been composed merely "for the sake of writing something"!

During the summer of 1893 Tchaikovsky worked assiduously, though without pleasure, on the new concerto (along with the *Pathétique* Symphony); and on 1 July, he wrote on the draft of the first movement "Finished—thank God! The revisions were begun June 23rd and finished July 1st, the day of Bob's[92] departure." By 10 July the sketches for all three movements were completed. Returning to Klin after having spent some time in Hamburg and St. Petersburg, Tchaikovsky settled down to orchestrating the new concerto. Having already discarded the *Andante* and *Finale* (see letters to Siloti and Stoyovsky, above, p. 163), he soon completed this task, and the finished manuscript was inscribed "3 Oct[ober] 1893. Klin."

Not surprisingly, Tchaikovsky's earlier reservations concerning the material of the aborted Symphony in E-flat developed almost into antipathy during its reconstruction as a concerto. Indeed, at one stage, Tchaikovsky expressed the intention (in a letter to Siloti dated 1 August 1893) of destroying it altogether if the opinion of Taneyev, to whom he intended to show the new concerto, proved unfavorable. Knowing that Tchaikovsky was quite capable of following this through—he had already destroyed the orchestral score of his symphonic ballad *Voyevoda* for similar reasons less than two years earlier[93]—Siloti wrote to Tchaikovsky imploring him to reconsider such drastic action: "As you write that the concerto's music is not bad, then it is always possible to create external brilliance. This will be quite easy to do, so long as the work is not particularly long."[94] It was probably Siloti's final remark that suggested to Tchaikovsky the idea of jettisoning the *Andante* and *Finale* movements, for it is in his reply (dated 25 September, see p. 000) that Tchaikovsky first mentioned the decision to publish the *Allegro brillante* on its own.

In the actual process of reconstruction, it is remarkable how closely Tchaikovsky adhered to the Symphony's original material.[95] Indeed, the only notable differences (apart from the addition of the piano part) occur in the orchestration—understandably modified to provide material for the soloist—and in the construction of the development's closing section.[96]

Remarkable also, considering its orchestral provenance, is the piano writing itself, which in many respects is superior to that of both the Second

Concerto and the *Concert Fantasia* (discussed on pp. 175–85). It must be remembered, of course, that as Tchaikovsky's finest piano music was fundamentally orchestral in concept, the task of extracting and developing potential keyboard figurations from existing symphonic material posed fewer problems than one might have expected, probably fewer than the creation of an "original" or "genuine" piano part. What pleasure it must have given Tchaikovsky to "transcribe" for piano the existing orchestration of the beautiful second subject, for example, a procedure identical to the corresponding passage (and many others) in the First Concerto, composed nearly twenty years earlier (see Exx. 4-1 and 4-53).

The third subject, on the other hand, is so amenable to pianistic treatment that commentators have perhaps understandably jumped to the conclusion that it had been composed "fresh for the concerto."[97] Certainly Tchaikovsky's skillful toccata-like treatment does little to discourage this view (see Ex. 4-54). The symphonic origin of the third subject is verified by Semeon Bogatyryev's reconstruction of the Symphony in E-flat, as it faithfully incorporates Tchaikovsky's original orchestration for most of the first

Ex. 4-53. Tchaikovsky: a. Symphony No. 7, in E-flat (reconstructed), first movement, ④, mm. 14-18; b. Piano Concerto No. 3, in E-flat, Op. 75, mm. 69-73.

Ex. 4-54. Tchaikovsky, Piano Concerto No. 3, mm. 100-102.

movement.[98] Bogatyryev outlined his intentions in the Editor's Note to the score:

> Altogether, the Editor's task was, first, to find in the sketches the continua-
> tion of the Symphony's first movement, 248 bars of which had been scored by
> the composer himself, and secondly, to orchestrate the music that had not
> been orchestrated (the end of the Development Section, the whole of the
> Recapitulation and the coda—157 bars in all. . . .[99]

What Tchaikovsky composed afresh for the Concerto was the Cadenza, which neatly slots into place between the orchestral ritornello of the development and the recapitulation. Indeed, like its counterparts in the First and Second Concertos, it contributes to the working-out of material from the exposition, in this instance, concentrating on the second subject (Ex. 4-53). The Cadenza of the Third Concerto has a certain repetitiveness, owing to an overindulgence in melodic sequences and arpeggio figurations in the accompanying passage-work and a tendency toward melodramatic effects, such as the "telescoping" of themes and undulating dynamics. Nevertheless it is a stunning *tour de force* of virtuosic piano writing, rivaling the First Concerto's principal cadenza musically and surpassing it in pianistic effectiveness. Some sections are spectacular in their virtuosity. In the *Allegro vivace*, for example, the second subject luxuriates in passage-work which fully exploits the extremes of the keyboard (Ex. 4-55).

Only occasionally does the piano writing in the Third Concerto exhibit the kind of clumsiness which Nikolai Rubinstein criticized (and Dann-reuther amended) in the First; significantly, the passages in question are very similar in layout (see Ex. 4-56).

Ex. 4-55.   Tchaikovsky, Piano Concerto No. 3, mm. 250-53.

Ex. 4-56. Tchaikovsky: a. Piano Concerto No. 1, first edition, first movement, m. 252; b. Piano Concerto No. 3, mm. 42-44; c. Piano Concerto No. 1, mm. 6-8; d. Piano Concerto No. 3, mm. 113-14.

For all its faults, the Third Concerto is superior to Tchaikovsky's other compositions for piano and orchestra with the exception of the First Concerto, which must be considered in a different class altogether. With its three strong melodic ideas, an exciting well-wrought development, and a cadenza of almost unprecedented virtuosity, the Third Concerto represents an undeservedly neglected Russian piano concerto of considerable appeal. Perhaps if Tchaikovsky had succeeded in composing two additional movements of comparable stature—three-movement concertos being invariably more popular than single-movement concertos—the Third might have secured a place in the repertoire.

Andante and Finale

It was this knowledge which encouraged Tchaikovsky's protégé Sergei Taneyev (to whom was entrusted the completion of Tchaikovsky's unfinished compositions) to undertake the task of reconstructing the sketches for the *Andante and Finale*, which had been handed to him by Modest Tchaikovsky shortly after the composer's death on 25 October 1893. The ever-diligent Taneyev began work without delay, noting, however, in a letter dated 3 November: "The *Andante* is delightful, though it is a pity that Peter Ilyich arranged it as a piano work and did not leave it for orchestra."[100]

Curiously, in his correspondence with Modest, not once did Taneyev refer to the two movements in terms more specific than "Konzertstück," "piano piece," or simply "piano composition." Whether his reluctance to attach a label to the work stemmed from a pious belief that his task involved solely the work's reconstruction, or whether he genuinely intended to reunite the two wayward movements with the published first movement (and thus complete the already titled "Third Piano Concerto") is not known. However, when the possibility of publication eventually arose, the question of a title for the two movements proved too difficult for the publisher, Beliaev, and he appealed to Taneyev for suggestions:

> I have one or two questions: in view of the fact that the first movement of Peter Ilyich's piano concerto has already been published by Jurgenson, what are we going to call the two unpublished movements? It is hardly convenient to call them the other two movements of the same concerto. But if it is to be a separate work then could it be the 4th concerto in 2 movements or the 2nd Concertstück? You were very close to Pyotr Il'ich and probably understood his intentions; I hope you won't withhold your ideas on this matter.[101]

After much deliberation, Taneyev decided to name the work, appropriately yet somewhat unimaginatively, *Andante and Finale*, the titles of the two individual movements. The score was published in 1897.

From the outset, Taneyev's intentions, naturally enough, were to recreate as closely as possible the style of instrumentation Tchaikovsky would have adopted. Thus, Taneyev scored the *Finale* for the same instruments as the already completed first movement (with the addition of cymbals and side-drum to underline the martial character of the music) and whittled down the scoring of the *Andante* to woodwind, horns, and strings. Apart from one or two miscalculations, such as the somewhat Rubinsteinesque doubling of the horns and first violins beginning at m. 24 of the *Andante*, and the occasional patch of inappropriate unison and octave doublings, the instrumentation is, on the whole, admirably carried out. Particularly fine is the opening of the central *Più mosso* section of the *Andante*, which is reminiscent in its scoring for solo violin, viola, and piano of the closing section of the Second Piano Concerto's *Andante non troppo* movement (this was probably Taneyev's intention: compare Exx. 4-46 and 4-57).

Taneyev also incorporated other subtle characteristics of Tchaikovsky's symphonic style: thematic material in double octaves in the upper strings, liberal use of horns to enrich the middle registers of the orchestral texture, the introduction of subsidiary material (usually solo cello) to add variety and interest to the recapitulation of a principal subject. Though Taneyev's instrumentation is resourceful, his efforts did little to disguise the appalling triviality of much of the material he was working with. The *Andante* and

Ex. 4-57.   Tchaikovsky, *Andante and Finale*, Op. 79, *Andante*, mm. 53-58.

particularly the *Finale* are characterized by long stretches of unremitting diatonic harmony over tonic pedals, contrived counterpoint, rambling passages of pseudo-developmental intent (particularly in the coda of the *Finale*), and, worst of all, melodies of truly astonishing banality (as in Ex. 4-58).

In addition to the poverty of invention, Tchaikovsky's piano writing is dull and unimaginative. Not only is it predominantly superfluous to the musical ideas it accompanies—which is damning enough—but it does not even offer the secondary attraction of virtuosity (apart from, perhaps, the opening theme of the *Finale*—a curious blend of Brahms and Schumann spiced with chromatic figurations derived from Liszt). Clearly recognizing the futility of pianistically elaborating a work which he rightly acknowledged to be inferior, Tchaikovsky decided that Siloti's suggestion of adding "outward brilliance"[102] was not practicable after all. In any case, disenchantment and apathy set in long before the work had been completed, judging from the apparently unfinished soloist's part in the coda of the *Andante* (see Ex. 4-59).

Taneyev, however, thought differently about the possibilities of revitalizing the existing piano part. After giving the first performance of the *Andante and Finale* in St. Petersburg on 8 February 1896, he set to work recomposing much of the solo writing of the *Andante* (the *Finale* is left unchanged, apart from some seventeen bars in the first episode; see Ex. 4-64). He completed it in time for a performance on 17 October 1898 at one of Beliaev's "Russian" concerts (conducted by Rimsky-Korsakov). Two weeks earlier, Taneyev wrote to Modest Tchaikovsky about the forthcoming concert and his new version of the work:

> I am playing the *Andante and Finale* and hope that you will be able to come and hear it. I have made a revision of the piano part and it seems to me to be effective. It preserves everything composed by Peter Ilyich, but also shows off the pianist to greater advantage, and I think perhaps the concerto will be more successful in this form.[103]

In the short term Taneyev was proved right, for the performance was a considerable success, as he proudly informed Modest toward the end of

Ex. 4-58. Tchaikovsky, *Andante and Finale*, Finale: a. first episode, mm. 48-55; b. second episode, mm. 117-21.

Ex. 4-59. Tchaikovsky, *Andante and Finale, Andante,* mm. 197-215.

October. However, contemporary performances of Taneyev's version have been rare, though in the Soviet Union it was occasionally played by L. Lukomsky and A. Iokheles (both professors at the Moscow Conservatory).

At first glance, Taneyev's revisions—which involve some eighty bars of the *Andante* and seventeen in the *Finale*—suggest a fairly conventional virtuosic reappraisal of Tchaikovsky's awkward and ineffectual piano writing, as illustrated by the beginning of Taneyev's *Ossia* (Ex. 4-60). On closer examination, however, it becomes apparent that a great deal of Taneyev's revised piano solo, in addition to incorporating Tchaikovsky's original figurations, embraces a considerable amount of thematic material formerly and exclusively assigned to the orchestra (see Ex. 4-61).[104] It could be argued that Taneyev had merely replaced the superfluous with the superabundant. On the other hand, whatever Taneyev was capable of devising, it could hardly be considered inferior to the paltry token of a piano part provided by Tchaikovsky.

Taneyev was not invariably justified in implementing his often drastic revisions, nor was he always entirely successful. It is questionable, for example, whether his arpeggiated arrangement of the left hand of Tchaikovsky's piano part commencing at m. 69 represents an improvement. On the contrary, it could be considered that Tchaikovsky's treatment, though less grateful and effective from a purely pianistic point of view, is more appropriate within the context of a concerto-style work (see Ex. 4-62). These, however, are very isolated occurrences. Much to his

Ex. 4-60. Tchaikovsky, *Andante and Finale, Andante*, mm. 37-38: a. Taneyev's *Ossia*; b. Tchaikovsky's original.

Ex. 4-61. Tchaikovsky, *Andante and Finale, Andante*, mm. 82-83: a. Taneyev's *Ossia*; b. Tchaikovsky's original; c. orchestral part transcribed for piano.

credit, when confronted with a genuinely fine passage of Tchaikovskian piano writing (an even rarer occurrence!), Taneyev had the sense to leave well enough alone, as in Ex. 4-63. At this point in the score, Taneyev's revisions come to an abrupt halt and are not resumed until m. 47 of the *Finale*. In view of the large amount of recapitulated piano writing still to follow, his decision not to continue is most curious. Even more perplexing is his indifference to the apparently unfinished piano part in the coda of the *Andante* (see Ex. 4-59).

a.

b.

Ex. 4-62. Tchaikovsky, *Andante and Finale, Andante,* mm. 68-73: a. Taneyev's *Ossia*; b. Tchaikovsky's original.

Ex. 4-63. Tchaikovsky, *Andante and Finale, Andante,* mm. 118-23.

Despite there being plenty of scope for improvement elsewhere in the movement, Taneyev chose to confine his alterations in the *Finale* to the "twiddling little figures" (to quote Eric Blom[105]) which accompany the second episode's principal theme. Again, as in the *Andante,* he manages to preserve "everything composed by Peter Ilyich" (or nearly everything), and at the same time, provides a decorated version of thematic material originally found only in the orchestra (as in Ex. 4-64)

Whether Taneyev was musically successful in his virtuosic reappraisal of Tchaikovsky's piano writing, or whether he had merely added to his

Ex. 4-64. Tchaikovsky, *Andante and Finale, Finale,* mm. 48-51: a. Taneyev's *Ossia;* b. Tchaikovsky's original; c. orchestral part transcribed for piano.

original folly (i.e., his orchestration of the *Andante and Finale*), is a matter of taste. Indeed, the whole issue of whether the elaboration of material which is fundamentally inferior represents a valid contribution to music can only be assessed in purely subjective terms: *tot homines, tot sententiae*. Nevertheless it would be unfair to condemn his efforts too severely. At worst, Taneyev merely accentuated some of the more glaring defects in a piano part which, it must be remembered, was never intended for publication. At best, he marginally improved, from a performing point of view at least, a composition which is generally considered best forgotten.

Concert Fantasia

Like the Third Piano Concerto, Op. 75, the *Concert Fantasia* in G, Op. 56, was constructed around material originally intended for another work but rejected on grounds of unsuitability or inferior quality. Whereas the Third Concerto emerged, albeit half-heartedly, from the sketches of what was intended to be a seventh symphony (see p. 163), the initial idea for the *Concert Fantasia* (to be more precise, for a piano concerto—the idea for a two-movement work for piano and orchestra and the title came later) was conceived some three days *before* that of the parent work from which material was to be extracted, i.e., the Third Orchestral Suite, in G, Op. 55. This is evident from two entries Tchaikovsky made in his diaries for 1884. The first, on 13 April, reads. "Hit upon an idea for a piano concerto, but it turned out too weak and not original."[106] Three days later he wrote: "I've tried to lay the foundation of a new symphony. . . . As I strolled in the garden it was not a future symphony but a suite which germinated in my mind."[107]

It would be wrong, however, to assume, as one commentator has suggested, that the idea "hit upon" by Tchaikovsky on 13 April was "subsequently re-worked" and incorporated into the *Concert Fantasia*.[108] It is evident from the diary entry of 11 May that he was still preoccupied with the original concept of the Third Suite's first movement (on which the second movement, "Contrasts," of the *Concert Fantasia* was eventually to be based) and had, to all intents and purposes, forgotten about his earlier idea for a concerto: "The first movement of the Suite, called *Contrasts*, and its themes [Ex. 4-65] have become so repugnant to me that, after spending the whole day on it, I decided to discard it and write something else entirely different."[109]

Ex. 4-65.

Evidently his characteristic thrift regarding time and material momentarily overcame his growing antipathy for the work, for the following day
Tchaikovsky returned to the sketches, albeit reluctantly: "After tea I began
to busy myself again with the repugnant 'Contrasts,' suddenly a new idea
flashed into my mind and the work improved."[110] Precisely what this new
idea was is not known. But a month later, Tchaikovsky informed Mme.
von Meck (in a letter dated 16 June) that in addition to the Suite, he had
also begun a piano concerto,[111] so perhaps the new idea was to transform
the "repugnant 'Contrasts' " into something more congenial, i.e., a movement of a piano concerto.

During the following two weeks Tchaikovsky gradually formulated the
overall design of the new composition. In a letter dated 30 June, he wrote
to Taneyev about his intention to construct it in two movements only.[112]
Although work on the *Concert Fantasia* proceeded fairly rapidly (it was
finished on 15 August, according to a letter to Mme. von Meck, and the
orchestration was completed on 24 September), Tchaikovsky was unable to
devote his full attention to its composition. He was anxious over his sister
Alexandra's health and deeply concerned about his violinist friend Joseph
Kotek, who was suffering from tuberculosis and who died later that year in
Switzerland. In addition to these personal worries, Tchaikovsky was eager
to finish the Third Orchestral Suite, which necessitated composing a new
movement to replace "Contrasts." He decided on an *Elegy*, and the Suite
was finished in July 1884.

Tchaikovsky resumed work on the *Concert Fantasia* and wrote to Mme.
von Meck on 14 July about his progress.[113] He also deliberated at great
length on the merits and eligibility of various pianists he had in mind for
the first performance of the new work:

> I want to finish the piano concerto, which I wrote to you about, this autumn
> or winter. Of course I can no longer hope for an ideal performer such as N. G.
> Rubinstein—of whom I always thought when conceiving a concerto. There is,
> however, a pianist—a certain young man called D'Albert, who came to
> Moscow last winter and whom I have heard many times in concerts and
> private houses. In my opinion this brilliant pianist is the true heir to Rubin-
> stein. Taneyev (whom I place very highly as a musician-theorist, composer,
> and teacher) is, of course, a suitable performer as far as I'm concerned,
> though he is not a virtuoso. In regard to Siloti, between you and me, it seems
> to me (though perhaps I am mistaken) that he is just a somewhat puffed-up
> local celebrity. Not that his playing is without external brilliance and power in
> a material sense of the word, just that he didn't make a serious impression on
> me. . . . Perhaps this is because he is still very young. . . .[114]

Despite Tchaikovsky's reservations concerning Taneyev's playing (which
appear somewhat ungrateful and unwarranted, considering the apparently superb performances Taneyev had already given of Tchaikovsky's First
and Second Concertos), it was nevertheless Taneyev and not D'Albert to

whom Tchaikovsky turned when the possibility of the *Concert Fantasia*'s première arose: "I must play him [Taneyev] the newly completed concerto which he is going to perform for the Musical Society. He will start learning it straight away."[115]

The first performance took place in Moscow, with Taneyev as soloist, on 22 February 1885, under the direction of Max von Erdmannsdörfer as part of the tenth symphonic meeting of the Russian Musical Society.[116] Tchaikovsky wrote in glowing terms of Taneyev's playing and the performance as a whole: "I heard a splendid performance of my Fantasia given by Taneyev with the orchestra, and I am very pleased. It was a great success with the audience—more so than the Suite."[117]

When the subject of the dedication of the *Concert Fantasia* arose, Taneyev, despite his loyalty and tireless efforts on behalf of Tchaikovsky's music, was once again overlooked. The name inscribed on the two-piano arrangment, which was published in December 1884, was that of Anna Esipova, a pupil and later the second wife of Leschetizky. But her failure to play the work in public resulted in Tchaikovsky's changing the dedication when the full score was published in 1893. The new dedicatee, Sophie Menter, a Bavarian pianist at that time on the staff of the St. Petersburg Conservatory, proved a wiser choice, for she played it frequently and with notable success. In the original manuscript, however, no dedication is given.

Because of the feminine nature of these dedications the *Concert Fantasia* was dubbed the "Damen-Konzert" in Germany. The prodigious difficulties of the soloist's part, which in places surpass anything Tchaikovsky had hitherto written, can only testify to the immense technical competence of the two pianists concerned. The piano writing in the *Concert Fantasia* suggests a further reappraisal of the soloist's role in relation to the orchestra: In the First Concerto and, to a lesser extent, in the Second, the feeling is predominantly one of confrontation, while in the *Concert Fantasia* it is more one of collaboration, with the piano either assuming a purely decorative role or joining forces with the orchestra in the presentation of material. A significant outcome of this shift in emphasis is the perceptibly lighter texture of piano writing in passages where soloist and orchestra play together[118] and a considerably more refined and varied orchestration (as seen in Ex. 4-66).

Nevertheless, Tchaikovsky, as if anxious to compensate for the comparative economy of piano writing in the outer sections of the opening movement—and at the same time, continue the trend toward the segregation of piano and orchestra initiated by the Second Concerto—provides this movement with a central cadenza-style "solo" of unprecedented length, virtuosity, and magniloquence. Apart from the welcome entry of what appears to be a new melody but is merely a thematic lead into the principal subject (a function similar to the third subject of the Second Piano Concerto's opening movement), the "solo" is practically monothematic in

Ex. 4-66. Tchaikovsky, *Concert Fantasia*, Op. 56, first movement, "Quasi Rondo," mm. 33-34.

design and depends largely on contrasting virtuosic presentations of its theme to sustain interest. Lacking the kind of pianistic imagination and insight which enabled Balakirev, for instance, to manipulate and transform thematic material into new and interesting configurations (as in the Oriental fantasy *Islamey*), Tchaikovsky merely exhibits his scarcely altered theme in a series of virtuosic cameos (see Ex. 4-67). But since the principal theme resembles, whether intentionally or otherwise, the already sufficiently exposed first subject of the first movement (see Ex. 4-72), a feeling of monotony soon envelopes the "solo," despite the obvious appeal of its *bravura*.

Pianistically, Tchaikovsky drew upon his own somewhat limited repertoire of patterns and figurations and borrowed ideas from Liszt (as he had in the Second Concerto), not only for the more virtuosic passages in the "solo" but also for two sections of more poetic intent: the recitative-style link passage featuring a series of descending arpeggiated diminished-seventh chords, reminiscent of the corresponding section of Liszt's Transcendental Etude *Mazeppa*; and the quasi-impressionistic closing section of the "solo" (designated *Andante molto sostenuto*), which was possibly modeled on Liszt's remarkably prescient Transcendental Etude *Harmonies du Soir* (see Ex. 4-68). Elsewhere, however, Tchaikovsky's piano writing is fairly conventional and contributes nothing significant or original to the genre.

Structurally, on the other hand, the *Concert Fantasia* is highly unconventional and offers some interesting solutions to familiar problems. As already noted, it would be a mistake to assume that these innovations were undertaken in a spirit of fervent experimentalism, for unlike Liszt (to whom the development of new forms was an integral part of his musical creativity), Tchaikovsky adopted unfamiliar structures or radically altered existing ones as a means of avoiding what could be potentially troublesome. For example, his decision to construct the *Concert Fantasia* in two movements was prompted not so much by a desire to be radical or ex-

Ex. 4-67. Tchaikovsky, *Concert Fantasia*, first movement,: a. mm. 76-79; b. mm. 88-90; c. mm. 116-19.

perimental but by a recognition of the advantages in preserving the transplanted "Contrasts" movement intact, i.e., in its original single-movement format.[119] Tchaikovsky believed that, being substantially endowed with both slow, lyrical sections and brilliant scherzo-like passages, "Contrasts" was sufficiently varied and "contrasting" to take the place of the second and third movements of a conventional tripartite concerto format.

The most striking innovation of the individual movements is the complete omission of their development sections. In the first movement, some-

Ex. 4-68.   a. Tchaikovsky, *Concert Fantasia*, first movement, mm. 210-12; b. Liszt, *Harmonies du soir*, mm. 11-13.

what misleadingly entitled "Quasi Rondo" ("Quasi Sonata" would have been more appropriate), this structural modification enabled Tchaikovsky to side-step the thorny problems involved in the working-out of exposition material. In its place Tchaikovsky inserted the enormous "solo" cadenza, based, despite superficial similarities, on new material. This "cuckoo in the nest," being considerably larger than the unrelated "parent" sections which support it, threatens the stability of the somewhat fragile sonata structure which forms the basis of the movement (see Fig. V).

In the structurally more complex second movement, "Contrasts," Tchaikovsky does not even trouble to fill the void left by the absence of a development section. Consequently, the closing section of the exposition and the first subject of the recapitulation are juxtaposed without any formal link. Recognizing the need for some kind of musical development, even if it is only token, Tchaikovsky neatly combines the first and second subjects, with slight modifications to the quicker theme when the latter makes its appearance in the recapitulation (see Ex. 4-69).

Despite the ingenuity with which Tchaikovsky manipulates his thematic material, the result is not altogether convincing, as Eric Blom points out:

> As an achievement in neat thematic telescoping this piece may indeed be regarded as a "locus classicus." The only fault one may perhaps find with it, considered as such a feat, is that the quick theme is in itself rather wanting in spontaneity. One has the feeling that it may have been adjusted to fit in with the slow one by trial and error before work on the composition began in real earnest.[120]

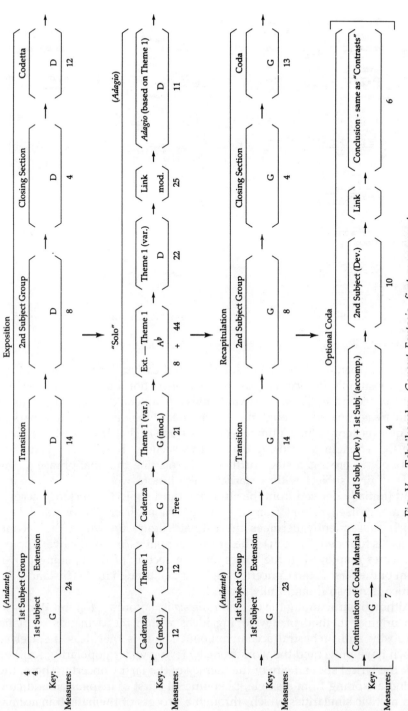

Fig. V. Tchaikovsky, *Concert Fantasia*, first movement

Ex. 4-69.   Tchaikovsky, *Concert Fantasia,* second movement, "Contrasts," mm. 340-47.

An anticipation of this procedure is found earlier in the movement, in the exposition's *Più mosso, quasi moderato assai* link passage between the first and second subjects. The two themes are dovetailed (i.e., fragments of them are alternated—though not, as yet, heard together) with four bars of the quicker tempo (in 2/4 time) set against one of the *Andante* (in 4/2 time) (see Ex. 4-70). In the closing bars of this section, Tchaikovsky takes the overlapping process a stage further by furnishing the final phrase of the *Andante* first subject with a staccato eighth-note woodwind accompaniment (initially derived from the attractive third subject's "rocking" accompaniment, itself cloned from the "love" theme from *Romeo and Juliet*), which subsequently becomes the ostinato figure on which the second subject is founded (Ex. 4-71). The process is reminiscent of the overlapping of themes employed in the corresponding section of the opening movement of the First Piano Concerto (see Ex. 4-24), though in this instance, the artifice is not so thoughtfully concealed.

Although structurally the *Concert Fantasia* is, according to John Warrack, "an original method of developing ideas within the demands of piano virtuosity and orchestral accompaniment,"[121] it is the ideas themselves which have prevented the work from achieving wider popularity, for they lack the lyrical spontaneity of the themes of the First Concerto. There, the melodies sprang from a single, phenomenal burst of inspiration and contain motivic similarities which, through a process of thematic transformation, subtly enhance the overall unity of the work. Motivic similarities are

Ex. 4-70.   Tchaikovsky, *Concert Fantasia*, second movement, mm. 56-58.

Ex. 4-71.   Tchaikovsky, *Concert Fantasia*, second movement, mm. 62-65.

also present in the thematic material of the *Concert Fantasia*, but Tchaikovsky's approach here is less spontaneous, and the material is less interesting. The employment of thematic unity is, in any case, a hazardous affair. At its best—as displayed in Rimsky-Korsakov's Piano Concerto, the finale of Rubinstein's Fourth Concerto, and, of course, Tchaikovsky's First Concerto—it can be a determining factor in the success of a work. If, however, the thematic fragments are not particularly distinctive or are not sufficiently developed or transformed, as in the *Concert Fantasia*, then a feeling of monotony gradually supercedes the original intention of creating structural unity. The thematic similarities in the *Concert Fantasia*—which in one instance also creates a link between the two movements—are tabulated in Ex. 4-72.

Tchaikovsky was acutely aware of the deficiencies of the *Concert Fantasia*, in particular, its second movement, for he took the novel and unprecedented step of furnishing the "Quasi Rondo" with an optional coda of considerable virtuosity in case the performer wished to jettison "Contrasts" and play the first movement on its own. Although this appendix is both a competent development of the tuneful second subject and an effective applause-raiser, it would be unwise to recommend its performance, whether or not "Contrasts" is incorporated, as one commentator has suggested,[122] for Tchaikovsky filched the final six bars from the coda to the "Contrasts" movement. To conclude both movements with identical material would only confuse the listener and could on no account be considered musically acceptable.

The *Concert Fantasia* has never managed to secure a permanent place in the repertoire, despite an encouraging reception when it was first performed by Taneyev in Moscow in 1885 and again a year later in St. Petersburg. Part of the blame for its neglect can be attributed, as noted, to its elegant though undistinguished thematic material. This material demonstrates the influence of ballet music—Tchaikovsky's principal interest at that time—and many of the *Fantasia's* melodies, being self-contained and without potential for development, are consequently unsuitable for the broader canvas of a concerto-style composition.

Audiences must also have been puzzled and discouraged by the structural eccentricities of the *Fantasia,* in particular, the huge and incongruous

Ex. 4-72.   Tchaikovsky, *Concert Fantasia.* First movement, "Quasi Rondo": a. first subject; b. "solo," principal theme; c., d. subsidiary themes. Second movement, "Contrasts": e. coda; f. first subject; g. subsidiary theme; h. third subject.

solo cadenza inserted into the heart of the opening movement. Perhaps audiences were right to be discouraged: the traditional cadenza was, after all, a perfectly logical and excitingly packaged means of further exploiting material stated earlier in the movement. Exciting though it may be, Tchaikovsky's "solo" is not logical—being grossly disproportionate in relation to its neighboring sections and constructed in a curious patchwork manner alien to large-scale symphonic composition—nor does it serve the important function of reminding the listener of the movement's principal ideas, since it is based on new material. Dare one suggest that, in his attempt to segregate soloist and orchestra still further and, at the same time, avoid the pitfalls of a conventional development, Tchaikovsky had blundered in his choice of an alternative?

What factors precipitated such a dramatic deterioration in Tchaikovsky's concerto writing, while his creativity in other genres—ballet, symphonies, etc.—remained unaffected? The principal cause was undoubtedly Nikolai Rubinstein's strictures concerning the First Concerto, so vociferously voiced on Christmas Eve 1874. Pieced together, fragments from Tchaikovsky's correspondence, diaries, and the concertos themselves suggest that the criticisms left a more profound and lasting impression on Tchaikovsky than has generally been acknowledged. Despite his defiant cry "I will not alter a single note!" after Rubinstein had finished demolishing the new work, Tchaikovsky lost both heart and confidence in writing piano concertos. It was only after Rubinstein had taken up the B-flat minor Concerto, in the late 1870s, that Tchaikovsky, as an act of conciliation, composed the Second, in G major, and dedicated it to him. After the immediate and spectacular success of the First Concerto, both in the United States and in Russia, there may also have been an element of "Look, you see? I *can* write decent piano concertos!" in that dedication. Rubinstein's lukewarm response to the Second Concerto was not quite what Tchaikovsky expected. He was infuriated and depressed, particularly as he knew, instinctively, that Rubinstein's cautious and measured comments had more than a grain of truth in them. The fact that Tchaikovsky could have contemplated, let alone realized, the 23-bar cut in the development of the first movement— something he would never have countenanced in the First Concerto—and sanctioned at least some of Siloti's amendments, suggests that he had less confidence in the Concerto than his correspondence would lead us to believe. That the cuts could be so painlessly administered, with little or no detrimental effect to the surrounding material or the structure as a whole, further indicates that Tchaikovsky perhaps had good reason to have reservations toward the new work.

Disenchantment with concerto composition, together with a loss of respect for the genre, soon set in following the completion of the Second Concerto. It was no accident that all Tchaikovsky's remaining works for piano and orchestra are in effect depositories of material originally intended for other works but rejected as being unsuitable or of inferior quality.

Conclusion

Consistent with its inauspicious beginnings, the Russian piano concerto's contribution to the development of the genre during the nineteenth century is predictably slight, representing an interesting, if numerically small addition to the repertoire. Nevertheless, its importance lies in its providing the foundations of a twentieth-century school of concerto composition of unparalleled brilliance and virtuosity, led by Rachmaninov and Prokofiev.

Although Prokofiev played and admired Tchaikovsky's First Concerto, it was Rimsky-Korsakov's tiny masterpiece which attracted him most: "I very much enjoyed working on the concerto," he wrote, after having performed it for his undergraduate examination at the St. Petersburg Conservatory in the spring of 1909. "There was something extremely good and picturesque about it."[1] In view of the structural peculiarities of his Concerto No. 1 in D-flat, Op. 10, composed in 1911–12, Prokofiev's study of Rimsky-Korsakov's Concerto proved to be not only pleasurable but also instructive, for it is likewise cast in a single-movement multisectional design of unusually brief duration (approximately fifteen minutes) and displays a similar mosiaclike approach in the development and elaboration of its thematic material. Nikolai Medtner's more substantial Piano Concerto in C minor, Op. 33 (1918), and Glazunov's two piano concertos (in F minor, Op. 92, and B major, Op. 100, composed in 1911 and 1917 respectively), also acknowledge Rimsky-Korsakov's experiments in structural condensation. This is particularly true of Glazunov's Op. 100, which is conceived, like Rimsky-Korsakov's concerto, in four interconnected and contrasted sections corresponding to conventional concerto movements. Rimsky-Korsakov's influence on Rachmaninov's concertos, however, is less evident, for although Rachmaninov considered Rimsky-Korsakov "possibly the greatest of Russian composers,"[2] he found the latter's piano concerto insufficiently "klaviermässig" to merit particular attention and remained indifferent to its structural innovations. Instead, Rachmaninov aligned himself with the more conservative tradition of concerto composition initiated by Anton Rubinstein and consolidated by Tchaikovsky, and brought it to a magnificent conclusion in his four concertos and the Rhapsody on a Theme of Paganini, Op. 43. Primary influences on Rachmaninov during his formative years include Rubinstein's Fourth Piano Concerto—the first movement of which he performed at a student concert in February

1891 and at the Moscow Electrical Exhibition in September 1892—and the Concerto in F minor, Op. 2, by his teacher Arensky. As Barrie Martyn[3] has pointed out, the Arensky Concerto may have guided Rachmaninov in the scoring and melodic writing of the opening of the slow movement of his own First Concerto. Tchaikovsky's concertos were, of course, of paramount importance, not only in the formation of Rachmaninov's piano style and treatment of soloist with orchestra, but also in matters relating to structural design. The idea of inserting a fast central episode of rapid octave sixteenth notes into the slow movements of his Second and Third Concertos was almost certainly inspired by the *prestissimo* section of the slow movement of Tchaikovsky's First Concerto, which was based on the French chansonette "Il faut s'amuser, danser et rire," itself modeled on the second movement of Rubinstein's Fourth Concerto.

However, these influences pale almost into insignificance compared to the impact of Grieg's Piano Concerto in A minor on Rachmaninov's First Concerto (though Rachmaninov hastened to disguise this fact while preparing the revised version in 1917). Indeed, the influence of Western composition, rather, the *dependence* on Western composition as a source of ideas, was a crucial factor in the development of the nineteenth-century Russian piano concerto, for hardly any were conceived without the scores of other composers being perused, analyzed, and occasionally plagiarized, particularly the concertos and solo piano works of Beethoven, Chopin, and Liszt. This leaning on Western composers was a direct consequence of the lack of a solid tradition of orchestral composition and subsequent inability of Russian composers to think in symphonic terms. In fact, the only tradition which Russian composers could draw upon with some degree of confidence was opera, for long before Glinka appeared on the scene, in the late 1830s, Russians had been gaining valuable experience playing in French and Italian opera theatre orchestras in St. Petersburg and Moscow, and in serf orchestras on private estates, where amateur operatic productions were staged by the Russian nobility. It is no coincidence, therefore, that opera, not symphonic music, became central to the creativity of almost every nineteenth-century Russian composer. Only Balakirev—under the spell of his idols, Liszt and Chopin—displayed a marked indifference, though he enthusiastically guided his *Moguchaia Kuchka* in their operatic projects and edited Glinka's operas for the publisher Jurgenson.

The substantial dependence of Russian composers on the music of others poses several tantalizing questions: what would Arensky's rather feeble piano concerto have been like without its generous borrowings from Chopin? Would Rimsky-Korsakov's concerto be so compact and masterfully composed had it not been "in all ways . . . a chip from Liszt's concertos?"[4] And, most intriguing of all: would Tchaikovsky have embarked on his Concerto No. 1 in B-flat minor if he had not had Anton Rubinstein's fine Concerto in D minor as a model?

Seen in their entirety, nineteenth-century Russian piano concertos can be said to exhibit almost all the weaknesses of their creators but only a few of their strengths. In the case of Rubinstein, for example, his carelessness, lack of self-criticism, and wild, incautious temperament encouraged him to compose in a bland, inconsequential manner in too great a quantity. Only his Fourth Concerto, which he uncharacteristically subjected to revisions after its completion, contains original ideas: his remaining works for piano and orchestra are derivative and often poorly composed. Arensky's stylistic derivativeness, on the other hand, was provoked by a lack of genuine creative individuality and a sometimes *blasé* attitude toward composition influenced by a life style which ran "a dissipated course between wine and card-playing,"[5] according to his former teacher Rimsky-Korsakov. The unprecedented degree of dependence on Chopin displayed in Arensky's Piano Concerto in F minor is either shameful or amusing, depending on one's viewpoint, and the work is no longer performed. Even more disappointing, considering his great talents as a pianist and composer, was Balakirev's uneven contribution to the concerto repertoire. Balakirev suffered from a restlessness, in both his creative and his personal life, which persistently interfered with his capacity to deal with the more practical aspects of composition. Most of his large-scale works were finished only after decades of procrastination, and not one of his three compositions for piano and orchestra was actually completed. Most tragic of all is the case of Tchaikovsky, whose peculiar personality trait of self-deception, combined with an almost pathological need to compose, encouraged him to work without inspiration "merely to fill lacunae which sporadically appeared in his creativity" (see above, p. 164). It was only in his first Concerto that Tchaikovsky remained faithful to his creative urges; significantly, this was the concerto he found most difficult to compose.

Notes

Introduction

1. Abraham Veinus, *The Concerto* (New York: Dover, 1964), p.236.
2. Sergei Bertensson and Jay Leyda, *Sergei Rachmaninoff* (London: Allen & Unwin, 1956), p.64.

1. The European Heritage

1. *Dni i gody Chaikovskogo* [Days and years of P.I. Tchaikovsky], edited by V. Yakovlev et al. (Moscow/Leningrad, 1940), pp.449–50.
2. Bortnyansky evidently made a favorable impression on Italian audiences, for the three operas he composed in Italy were staged with some success: "Creonte" (libretto by M. Coltellini) in Venice in 1776, "Quinto Fabio" in Modena and Venice in 1778, and "Alcide" (libretto by Metastasio).
3. Gerald Seaman, "The Rise of Russian Piano Music," *The Music Review* 27 (August 1966):180.
4. According to the inscription on the manuscript, cited in M. S. Druzin and Y. V. Keldysh, *Ocherki po istorii Russkoi Muzyki 1790–1825* [Essays on the history of Russian music 1790–1825] (Leningrad, 1956), p.309.
5. Coincidentally, Tchaikovsky also incorporated a French song (the chansonette "Il faut s'amuser, danser et rire") in the second movement of his Piano Concerto in B-flat minor (see p.133). It is doubtful, however, that Tchaikovsky was consciously following Bortnyansky's example, as the *Sinfonia Concertante* remained in manuscript until a facsimile copy was made in the Soviet Union in 1953.
6. Yuri Keldysh, *Russkaia Muzyka XVIII veka* [Russian music of the 18th century] (Moscow/Leningrad, 1965), p.424.
7. Very few Russian compositions of symphonic proportions were composed during the early nineteenth century. The most prolific composer was probably Alyabev, who sketched four symphonies: No. 1 in G major (c.1815), No. 2 in E-flat (c.1815), No. 3 in E minor (1830), and No. 4 (1850). The E minor symphony, of which only the first movement survives, was published in Moscow in 1955. It was begun on 30 October 1830 in Tobolsk, according to the manuscript, and is scored for woodwinds, four horns, two trumpets in B-flat, one trombone, timpani, and strings.
8. Among European piano manufacturers who established warehouses and showrooms in Russia during the early years of the nineteenth century were the firms of Clementi, Tischner, Schröter, Backers, and Diderichs. It was as salesman-demonstrator for Clementi's showroom in St. Petersburg, incidentally, that John Field first attracted the attention of the Russian public.
9. The sustaining pedal had been introduced in 1789 by the German builder Johann Andreas Stein (1728–92), an apprentice of Gottfried Silbermann. Before its use, Stein's fortepianos had been equipped with a knee lever.

10. Field also employed a second piano in his Fifth Concerto, "since one piano-forte alone would be too weak to express the storm" (quoted in Abraham Veinus, *The Concerto* [New York: Dover, 1964], p.217). The idea of doubling the soloist's instrument in the more dramatic episodes of a concerto originated with Steibelt, though he never put it into practice.

11. Field's First, Sixth, and Seventh Concertos incorporate nocturnes (the last two of which were published separately); and in later performances, Field often inserted a solo nocturne between the two movements of his Third Concerto (probably the Nocturne No. 5, as there exist sketches of an orchestral accompaniment to an extended version of this piece).

12. The influence of Field's pianistic style is particularly evident in the piano compositions of Parfeni Nikolaevich Engalichev (1769–1829), Lev Stepanovich Gurilyov (1770–1844), and Ivan Fyodorovich Laskovsky (1799–1855).

13. Field's innovative step of introducing a slow interlude into the first movement of the concerto may have inspired Schumann to adopt a similar procedure in his Fantasia in A minor, later to become the first movement of the Piano Concerto, Op. 54. Field's "Waltz" rondo finale may also have suggested to Schumann the incorporation of waltzlike passages in his own concerto finale.

14. M. I. Glinka, *Literaturnoe nasledie*, Vol. I: *Avtobiograficheskie i tvorcheskie materi-aly* [Literary heritage. Vol. 1, Autobiographical and creative materials], ed. V. Bogdanov-Berezovskii (Leningrad, 1952), p.75.

15. S. M. Lyapunov, "M. A. Balakirev," *Ezhegodnik imperatorskikh teatrov* [Year-book of the imperial theatres], VII (1910):44 (quoted in Edward Garden, *Balakirev* [London, 1967], p.23).

16. Just as Field had founded a tradition of piano playing in Russia, so Balakirev achieved the same in composition. His pupil Rimsky-Korsakov, probably the most important and influential teacher of his generation, included among his students Glazunov, Lyadov, Stravinsky, and Prokofiev. Glazunov also became Prokofiev's teacher and later played an important part in the musical development of Shostako-vich.

17. In German history, the period between the Congress of Vienna and the revolutions of 1848 has been dubbed the Biedermeier era after a collection of poems entitled "Auserlesene Gedichte von Weiland Gottlieb Biedermeier," published in the Munich journal *Fliegende Blätter* between 1855 and 1857. The fictitious author Biedermeier was created by Adolf Kussmaul and Ludwig Eichrodt as the personification of his age—an age of reconstruction after many turbulent years of revolution and war, of the rise of the bourgeoisie and the Protestant work ethic.

18. The idea of attaching the epithet "Biedermeier" to concertos composed during the period c.1810–35 is not new. The present author has followed the example of the Italian musicologist Piero Rattalino, in his useful and informative handbook *Il Concerto per Pianoforte e Orchestra* (Milan: Ricordi-Giunti, 1988).

19. The early decades of the nineteenth century witnessed, in effect, the birth of the modern piano. Three important innovations were introduced that revolution-ized the piano's technical and expressive capabilities: the double-escapement action perfected by the Frenchman Sébastien Erard and patented by his nephew Pierre in 1821; the adoption of an all-metal frame by Alpheus Babcock of Boston in 1825; and the introduction of felt hammers by Henri Pape of Paris in 1826.

20. Field, for example, introduced into his concertos instruments and orchestral effects formerly and exclusively reserved for the opera theatre, including tremolo strings, tam-tam, triangle, and bell pedal.

21. Veinus, p.154.

22. Although the employment of folk or folklike material was an important feature of the "Biedermeier" concerto (for example, Moscheles' No. 2, Op. 56; Cramer's No. 5, Op. 48; and Chopin's Opp. 11 and 21), it was by no means a

nineteenth-century innovation. Haydn had already composed a "Rondo all'un-
gherese" for his Piano Concerto in D major, and Josef Stéphan (1726–97) employed
Bohemian folk characteristics in many of his 42 harpsichord concertos.

23. Beethoven's *Missa Solemnis* was given its world première by the St. Petersburg Philharmonic Society on 26 March 1824 in a benefit concert for musicians'
widows. The conductor was Prince Nikolai Galitzin.

24. It could be conjectured that the "extremely variable" quality of instrumentalists also encouraged "Biedermeier" composers to write simpler orchestral parts, a practical consideration never far from the minds of baroque composers.
Indeed, the idea of dividing the orchestra into two sections—the *ripieno* and the
smaller, more-virtuosic *concertante*—was in part born out of the necessity to
accommodate both skilled, often professional, players and the less-experienced
"rank and file."

25. Chopin has often been criticized for the weak, unadventurous orchestration
of his concertos and the exaggerated importance given to the soloist's part. But
Chopin, like Weber, Field, and many others, was merely following the then
dominant trend in concerto composition, a trend which encouraged the subordina-
tion of the orchestra by the soloist. Seen in this light, Chopin's concertos merit a
critical reappraisal and their "faults" should be reassessed accordingly.

26. One of Alyabev's songs, "The Nightingale," achieved international recognition when Rossini introduced it into the singing lesson scene of his opera *Il barbiere
di Siviglia*. Liszt subsequently made a transcription of the song for piano solo,
published in 1842 as the first of "Deux Mélodies russes, Arabesques."

27. Seaman, p.183.

28. Seaman, pp.182–83, analyzes a typical set of Kashin's variations based on the
folk song "Akh, Seni moi, seni novye moi": "It is remarkable that each of these
variations has the character of a Russian dance. No. 1, for instance, is typical of a
folk instrumental accompaniment as the dancers move slowly round. No. VI
suggests the sound of stamping, while variation IX seems to be evocative of a dance
'v prisyadku'—the lively Russian dance executed in a squatting position with
folded arms. The character of the last is underlined not only by a *Sforzando* but by
the introduction of stronger harmonies. . . . Generally speaking, the whole set
conveys the impression of a folk-scene and is an interesting precursor of the type of
folk picture employed so successfully by Tchaikovsky at a later date."

29. In 1840, the year before his death, Kashin established a music school in
Moscow. Like his concerts, the school was open to all classes of Russians. Tuition
fees were modest, and free lessons were given to those unable to pay. To what
extent Kashin's humanitarian initiatives influenced Gavril Lomakin's decision to
establish his more-celebrated Free Music School in St. Petersburg more than twenty
years later is not known. Their objectives however, were identical: to provide basic
musical education for ordinary Russian people.

30. Coincidentally, Balakirev also wrote an operatic fantasia, the *Fantasia on
Themes from Glinka's opera "A Life for the Tsar"* (composed 1854–55, revised 1899).

2. The Piano Concertos of Anton Rubinstein

1. "I regard Brahms as the successor of Schumann," Rubinstein once pro-
claimed, "and myself as the successor of Schubert and Chopin—we two conclude
the third epoch of musical art." Anton Rubinstein, *Gedankenkorb* [Thought basket],
ed. H. Wolff (Leipzig, 1897); translated as *Thoughts and Aphorisms* (St. Petersburg,
1903).

2. *Biblioteka dlia Chteniia* [Reading library] (St. Petersburg) 118 (April 1853): 79–
80.

3. Letter to Rubinstein, dated 19 November 1854, quoted in *Franz Liszts Briefe* [Letters of Franz Liszt], ed. La Mara, 8 vols. (Leipzig, 1893–1904), vol. 6, pp.177–78.

4. Quoted in L. A. Barenboim, *Anton Grigorevich Rubinstein* (Leningrad: Gosudarstvennoe muzykal'noe izdatel'stvo, 1957), vol. 2, p.153.

5. The F-major Concerto was lost soon after its first performance in 1848.

6. Rubinstein's first public performance on 11 July 1839, favorably reviewed in the Moscow journal *Galathea*, was of a movement from Hummel's Piano Concerto in A minor, Op. 85.

7. In 1845, Anton Rubinstein, together with his younger brother, Nikolai, was taken to Berlin, on Meyerbeer's recommendation, to study theory, harmony, and counterpoint with Siegfried Dehn, a pedagogue whose teaching was firmly entrenched in the conservative traditions of German Classical and early Romantic Music. Among Dehn's pupils were Kullak, Cornelius, and Glinka.

8. During the years 1852–55, Anton Rubinstein composed one full-scale opera, *Dmitry Donskoy or The Battle of Kulikovo*, and three one-act operas "depicting the different peoples of Russia": *Hadji-Abrek* (to a poem by Lermontov), *The Siberian Hunters*, and *Fomka the Fool*. Supporters of the Nationalists, led by the critic Vladimir Stasov, bitterly resented the comparisons made between *Fomka the Fool* and Glinka's *Ruslan* and *A Life for the Tsar* and viewed Rubinstein's opera as a deliberate parody. The ensuing hostility unnerved Rubinstein, and he ceased to compose in a national vein—apart from a turgid concert overture *Ivan the Terrible* (1868)—until the appearance of the *Russian Capriccio* for piano and orchestra, Op. 102, in 1878. About this time Rubinstein also composed two of his finest works, also nationalist in character: the Fifth Symphony in G minor, Op. 107, and the opera *The Merchant Kalashnikov*.

9. In one of his last reviews as editor of *Neue Zeitschrift für Musik*, Schumann wrote of "the talented boy who had acquired a great reputation as a pianist," and despite finding fault with a harmonic progression, stated that "perfection and originality could not be expected from such a young composer." Schumann also saw, in the proliferation of melodic ideas, the "promise of significant development." (*Gesammelte Schriften über Musik und Musiker*, vol. 4 [Leipzig, 1854] pp.244–45.)

10. Alexander Serov, *Izbrannye stat'i* [Selected articles], ed. Georgii Khubov (Moscow and Leningrad, 1950–57), p.584.

11. Letter to Karl Franz Brendel (successor to Schumann as editor of *Neue Zeitschrift für Musik*), quoted in *Letters of Franz Liszt*, ed. Constance Bach (London, 1894), vol. 1 (translation of vols. 1 and 2 of *Franz Liszts Briefe*), p.219.

12. In the third edition of Tchaikovsky's First Piano Concerto, the version generally performed today, the opening theme's celebrated chordal accompaniment in the soloist's part (Ex. 2-30a) is so similar to the two passages quoted here (Exx. 2-6a,b) that it is possible that Tchaikovsky, or whoever was responsible for the changes incorporated into this edition, was encouraged to adopt a similar layout. The original inspiration, however, was almost certainly Rachmaninov's unpublished Nocturne in C minor (see p.123).

13. The final piece in Liszt's tripartite appendix to his *Années de Pèlerinage: Deuxième Année (Italie)*.

14. The initial idea of incorporating a tarantella finale into his Fifth Piano Concerto probably resulted from Rubinstein's close involvement in the conception of Saint-Saëns' Piano Concerto No. 2, in G minor, which also contains a tarantella finale. Rubinstein conducted the first performance of this concerto, with Saint-Saëns as soloist, in the Salle Pleyel, Paris, on 13 May 1868. Although there are a few superficial similarities in the two finales, it is apparent that Rubinstein was indifferent to Saint-Saëns' masterly treatment of this delicate yet spirited Italian dance. Had he not been so, the somewhat elephantine finale of his Fifth Concerto might have been tempered to a more appropriate texture.

15. Anton Rubinstein, *Autobiography*, trans. Aline Delano (Boston: Little, Brown and Co., 1890), pp.75–76.

16. Quoted in James Bakst, *A History of Russian-Soviet Music* (New York: Dodd, Mead and Co., 1966), p.169.

17. Anton Rubinstein, *Music and Its Masters*, trans. Mrs. John P. Morgan (London: Augener, 1920?), p.78.

18. The Piano Concerto in E minor, Op. 25, was composed in 1850 and published in 1858. It was dedicated to Rubinstein's teacher Alexandre Villoing.

19. The Piano Concerto in G, Op. 45—composed in 1853–54 and published in 1858—was first performed on 18 May 1857 in London by the London Philharmonic Orchestra with Rubinstein as soloist. That this work, the most structurally adventurous of all Rubinstein's concertos, is dedicated to Moscheles is not without significance, for Moscheles was one of the pioneers of the multisectional single-movement concerto and an early exponent of cyclic form and thematic recall.

20. John Culshaw, *The Concerto* (London: Max Parrish & Co., 1949), p.47.

21. Rubinstein, *Gedankenkorb*, p.44; also quoted in Barenboim, vol. I, p.128.

22. Field's Second Piano Concerto, in A-flat, composed around 1811, was greatly admired by Schumann, who considered it "divine," and by Chopin, who introduced it into his teaching material and may have used it as a model for his own F-minor Concerto. Field's Concerto soon entered into the virtuoso's repertoire and was performed throughout the nineteenth century. In Russia, it was frequently played by Rubinstein's brother Nikolai. The inclusion of a fugato in the rondo finale may be attributed to the fact that Field was then studying counterpoint with the theoretician J. H. Miller, who also taught Glinka.

23. Edward Garden, "Three Russian Piano Concertos," *Music and Letters* 60/2 (1979):167.

24. A fugato is also incorporated into the development section of the finale of Balakirev's Concerto in E-flat.

25. Toward the middle of the rondo finale of his Piano Concerto in E-flat, Beethoven recalls the anticipatory fragments of the rondo theme as they appeared in the closing section of the slow movement. Other significant examples of thematic recall include Schumann's Piano Quintet in E-flat, Op. 44, in which the principal theme of the first movement is "recalled" in the coda of the finale and involved in a double fugue with the principal theme of the finale; Berlioz's *Harold in Italy*, in which the finale, "The Orgy of Brigands," begins with numerous reminders of previous movements; Schumann's Symphony No. 3, in E-flat, Op. 97 ("Rhenish"); Mendelssohn's Symphony No. 3, in A minor/major, Op. 56 ("Scottish"); and Beethoven's Symphony No. 9, in D minor, Op. 125 ("Choral").

26. The first three quotations in Ex. 2-17 were correlated by Barenboim, vol. 1, p.324.

27. A. D. Alekseev, *Russkaia fortepiannaia muzyka* [Russian piano music] (Moscow: Izdatel'stvo Akademii Nauk, 1963), p.129.

28. Quoted in Bakst, p.170.

29. Barenboim, vol. 1, p.322.

30. Ibid.

31. César Cui, *Izbrannye stat'i ob ispolniteliakh* [Selected articles on performers] (Moscow: Gosudarstvennoe muzykal'noe izdatel'stvo, 1957), p.152.

32. Modest Tchaikovsky, *The Life and Letters of Peter Ilyich Tchaikovsky*, ed. Rosa Newmarch (London: John Lane, The Bodley Head, 1906), p.592.

33. Tchaikovsky also arranged Rubinstein's orchestral piece *Ivan the Terrible* for Bessel in 1869 and translated the texts of Rubinstein's *Persian Songs*, Op. 34, from the original German into Russian.

34. Rubinstein's opera *Nero* was published in 1879. The libretto is by J. Barbier.

35. Quoted in Vladimir Volkoff, *Tchaikovsky: A Self-Portrait* (London: Robert Hale and Company, 1975), p.79.

36. Garden, p.167.

37. In his diatribe aimed at Tchaikovsky's First Concerto (described in detail in a letter from Tchaikovsky to his patron, Nadezhda von Meck, dated 21 January 1878; see pp.116–17), Nikolai Rubinstein accused Tchaikovsky of "stealing from others." In view of the evidence presented in this study, Rubinstein was probably referring to Tchaikovsky's borrowing of pianistic ideas from the piano concertos of Rubinstein's brother, Anton.

38. It is not known why, in November 1874, Tchaikovsky embarked on a piano concerto. The reason must have been very persuasive, as, according to his friend the music critic Herman Laroche, Tchaikovsky had stated many times during his student days at the St. Petersburg Conservatory that "he would never write a work for solo piano and orchestra." (David Brown, *Tchaikovsky: A Biographical and Critical Study*, vol. 1, *The Early Years* [London, 1978], p.71.)

39. A. A. Nikolaev, *Fortepiannoe nasledie Chaikovskogo* [The piano heritage of Tchaikovsky] (Moscow, 1958), p.42; also quoted in Barenboim, vol. 1, p.325.

40. Alekseev, p.139.

41. Ulrich Niebuhr, "Der Einfluss Anton Rubinsteins auf die Klavierkonzerte Peter Tschaikowskys," *Die Musikforschung* XXVII/4 (1974):412–34.

42. Tchaikovsky may also have been influenced by the vibrant opening theme of the finale of Rubinstein's Fourth Concerto (see Ex. 2–19b), which is visually dissimilar but closer in character, particularly from a rhythmic point of view.

43. V. A. Rubinstein, *Oskolki proshlogo* [Fragments of the past] (n.p., n.d.), pp.29–32; also quoted in Barenboim, vol. 1, pp.392–93.

44. Quoted in Bakst, p.170.

45. See Robert C. Ridenour, *Nationalism, Modernism, and Personal Rivalry in Nineteenth-Century Russian Music* (Ann Arbor: UMI Research Press, 1981).

46. Alexander Serov, *Kriticheskie stat'i* [Critical articles], ed. N. Stoianovskii et al. (St. Petersburg, 1892–95), vol. 2 (1893), p.602. César Cui also refused to acknowledge Rubinstein's symphonies for the very same reason. In his opinion, "the first Russian symphony was by Rimsky-Korsakov" (*Izbrannye stat'i*, pp.66–68).

47. Cui, p.120.

48. Hans von Bülow, *Briefe und Schriften* [Letters and writings] (Leipzig, 1895), vol. 4, p.218.

49. Quoted in Barenboim, vol. 2, p.47.

50. Alekseev, p.139.

51. Gerald Abraham, in "Anton Rubinstein: Russian Composer," *Slavonic and Romantic Music* (London: Faber, 1968), pp.99–106, includes the *Capriccio* in his list of Rubinstein's "Russian" compositions. However, he considers Rubinstein's "Russian" period "about 1879–82 to be precise," in which case the *Capriccio* and the opera *The Merchant Kalashnikov*, both of which were composed in 1878, are excluded chronologically.

52. Quoted in Barenboim, vol. 2, p.203.

53. Emil Sauer, *Meine Welt, Bilder aus dem Geheimfach meiner Kunst und meines Lebens* [My world, images from a secret drawer of my art and my life] (Stuttgart, 1901), p.109.

54. Abraham, p.103.

55. S. Kruglikov, "Kontserty Rubinsteina" [Rubinstein's concerts], *Artist* 2 (Moscow, 1892):125.

3. The Piano Concertos of the Nationalists and the Eclectics

1. Balakirev admired the compositions of Henselt, or at least acknowledged him as a composer of some merit. In 1884 Balakirev composed his study-idyll *Au jardin*,

for piano, in a deliberately Henseltian manner and dedicated the piece to the Bavarian composer. Four years later, on the fiftieth anniversary of his debut as a pianist, Balakirev published an article on Henselt under the pseudonym Valerian Gorshkov in the journal *New Times*. During the same year, Balakirev recommended as a model concerto movement the *Larghetto* from Henselt's Piano Concerto in F minor, Op. 16, to his protégé Sergei Lyapunov, who was having difficulties with the slow movement of his own concerto (No. 1, in E-flat minor, Op. 4).

2. See Richard Davis, "Henselt, Balakirev and the piano," *The Music Review* 28 (August 1967):173–208.

3. The idea of arranging his very earliest work as an octet probably resulted from Balakirev's acquaintance with Rubinstein's Octet, Op. 9, itself a rescoring of an earlier sketch for a piano concerto in D minor composed in 1849. The ensemble of instruments used seems to indicate this, being identical except for Balakirev's oboe in place of Rubinstein's clarinet.

4. In 1853, Balakirev left the Alexandrovsky Institute, in Nizhny-Novogorod, and entered the University of Kazan.

5. On the manuscript, next to the initial orchestral statement of this folk tune, Balakirev wrote in pencil the following two lines, presumably taken from the original song: "Ah, clear in the mist the sun is not eclipsed, The poor maiden fair weeps having been deceived, deceived . . ." (translated from the Russian).

6. See V. Stasov, *Selected Essays on Music*, ed. Gerald Abraham (London: Barrie and Rockliff, 1968). pp.93–96.

7. Alexander Serov, *Kriticheskie stat'i* [Critical articles], ed. N. Stoianovskii et al. (St. Petersburg, 1892–95), vol. 1 (1892), p.455.

8. On p.18 of the manuscript, Balakirev wrote "S. Peterburg, 26 ianvaria 1856 goda, dom Butyrin" [St. Petersburg, 26 January 1856, Butyrin's house] and on the following page "Konets" [The end]. It is probable that he later returned to the work to undertake some revisions, for p.18 also carries the date 29 June 1857.

9. Ulybyshev was a local landowner, amateur musician, and writer who was introduced to Balakirev by Balakirev's music teacher Karl Eisrich.

10. A few months before his death, in May 1910, Balakirev re-orchestrated Chopin's E-minor Concerto for the centenary celebrations of the Polish composer's birth.

11. Anton Arensky apparently thought otherwise, for he incorporated a variant of Balakirev's second subject in his Piano Concerto in F minor, Op. 2, composed thirty years later (see Ex. 3-28).

12. *Perepiska M. A. Balakireva s. V. V. Stasovym* [Correspondence of M. A. Balakirev and V. V. Stasov], vol. 1, 1858–69 (Moscow, 1935), p.74.

13. The curious history of the concerto is definitively chronicled in Edward Garden, "Three Russian Piano Concertos," *Music and Letters* 60/2 (1979):166–79.

14. Ibid., p.167.

15. M. Balakirev, *Polnoe sobranie sochineniy dlia fortepianno* [Complete piano compositions], ed. K. S. Sorokin, vol. 3 (Moscow/Leningrad: Gosudarstvennoe muzykal'noe izdatel'stvo, 1954), p.269.

16. *Perepiska M. A. Balakireva s V. V. Stasovym*, vol. 1, p.400.

17. Ibid.

18. One of these performances was mentioned by César Cui in an unpublished letter dated 28 October 1863 (deposited in the Leningrad Conservatory).

19. Edward Garden, *Balakirev* (London: Faber, 1967), p.254. The composition referred to as "Lear" is Balakirev's *Overture and Incidental Music for Shakespeare's* "King Lear" (1858–61, revised and rescored 1902).

20. Nikolai Rimsky-Korsakov, *Polnoe sobranie sochineniy* [Complete edition], vol. 1, *Letopis' moei muzykal'noi zhizni* (Moscow, 1963), p.22; English translation as *My Musical Life* (New York: Alfred A. Knopf, 1942), p.63.

21. According to Rimsky-Korsakov, Balakirev was making sketches for "an octet or nonet with piano in F major" (ibid. [English translation], p.64) around the same time as the concerto.
22. Garden, "The Russian Piano Concertos," p.169.
23. Ibid.
24. No. 18 in Balakirev's collection of *40 Russian Folk Songs*, published by Johansen in 1866.
25. Garden, *Balakirev*, p.255.
26. Balakirev also used this theme in his anthem "Rest with the Holy Ones."
27. Whether Balakirev was influenced by Musorgsky in this passage is not known, as it may have been introduced into the finale by Lyapunov after Balakirev's death.
28. In common with the first movement, the finale's development contains a fugato. In this instance it is more skillfully contrived and is predominantly constructed on the second bar of the second subject (i.e., the bar which had previously been omitted in much of the previous "working-out" of the theme).
29. Quoted in Abraham Veinus, *The Concerto* (New York: Dover, 1964), p.211. Liszt was also striving toward a more symphonic approach in his concertos: No. 2 was even inscribed *Concerto symphonique*, and No. 1 was dedicated to Litolff. Liszt's approach, however, was somewhat different from Litolff's, for instead of diminishing the importance of the soloist's role, his intention was to enhance the orchestral part through symphonic means.
30. Garden, "Three Russian Piano Concertos," p.170.
31. Rimsky-Korsakov, *My Musical Life*, p.73.
32. M. D. Calvocoressi, *Mussorgsky* (London: Dent, 1946), p.176.
33. Ibid.
34. The fantasy is first mentioned in a letter to Balakirev dated 20 April 1866, one month after Musorgsky had heard *Todtentanz* in a performance conducted by Balakirev.
35. For a full account of Rimsky-Korsakov's revisions to Musorgsky's *St. John's Eve*, see Edward Garden, "Three Nights on Bare Mountain," *The Musical Times* 129/1745 (July 1988):333–35.
36. Rimsky-Korsakov, *My Musical Life*.
37. Edward R. Reilly, "The First Extant Version of Night on Bare Mountain," in *Musorgsky: In Memoriam 1881–1981*, ed. Malcolm Hamrick Brown (Ann Arbor: UMI Research Press, 1981), p.139.
38. Rimsky-Korsakov, *My Musical Life*, p.382.
39. The concerto is listed as No. 19 of the complete register of Taneyev's works in *Sergei Ivanovich Taneiev, His Personality and Creative Work* (Moscow: State Publishing Bureau, Music Sector, 1925), pp.120–23.
40. Only two movements were composed, the second of which was left in short score. It was later orchestrated by V. Shebalin after Taneyev's death.
41. *P. I. Chaikovskii: S. I. Taneev. Pis'ma* [Letters], ed. V. A. Zhdanov (Moscow: Muzykal'noe izdatel'stvo, 1951), p.4.
42. Peterson was at one time the proprietor of Bekker's piano factory.
43. David Brown, "Taneyev," in *The New Grove Dictionary of Music and Musicians*, ed. Stanley Sadie (London: Macmillan, 1980), states that until 1878 Taneyev kept his compositions a secret from everyone except Tchaikovsky. The statement above suggests otherwise; indeed, Taneyev appears to have been most enterprising in his efforts to promote his music or, rather, in seeking advice on how to improve it.
44. *P. I. Chaikovskii: S. I. Taneev. Pis'ma*, p.5.
45. Ibid., p.6.
46. Ibid.
47. Ibid., p.11.

48. As already noted in chapter 2, regarding Rubinstein's compositions, it was only in his diaries that Tchaikovsky expressed his true opinions concerning the music of other composers. It is unlikely, for example, that he "greatly appreciated [Taneyev's] concerto" or that he considered it "abounding in first-rate, beautiful passages" (as Yagolim suggests in the Preface to the full score).

49. Quoted in S. Bertensson and J. Leyda, *Sergei Rachmaninov* (London: George Allen and Unwin, 1956), p.246.

50. Taneyev also gave the Moscow première of the Concerto on 21 November 1875.

51. In January 1875, the year before he composed his Concerto in E-flat, Taneyev performed Brahm's D-minor Piano Concerto at an R.M.S. concert in Moscow with Nikolai Rubinstein as conductor.

52. Brown, "Taneyev."

53. Among Taneyev's more important writings are *Podvizhoi kontrapunkt strogovo pis'ma* [Invertible counterpoint in the strict style] (Leipzig and Moscow, 1909; English translation, 1962); and *Uchenie o kanone* [The study of canon] (Moscow, 1929).

54. One of the fantasias, probably Op. 39, was performed at a concert under the aegis of the R.M.S. as part of an all-Russian Exposition in Moscow, in late summer 1881. Rimsky-Korsakov organized the event and conducted the fantasia.

55. Quoted in G. M. Tsuipin, *A. S. Arenskii* [A. S. Arensky] (Moscow: Izdatel-'stvo muzyka, 1966), p.79.

56. With one notable exception: the closing phrase of Arensky's second subject is borrowed from the principal theme of the *Allegretto vivace* section of Liszt's Concerto.

57. Arensky's collection of piano pieces *Logaoedics: Essays on Forgotten Rhythms*, Op. 28, is prefaced by a chart which attempts to clarify the rhythmic complexities of the following pieces, exotically entitled "Logaèdes," "Péons," "Ioniques," "Sarimetre des chansons persanes," "Strophe alcéene," and "Strophe sapphique." According to the score, they are based on "les poesies antiques des grecs, des romains et d'autres peuples." The collection itself has now been forgotten.

58. Modest Tchaikovsky, *The Life and Letters of Peter Ilyich Tchaikovsky* (London: John Lane, The Bodley Head, 1906), pp.496–97.

59. Rimsky-Korsakov's *Sadko* and Stravinsky's *Firebird*, among others.

60. Tsuipin, p.79.

61. Boris Asaf'ev, *Russkaia muzyka*, p.228 (quoted in Tsuipin, p.87).

62. Rimsky-Korsakov, who openly admitted to being influenced by "bylini" in his opera *Sadko* and who apparently heard Riabinin in St. Petersburg the same year as Arensky, indirectly gave an apt definition of the genre in his autobiography: "This recitative is not conversational language, but a sort of conventionally regulated narration of parlando singing of which the prototype may be found in the declamation of Riabinin's bylinas" (*My Musical Life*, pp.364–65).

63. Cited in a dissertation by I. Isobov, "A. S. Arenskii," deposited in the Moscow Conservatory; quoted in Tsuipin, p.88.

64. Both songs are quoted in T. V. Popov, *Russkoi narodnoi muzykal'noi tvorchestvo* [Russian folk music], vol. 1 (Moscow, 1955), pp.146, 152.

65. Tsuipin, p.94.

66. Goldenweizer was by no means a stranger to Arensky's music. In 1897, he performed Arensky's Piano Concerto in F minor at one of Beliaev's Russian Symphonic Concerts.

67. Garden, "Three Russian Piano Concertos," p.173.

68. Tchaikovsky's Third Concerto, Op. 75, and his Concert Fantasia, Op. 56, are both superior to the conventional three-movement Second Concerto, in G major, Op. 44, yet performances of these attractive works are far less frequent.

69. In the spring of 1882 Rimsky-Korsakov supervised the composition of Arensky's Concerto, and in August he conducted Tchaikovsky's First Piano Concerto and Napravnik's Fantasia on Russian Themes at two concerts—the programs of which were chosen by him—given by the R.M.S. for the All-Russian Exposition in Moscow.

70. Rimsky-Korsakov, *My Musical Life*, p.263.

71. Ibid., pp.66–67.

72. Ibid., p.263.

73. M. F. Gnessin, *Mysli i vospominaniia o N. A. Rimskom-Korsakove* [Thoughts and reminiscences of N. A. Rimsky-Korsakov] (Moscow, 1956), p.79; quoted in Garden, "Three Russian Piano Concertos," p.263.

74. Rimsky-Korsakov, *My Musical Life*, p.263.

75. Rachmaninov was well acquainted with Rimsky-Korsakov's Concerto, certainly well enough to declare that it was not "klaviermässig" (see p.93).

76. The most important and extensive use of canon in the Concerto, however, is Rimsky-Korsakov's treatment of the *Allegretto quasi polacca* theme (Ex. 3-33e).

77. "New Lights on the Art of the Piano," *The Etude* (April–May 1923); quoted in Bertensson and Leyda, p.231.

78. César Cui, *Izbrannye stat'i* [Selected articles], (Leningrad: Gosudarstvennoe muzykal'noe izdatel'stvo, 1952), pp.336–37.

79. Letter from Balakirev to Lyapunov, dated 20 June 1888, quoted in M. E. Shifman, *S. M. Liapunov: zhizni tvorchestvo* [S. M. Lyapunov: life and works] (Moscow, 1960), p.35.

80. Balakirev re-orchestrated sections of Lyapunov's First Symphony and incorporated additional material in the score.

81. A. Lyapunova, "Iz Istorii tvorchestvikh sviazei M. Balakireva i S. Liapunova" [On the creative relationship of M. Balakirev and S. Lyapunov], in *Balakirev, issledovaniia i stat'i* [Balakirev, research and articles] (Leningrad, 1961), p.392.

82. M. D. Calvocoressi and Gerald Abraham, *Masters of Russian Music* (London: Duckworth, 1936), p.437.

83. The concert, which took place at the Free Music School in St. Petersburg, was conducted by Balakirev, with A. I. Borovka as soloist.

84. The sixteen-year-old Rachmaninov was studying composition with Arensky and Taneyev at the Moscow Conservatory during the academic year 1888–89.

85. The first movement, in fact, had been finished the previous year and was begun as early as 8 June 1890.

86. S. V. Rakhmaninov, *Pis'ma* [Letters], ed. Z. A. Apetian, (Moscow: Gosudarstvennoe muzykal'noe izdatel'stvo, 1955), p.42.

87. Ibid., p.54. See also Bertensson and Leyda, pp.36–37.

88. A. H. C., in *Dnevnik artista* [Artist's journal] 1 (Moscow, 1892):39.

89. Varvara Arkadevna Satina was the sister of Rachmaninov's father. She had four children: Alexander, Natalia, Sophia, and Vladimir.

90. Rachmaninov, however, conducted a performance of Grieg's Concerto on 26 January 1908 in St. Petersburg, with his cousin Alexander Siloti as soloist. The concert also included the première of his Second Symphony, Op. 27.

91. This was largely due to Tchaikovsky, for it was through his influence that Rachmaninov obtained an important contract with Gutheil in 1893, which led to his works being published without delay. Naturally eager to see his compositions in print and keen to earn money other than by teaching, which he loathed, Rachmaninov hurried into publication music which was in need of further refinement, such as the First Piano Concerto, Op. 1, or was of the "pot-boiler" variety composed for the *fin-de-siècle* Russian salon.

92. Rakhmaninov, p.344; see also Bertensson and Leyda, p.145.

93. A detailed description of Rachmaninov's revisions to the First Piano Con-

certo is outside the chronological scope of this volume. However, Fritz Butzbach, *Studien zum Klavierkonzert Nr. 1, fis-moll, Op. 1 von S. V. Rachmaninov* (Regensburg: Bosse, 1979), gives an exhaustive, bar-by-bar account of Rachmaninov's alterations and excisions, and must be considered the definitive study in this musicological field. A less weighty account outlining Rachmaninov's intentions is Geoffrey Norris, "Rakhmaninov's Second Thoughts," *The Musical Times* 114 (1973):364–68. Norris's book *Rakhmaninov*, Master Musicians series (London: Dent, 1978), also contains a section devoted to the First Concerto's revisions (pp. 110–15).

94. There also exists a juvenile work left in short score, Fantasy for Piano and Orchestra, composed in 1887–88, during Scriabin's first year at the Moscow Conservatory. It was orchestrated by G. Zinger and published posthumously.

95. Letter of 17 December 1896 to M. P. Beliaev; quoted in A. N. Scriabin, *Pis'ma* [Letters], ed. A. V. Kashperov (Moscow: Izdatel'stvo muzyka, 1965), p. 160.

96. The arrangement was published by Beliaev in 1897, but, shamefully, no acknowledgment was given to Vera Isaakovich for her contribution. The title page merely reads "Arrangement for two pianos by the author."

97. Scriabin, pp. 168–69.

98. Quoted in Faubion Bowers, *Scriabin*, vol. I (Tokyo and Palo Alto: Kodansha International, 1969), p. 235.

99. Scriabin, pp. 172–73; Bowers, *Scriabin*, p. 236.

100. Bowers, *Scriabin*, p. 237.

101. Rimsky-Korsakov, *My Musical Life*, p. 379.

102. Bowers, *Scriabin*, p. 238. The period of Rimsky-Korsakov's involvement with Scriabin's Concerto coincided with the composition of his opera *Mozart and Salieri*. It is possible that Rimsky-Korsakov's irrational attitude toward Scriabin and his music was in part due to his deep involvement in the plot of Pushkin's drama and his identification with the character of Salieri.

103. Scriabin, p. 183.

104. Bowers, *Scriabin*, p. 244.

105. Ibid.

106. Quoted in Faubion Bowers, *The New Scriabin* (London: David & Charles, 1974) pp. 34–37.

107. Bowers, *Scriabin*, p. 240.

108. Hugh MacDonald considers the Concerto's three movements "thematically unrelated" (*Skryabin* [London: Oxford University Press, 1978], p. 28).

109. In the Third Sonata, Op. 23, the principal theme of the third movement is apotheosed in the climatic *maestoso* passage in the closing pages of the finale; and in the Fourth Sonata, Op. 30, the delicate Wagnerian opening theme (*Andante*) is expanded to the very limits of piano sonority. Other examples of "recall" or thematic "apotheosis" are found in the Fifth and Ninth Sonatas (Opp. 53 and 68 respectively).

4. The Piano Concertos of Peter Tchaikovsky

1. P. I. Tchaikovsky, *Perepiska s N. F. von Meck* [Correspondence with N. F. von Meck] 3 vols., ed. V. A. Zhdanov and N. T. Zhegin (Moscow/Leningrad, 1934–36), vol. 2, p. 439, as quoted in John Warrack, *Tchaikovsky* (London: Hamish Hamilton, 1973), p. 164.

2. According to Herman Laroche, a fellow student, Tchaikovsky had frequently declared during his years at the St. Petersburg Conservatory that he would never compose a piano concerto. (See David Brown, *Tchaikovsky: A Biographical and Critical Study*, vol. 1, *The Early Years* [London: Victor Gollancz, 1978], p. 71.)

3. Despite many references to the Piano Concerto in B-flat in his correspondence,

Tchaikovsky makes no mention of having difficulty in coping with its formidable technical demands. Moreover, the version he played for Rubinstein, which was subsequently to become the first edition, is even more demanding than the version performed today, being peppered with unnecessarily awkward passages.

4. M. I. Tchaikovsky, *Zhizn' Petra Il'icha Chaikovskogo* [The Life of Peter Ilyich Tchaikovsky] (Moscow, 1900–1902), vol. 1, p.451.

5. *Dni i Gody P. I. Chaikovskogo: Letopsis' zhizni i tvorchestva* [Days and years of P. I. Tchaikovsky: Chronicle of his life and words], ed. V. Yakovlev, (Moscow/Leningrad, 1940) p.118.

6. M. I. Tchaikovsky, *The Life and Letters of Peter Ilyich Tchaikovsky*, ed. Rosa Newmarch (London, 1906), p.162.

7. M. I. Tchaikovsky, *Zhizn' Petra Il'icha Chaikovskogo*, vol. 1, p.451.

8. *Perepiska s N. F. Von Meck*, vol. 1, pp.173–74 (as quoted in Wilson Strutte, *Tchaikovsky* [Tunbridge Wells: Midas, 1979], pp.44–45).

9. Ibid.

10. According to a letter dated 20 January 1878 to his brother Anatoli, Tchaikovsky had discovered that Rubinstein had been to see his patron Nadezhda von Meck to dissuade her from bestowing an annuity on Tchaikovsky. Apparently Rubinstein feared that with this not inconsiderable boost to his financial situation, Tchaikovsky might contemplate resigning from the Conservatory. He also believed that the annuity would "foster idleness" (see James Friskin, "The Text of Tchaikovsky's B Flat Minor Concerto," *Music and Letters* 50/2 [1969]:246–51).

11. *Perepiska s N. F. von Meck*, vol. 1, pp.173–74 (Strutte, p.45).

12. Curiously enough, the conductor was none other than Nikolai Rubinstein. Favorable remarks about the première by Tchaikovsky suggest that to some extent he had settled his differences with his volatile colleague: "The present writer could not wish to hear a better performance of the piece than this one, for which he is indebted to the sympathetic talent of Mr. Taneyev and Mr. Rubinstein's mastery as a conductor" (G. Dombaev, *Tvorchestvo P. I. Chaikovskogo* [Tchaikovsky's works] [Moscow, 1958], p.447).

13. P. I. Tchaikovsky, *Polnoe sobranie sochineniy, II; Literaturnie proizvedeniia i perepiska* [Complete edition; literary works and correspondence] (Moscow, 1953), pp.292–93.

14. Friskin, pp.246–51.

15. The score of the Concerto in B-flat in which Dannreuther scribbled these amendments still survives and is deposited in the British Museum.

16. The amendments, which in the Soviet Complete Edition of Tchaikovsky's works take the form of an *ossia*, involve mm. 6–25, 71–84, 129–45, 219–22, 228–50, 261, 426–39, 491–531, 620–39, and 646–56 of the first movement.

17. As mentioned on p.43, it was not until the third edition (1889) that the soloist's famous octave chords, covering the entire range of the keyboard, were incorporated.

18. What prompted Tchaikovsky to embark on a third edition of his First Piano Concerto is not known. Perhaps his renewed acquaintance with his former fiancée, Desirée Artôt, after nearly twenty years, reawakened his interest in the First Concerto, a work which, according to David Brown, is dedicated to Artôt in all but name (*Tchaikovsky*, vol. 1, *The Early Years 1840–1874* [London: Gollancz, 1978], pp. 197–200). Tchaikovsky also heard an excellent performance of the Concerto given by Siloti in Berlin, shortly before he set about the revisions.

19. Brown, *Tchaikovsky*, vol. 2: *The Crisis Years 1874–1878* (London: Gollancz, 1982), pp.22–24.

20. Friskin, p.250.

21. Ibid.

22. Dannreuther was intimately acquainted with two of the three concertos most likely to have influenced the introductory chords of Tchaikovsky's concerto: Liszt's

Second Piano Concerto (see Ex. 4-6) and Grieg's Concerto in A minor (the third was Rubinstein's Fifth Concerto, Op. 94). In fact, Dannreuther gave the English premières of both works. Furthermore, it is probable, considering the importance of the event, that Dannreuther was present when Grieg made his London debut playing his Concerto at St. James Hall, London, on 3 May 1888. The work was an unqualified success with both critics and audience. Perhaps the stunning octave chords in the introduction of Grieg's Concerto prompted Dannreuther to suggest to Tchaikovsky a reappraisal of the soloist's role in his own introduction.

23. Rubinstein's accusation could not, of course, have applied to Tchaikovsky's final version of the introductory chords (Ex. 4-6b), as they were not incorporated in the score until 1889.

24. Eric Blom, "Works for Solo Instrument and Orchestra," in *Tchaikovsky: A Symposium*, ed. Gerald Abraham (London: Lindsay Drummond, 1945), p.51.

25. Ibid.

26. However, the comparative ease with which these two themes combine ties in neatly with Henry Zajaczkowski's belief that they may have been derived from the same source, i.e., the Russian folk song "Podoydu, podoydu vo Tsar-Gorod," No. 30 in Tchaikovsky's collection of 50 Russian folk songs (1868–69), published by Jurgenson. (For a more detailed account see p.133.)

27. Blom, p.52.

28. Ibid.

29. A. Orlova, *Pyotr Il'ich Chaikovskii* [Peter Ilyich Tchaikovsky] (Moscow: Izdatel'stvo Muzyka, 1980), p.55.

30. A. D. Alekseev, *Russkaia fortepiannaia muzyka konets XIX nachalo XX veka* [Russian piano music from the end of the 19th to the beginning of the 20th century] (Moscow: Izdatel'stvo Nauk, 1969), p.64.

31. This is corrected in the Eulenburg score so as to conform with the other statements of the theme.

32. Alekseev, p.64.

33. Edward Garden, "A Note on Tchaikovsky's First Piano Concerto," *Musical Times* 122/1658 (April 1981):238–39; and Brown, *Tchaikovsky*, vol. 2, pp.22–24.

34. For a detailed account of these discoveries, see Brown, *Tchaikovsky*, vol. 1, pp.197–200.

35. Brown, vol. 2, p.24.

36. In anticipation of the exposition, the piano part in this closing section toys with the sinuous contours of the Ukrainian folk song's first subject, which immediately follows.

37. Edward Garden, "Three Russian Piano Concertos," *Music and Letters* 60/2 (1979):176.

38. According to Tchaikovsky, this folk song was sung by "every blind Ukrainian singer" (letter to Nadezhda von Meck, 21 May 1879, *Perepiska s N. F. von Meck*, vol. 2, p.116).

39. Blom, p.53.

40. A fragment of this Ukrainian folk song also appears in the first piece, entitled "Song," in Aram Khachaturian, *Scenes from Childhood*, a collection for piano solo.

41. In his biography, *Zhizn' Petra Il'icha Chaikovskogo* [Life of Peter Ilyich Tchaikovsky], Tchaikovsky's brother Modest refers to the chansonette as a tune "which my brother Anatoli and I were constantly singing at the beginning of the '70s" (quoted in Gerald Abraham, Foreword to the Eulenburg Score, p.v). It was also an acknowledged favorite of the Belgian soprano Désirée Artôt, to whom Tchaikovsky was briefly engaged during the winter of 1868–69. Tchaikovsky dedicated his Romance for piano, Op. 5, and the Six Romances, Op. 65, to Artôt, and there is evidence to suggest that several of the more important melodies in the symphonic poem *Fatum* and the First Piano Concerto are in part cipher-generated from Artôt's name (see Brown, *Tchaikovsky*, vol. 1, pp.197–200).

42. Henry Zajaczkowski, letter, *Musical Times* 123/1668 (February 1982):89.

43. This folk song is the same one that Balakirev used in his second *Overture on Three Russian Themes* (composed in 1863–64 and later to become the symphonic poem *Russia*). Perhaps his well-documented dislike of the finale's second subject was not so much a criticism of Tchaikovsky's melodic writing (he greately admired the equally passionate and effusive "love theme" in Tchaikovsky's overture *Romeo and Juliet*) as a disapproval of Tchaikovsky's treatment of the folk song "Podoidu, podoidu vo Tsar-Gorod." It may even have been Balakirev who suggested the employment of the folk song in the first place (as he did for Rimsky-Korsakov's Piano Concerto).

44. Brown, vol. 1, pp.287–88.

45. John Warrack, *Tchaikovsky Symphonies and Concertos* (London: BBC Publications, 1974), pp.8–9.

46. Letter of 24 June 1878 to Nadezhda von Meck, *Perepiska*, vol. 1, pp.377–78.

47. Blom, p.54.

48. Garden, "A Note," pp.238–39.

49. Brown, vol. 2, p.26.

50. In a letter to K. N. Igumrov dating from 1912 (published in *Sovetskaia Muzyka* 14/1 (1946):88–89), Taneyev argues that the original marking, *Allegro vivace assai,* is in fact the correct tempo and that the indication *Prestissimo* is too fast. The Soviet musicologist Yuri Tyulin is presumably of the same opinion, for in his analysis of the *Andantino semplice* movement he refers to the central section only as *Allegro vivace assai.* (Yuri Tyulin, *Proizvedeniia Chaikovskogo, structurniy analyz* [Structural analysis of Tchaikovsky's works] [Moscow: Izdatel'stvo Muzyka, 1973], p.195.)

51. Brown, vol. 2, p.21.

52. Though as Alekseev suggests, the inconsistency concerning the first bar of the opening theme hints at a possible link with the introductory theme of the Concerto.

53. Schubert's influence is also evident in the first and third movements of Tchaikovsky's String Quartet in D, Op. 11.

54. Eulenburg miniature score.

55. Blom, p.55.

56. Warrack, p.43.

57. Tyulin, p.197.

58. Brown, vol. 2, pp.21–22.

59. The otherwise splendid finale of Balakirev's Piano Concerto in E-flat (reconstructed from sketches by Lyapunov) suffers to a certain extent from the inappropriate application of sonata-form principles.

60. The motif used by the strings is an inversion of the final bar of the movement's four-bar introduction, also indicated *pizzicato.*

61. Garden, "Three Russian Piano Concertos," p.176.

62. Ibid.

63. A. A. Al'shvang, *P. I. Chaikovskii* [P. I. Tchaikovsky] (Moscow: Gosudarstvennoe muzykal'noe izdatel'stvo, 1959), p.213.

64. Edward Garden, *Tchaikovsky* (London: Dent, 1976), pp.91–106.

65. *Perepiska s N. F. von Meck*, vol. 1, pp.371–75 (as quoted in Strutte, pp.149–50).

66. Ibid., vol. 2, p.231 (as quoted in David Lloyd-Jones, Foreword to the Eulenburg miniature score, p.i).

67. P. I. Tchaikovsky, *Polnoe sobranie: sochineniy dlia fortepianno s orchestrom* [Complete edition: works for piano and orchestra] (Moscow: Gosudarstvennoe muzykal'noe izdatel'stvo, 1955), p.xiii.

68. Blom, p.58.

69. John Warrack, *Tchaikovsky* (London: Hamish Hamilton, 1973), p.164.

70. It is significant that during this period, almost all of Tchaikovsky's major

instrumental works, including the *Italian Capriccio*, Op. 45, and the *Serenade for Strings*, Op. 48, eschew complex structural designs such as sonata form.

71. Garden, *Tchaikovsky*, p.101.

72. Tchaikovsky, *Polnoe sobranie: sochineniy dlia fortepianno s orchestrom*, p.xiv.

73. Tyulin, p.197.

74. Roger Fiske, "Tchaikovsky's later piano concertos," *Musical Opinion* 62 (October 1938):18.

75. P. I. Tchaikovsky, *Perepiska s P. I. Jurgensonom* [Correspondence with P. I. Jurgenson] (Moscow, 1938), vol 1, pp.139–40 (as quoted in David Lloyd-Jones, Foreword to the Eulenburg miniature score, p.ii).

76. *Istoriia russkoi muzyki b issledovaniiakh i materialakh* [History of Russian music in research and materials], ed. K. A. Kuznetsova (Moscow, 1924), vol. 1, p.181.

77. *Perepiska s P. I. Jurgensonom*, vol. 1, p.164.

78. Kuznetsova, p.182.

79. An obvious reference to the Piano Concerto in B-flat minor.

80. Tchaikovsky, *Polnoe sobranie: sochineniy dlia fortepianno s orchestrom*, p.xiv (Lloyd-Jones, p.iv).

81. Tchaikovsky, *Polnoe sobranie: sochineniy dlia fortepianno s orchestrom*, pp.xiv–xv.

82. Lloyd-Jones, pp.iv–v.

83. *P. I. Chaikovskii: S. I. Taneev. Pis'ma* [P. I. Tchaikovsky: S. I. Taneyev, Letters] (Moscow: Muzykal'noe izdatel'stvo, 1951), p.80 (as quoted in Lloyd-Jones, pp.iv–v).

84. The cuts—the only ones sanctioned by Tchaikovsky—involve mm. 319–42 in the first movement, and mm. 247–81, 310–26 (piano), and 327 (orchestra) in the *Andante*.

85. Tchaikovsky, *Polnoe sobranie: sochineniy dlia fortepianno s orchestrom*, p.xv.

86. Tchaikovsky, *Perepiska s P. I. Jurgensonom*, vol. 2, p.210.

87. Ibid. (as quoted in Lloyd-Jones, p.vi).

88. Quoted in the Editor's Note to P. I. Tchaikovsky, *Symphony in E flat major*, restored, orchestrated and edited by S. Bogatyrev (Moscow, 1961), p.12 (original source: *P. I. Chaikovskii: S. I. Taneev, Pis'ma* p.249).

89. The French pianist and composer Louis Diémer (1843–1919), to whom the Third Concerto is dedicated, studied at the Paris Conservatoire with Bazin, Marmontel, and A. Thomas, and in 1888 he joined the staff as professor of piano. He performed Tchaikovsky's *Concert Fantasia* in Paris on 4 March 1888, conducted by the composer.

90. Bogatyrev, p.12.

91. P. I. Tchaikovsky, *Pis'ma k Blizkim: Izbrannoe* [Letters to relations: selection], ed. V. A. Zhdanov (Moscow: Izdatel'stvo Muzyka, 1955), p.523, letter No. 644.

92. Tchaikovsky's nephew Vladimir Davidov.

93. Coincidentally, it was Siloti who preserved the orchestral parts of the *Voyevoda*, thus rescuing one of Tchaikovsky's finest symphonic works from oblivion.

94. Tchaikovsky, *Polnoe sobranie: sochineniy dlia fortepianno s orchestrom*, p.ix.

95. Tchaikovsky also retained the original scoring.

96. In the Concerto, at m. 235, the soloist embarks on a large-scale cadenza of some 88 bars, whereas in the symphony, the development continues for another twenty measures.

97. Roger Fiske, "Tchaikovsky's later piano concertos," *Musical Opinion* 62 (December 1938):209.

98. The manuscript is preserved in the Tchaikovsky Museum at Klin.

99. Bogatyrev, p.15.

100. Tchaikovsky, *Polnoe sobranie: sochineniy dlia fortepianno s orchestrom*, p.x.

101. Ibid.

102. See letter quoted on p.164.

103. Tchaikovsky, *Polnoe sobranie: sochineniy dlia fortepianno s orchestrom*, p.xi.

104. The comparatively complex texture that results is characteristic of Taneyev's own composition at that time and reflects his growing preoccupation, during the 1890s, with contrapuntal studies.

105. Blom, p.67. Blom seems to show some confusion here, attributing these "twiddling little figures" to *either* Tchaikovsky or Taneyev and stating that they are "nothing for either of them to be proud of, or for the player to enjoy, for they have not even the attraction of difficulty." This statement suggests that Blom was unaware of Taneyev's version, which, whatever one's opinion from a musical point of view, undeniably provides the soloist with a part both technically attractive and rewarding to play (see Ex. 4-64). Blom nevertheless mentions the "great deal of pianistic embroidery" of the *Andante*, the keyboard writing of which "shows how intimately Taneyev understood the peculiar Tchaikovskian way of pianistic treatment. . . ." These observations imply that Blom, although acquainted with Taneyev's version, somehow failed to notice the seventeen-bar *ossia* in the Finale.

106. Vladimir Lakond, trans., *The Diaries of Tchaikovsky* (New York: Norton, 1945), pp.23–24.

107. Garden, *Tchaikovsky*, p.105.

108. Lakond, footnote, p.24.

109. Ibid., pp.33–34.

110. Ibid., p.34.

111. *Perepiska s N. F. von Meck*, vol. 3, p.285.

112. *P. I. Chaikovskii: S. I. Taneev, Pis'ma*, p.108.

113. Curiously, in his correspondence with von Meck, Tchaikovsky persistently refers to the new work as a "piano concerto."

114. *Perepiska s N. F. von Meck*, vol. 3, p.289.

115. Ibid., p.307.

116. Taneyev also gave the St. Petersburg première of the *Concert Fantasia* on 5 April 1886, with Hans von Bülow conducting.

117. *Perepiska s P. I. Jurgensonom*, vol. 2, p.28.

118. According to Roger Fiske ("Tchaikovsky's later piano concertos," *Musical Opinion* 62 [November 1938]:114), this lightening of texture may have resulted from the withdrawal of Nikolai Rubinstein's influence, following his death in 1881.

119. Fiske believes that in its present form "the movement could hardly have been designed to begin the work. Perhaps the sketch was for the Andante section only" (ibid.). However, the fact that the themes for both the *Andante* and the *Molto vivace* sections were quoted in Tchaikovsky's diaries suggests otherwise (see Ex. 4-65).

120. Blom, pp.62–63.

121. Warrack, p.48.

122. Fiske, p.115, states, "there seems no reason why the pianist should not play it in any case."

Conclusion

1. Sergei Prokofiev, *Prokofiev by Prokofiev*, trans. Guy Daniels (London: Macdonald General Books, 1979), pp.169–70.

2. Sergei Rachmaninov, "New Lights on the Art of the Piano," *The Etude*, April–May 1923 (quoted in Sergei Bertensson and Jay Leyda, *Sergei Rachmaninov* [London: Allen & Unwin, 1956], p.231).

3. Barrie Martyn, *Rachmaninov* (Aldershot: Scholar Press, 1990), p.49.

4. Nikolai Rimsky-Korsakov, *My Musical Life*, trans. Judah A. Joffe (New York: Alfred A. Knopf, 1952), p.263.

5. Ibid., p.417.

Chronological List of Works Analyzed

Dmitri Bortnyansky, *Sinfonia Concertante* (scored for fortepiano, harp, two violins, viola da gamba, bassoon, and cello). Composed in 1790. Dedicated to "son Altresse impériale Madame La Grande Duchesse de Russie." Facsimile published by USSR-State Music Publishers, 1953.

Alexandre Villoing, Piano Concerto in C minor, Op. 4. Composed in 183? Dedicated to the Royal Academy of Music, Stockholm.

Anton Rubinstein, Piano Concerto No. 1, in E minor, Op. 25. Composed in 1850. Dedicated to Alexandre Villoing. Published in Leipzig by Bartholf Senff, 1858. Later publishers include C. F. Peters and Edwin A. Fleisher.

———, Piano Concerto No. 2, in F major, Op. 35. Composed in 1851. Dedicated to Charles Levy. Published by Senff in 1858. Also published by Cranz.

Mily Balakirev, *Grande Fantaisie on Russian Folksongs,* for piano and orchestra, Op. 4. Composed in 1852. Dedicated to Charles Eisrich. Published by USSR-State Music Publishers, 1954.

Anton Rubinstein, Piano Concerto No. 3, in G major, Op. 45. Composed in 1853–54. Dedicated to Ignaz Moscheles. Published by Senff in 1858. First performed on 18 May 1857 in London by the composer with the London Philharmonic Orchestra. Later publishers include Bote & Bock and Carl Fischer.

Mily Balakirev, Concerto Movement in F-sharp minor. Composed in 1855–56. First performed on 12 February 1856 at a St. Petersburg University concert by the composer. Published by USSR-State Music Publishers, 1954.

Anton Rubinstein, Piano Concerto No. 4, in D minor, Op. 70. Composed in 1864. Dedicated to Ferdinand David. First and second editions (1866 and 1872 respectively) published by Senff. Later publishers include Kalmus, G. Schirmer, Simrock, Sirkorski, and USSR-State Music Publishers.

———, Fantasy in C major, Op. 84. Composed in 1869. Published by Senff. First performed by the composer in Moscow in December 1869.

Peter Tchaikovsky, Piano Concerto No. 1, in B-flat minor, Op. 23. Composed in 1874–75. Dedicated to Hans von Bülow. The orchestral parts of the first edition and a version for two pianos were published by Jurgenson in 1875. The full score, "revised and corrected by the composer," was brought out as a second edition by Jurgenson in August 1879. A third edition followed in 1889 after consultation with the pianist Alexander Siloti. The full score of the original version was published in 1955 in vol. 28 of the Soviet Complete Edition. First performed by Hans von Bülow in Town Hall, Boston, on 25 October 1875, conducted by Benjamin Johnson Lang. Later publishers include Edizioni Curci, Eulenburg, Wilhelm Hansen, Kalmus, International Music Co., C. F. Peters, G. Schirmer, and Zen-On.

Anton Rubinstein, Piano Concerto No. 5, in E-flat, Op. 94. Composed in 1875. Dedicated to Charles-Henri-Valentin Alkan. Published by Senff in 1875. Later publishers include Leduc and Rozsavolgyi.

Sergei Taneyev, Piano Concerto in E-flat (unfinished). Composed in 1876. Taneyev abandoned the work soon after, and the existing two movements—the first in full score and the second arranged for two pianos—was published by the USSR-State Music Publishers in 1957, edited by Pavel Lamm. The second movement was subsequently orchestrated by V. Shebalin.

Anton Rubinstein, *Russian Capriccio,* in C minor, Op. 102, for piano and orchestra. Composed in 1878. Dedicated to Anna Esipova. Published by Senff in 1879.

Peter Tchaikovsky, Piano Concerto No. 2, in G major, Op. 44. Composed in 1879–80. Dedicated to Nikolai Rubinstein. An arrangement for two pianos was published by Jurgenson in October 1880, and the full score and orchestral parts in February 1881. A second edition was brought out after Tchaikovsky's death by Jurgenson in 1897; it was heavily revised by Siloti and bears the ignominious title "Nouvelle Edition, revue et diminuée d'après les indications de l'auteur par A. Ziloti." First performed by Madeleine Schiller in a concert conducted by Theodore Thomas, 12 November 1881, in New York. Later publishers include Alkor, Eulenburg, Carl Fischer, Paragon, C. F. Peters, Rahter, and USSR-State Music Publishers, 1955.

Anton Arensky, Piano Concerto in F minor, Op. 2. Composed in 1881–82. Dedicated to Carl Davidov. Published in 1883 by Paul Pabst-Rahter. First performed by Pabst. Later publishers include Edwin A. Fleischer and USSR-State Music Publishers (1975).

Nikolai Rimsky-Korsakov, Piano Concerto in C-sharp minor, Op. 30. Composed in 1882–83. Dedicated to Franz Liszt. Published in Leipzig by Beliaev, 1886. First performed by N. S. Lavrov at a Free School concert in St. Petersburg on 27 February 1884. Later publishers include Boosey and Hawkes, International Music Co., and USSR-State Music Publishers.

Peter Tchaikovsky, *Concert Fantasia,* Op. 56. Composed in 1884. Published by Jurgenson in December 1884 as an arrangement for two pianos and initially dedicated to Anna Esipova. Full score published by Jurgenson in 1893, with the dedicatee changed to Sophie Menter. First performed by Taneyev on 22 February 1885 at an R.M.S. concert conducted by Max von Erdmannsdörfer. Later publishers include Carl Fischer, Hinrichsen, Kalmus, Paragon, and USSR-State Music Publishers, 1955.

Anton Rubinstein, *Concertstück* in A-flat, Op. 113. Composed, published (by Senff), and performed by Rubinstein for his fifty-year jubilee celebration in 1889. Also published by Carl Fischer.

Sergei Lyapunov, Piano Concerto No. 1, in E-flat minor, Op. 4. Composed in 1888–90. Published by Bote & Bock in 1892. First performed by A. I. Borovka on 8 April 1891 in St. Petersburg, conducted by Balakirev.

Sergei Rachmaninov, Piano Concerto in F-sharp minor, Op. 1. Composed in 1891. Dedicated to Alexander Siloti. Published in an arrangement for two pianos by Gutheil in 1893. Full score published by Muzyka in 1971 (eds. I. Iordan and G. Kirkor). First performed on 17 March 1892 by Rachmaninov at a student concert at the Moscow Conservatory conducted by Vasily Safonov.

Anton Arensky, *Fantasia on Themes of I. T. Riabinin,* Op. 48. Composed in 1892. Published by Jurgenson, 1899, and by USSR-State Music Publishers, 1979.

Peter Tchaikovsky, Piano Concerto No. 3, in E-flat, Op. 75. Composed in 1893. Dedicated to Louis Diémer. Published by Jurgenson in 1894. First performed by Taneyev on 7 January 1895. Later published by Kalmus, Sikorski, and USSR-State Music Publishers, 1955.

———, *Andante and Finale,* Op. 79. Composed in 1893. Orchestrated by Taneyev after Tchaikovsky's death, 1893–95, and published by Beliaev in 1897. First performed on 8 February 1896 in St. Petersburg with Taneyev as soloist. Later publishers include Kalmus and Paragon. Taneyev's revised version (1896–98) premiered 17 October 1898 at one of Beliaev's "Russian" concerts, conducted by Rimsky-Korsakov. Both versions published by USSR-State Music Publishers, 1955.

Alexander Scriabin, Piano Concerto in F-sharp minor, Op. 20. Composed in 1896–97. Published by Beliaev in 1898. First performed on 11 October 1897 in Odessa by the composer with Safonov conducting. Later publishers include Boosey and Hawkes, Music Corporation of America, Kalmus, Broude Brothers Study Score, and Eulenburg.

Mily Balakirev, Piano Concerto in E-flat. Composed in 1861–1910 (completed by Lyapunov). Dedicated to Boris Zhilinski. Published by Zimmermann in 1911. First performed on 4 December 1910 in Berlin by L. Kreutzer, with Safonov as conductor. Also published by USSR-State Music Publishers 1954.

Selected Bibliography

PRIMARY SOURCES IN RUSSIAN

Balakirev, Mily. *Polnoe sobranie sochineniy dlia fortepianno*, ed. K. S. Sorokin, vol. 3. Moscow/Leningrad: Gosudarstvennoe muzykal'noe izdatel'stvo, 1954.

Glinka, M. I. *Literaturnoe nasledie*, vol. 1, *Avtobiograficheskie i tvorcheskie materialy*, ed. V. Bogdanov-Berezovskii. Leningrad, 1952.

Karenin, Vladimir, ed. *Perepiska M. A. Balakireva s V. V. Stasovym*, vol. 1. Moscow, 1953.

Kunin, N. N. A. *Rimskii-Korsakov, Zhizn' i tvorchestvo v vospominaniiakh, pis'makh i kriticheskikh otzyvakh*. Moscow: Vsesoyuznoe izdatel'stvo sovetskii kompositor, 1974.

Kuznetzova, K. A., ed. *Istoriia russkoi muzyki v issledovaniiakh in materialakh*. Moscow, 1924.

Rachmaninov, Sergei. *Pis'ma*, ed. Z. A. Apetian. Moscow: Gosudarstvennoe muzykal'noe izdatel'stvo, 1955.

Rimsky-Korsakov, Nikolai. *Polnoe sobranie sochineniy*, vol. 1: *Letopis' moei muzykal'noi zhizni'*. Moscow, 1963.

Rubinstein, Anton. *Izbrannye pis'ma*. Moscow, 1954.

Scriabin, Alexander. *Pis'ma*, ed. A. V. Kashperov. Moscow: Izdatel'stvo Muzyka, 1965.

Serov, Alexander. *Izbrannye stat'i*, ed. Georgii Khubov. Moscow and Leningrad: Gosudarstvennoe muzykal'noe izdatel'stvo, 1950–57.

———. *Kriticheskie stat'i* [Critical articles], ed. N. Stoianovskii et al. St. Petersburg, 1892–95.

Tchaikovsky, I. I., ed. *Dnevniki P. I. Chaikovskogo*. Moscow/Petrograd, 1923.

Tchaikovsky, Modest. *Zhizn' Petra Il'icha Chaikovskogo*, vol. 1. Moscow, 1900–1902.

Tchaikovsky, Peter Ilyich. *Perepiska s P. I. Jurgensonom*, vol. 1. Moscow, 1938.

———. *Perepiska s N. F. von Meck*, ed. V. A. Zhdanov and N. T. Zhegin. Moscow/Leningrad, 1934–36.

———. *Pis'ma k Blizkim: Izbrannoe*, ed. V. A. Zhdanov. Moscow: Izdatel'stvo Muzyka, 1955.

———. *Polnoe sobranie sochineniy*, vol. 2: *Literaturnie proizvedeniia i perepiska*. Moscow, 1953.

———. *Polnoe sobranie: sochineniy dlia fortepianno s orchestrom* [Complete edition: works for piano and orchestra]. Moscow: Gosudarstvennoe muzykal'noe izdatel'sto, 1955.

———, and Taneyev, S. I. *Pis'ma*, ed. V. A. Zhdanov. Moscow: Muzykal'noe izdatel'stvo, 1951.

Yakovlev, V. *Dni i Gody P. I. Chaikovskogo: Letopis' zhizni i tvorchestva*, compiled by E. Zaidenshnur, V. Kiselev, A. Orlova, and N. Shemanin. Moscow/Leningrad, 1940.

SECONDARY SOURCES IN RUSSIAN

Alekseev, A. D. *Russkaia fortepiannaia muzyka*. Moscow: Izdatel'stvo Akademii Nauk, 1963.

————. *Russkaia fortepiannaia muzyka konets xix–nachala xx veka*. Moscow: Izdatel'stvo Nauk, 1969.
Al'shvang, A. A. *P. I. Chaikovskii*. Moscow: Gosudarstvennoe muzykal'noe izdatel'stvo, 1959.
Barenboim, L. A. *Anton Grigorevich Rubinstein*. 2 vols. Leningrad: Gosudarstvennoe muzykal'noe izdatel'stvo, 1957.
Cui, César. *Izbrannye stat'i ob ispolniteliakh* [Selected articles on performers]. Moscow: Gosudarstvennoe muzykal'noe izdatel'stvo, 1957.
Druzin, M. S., and Keldysh, Y. V. *Ocherki po istorii russkoi muzyki 1790–1825*. Leningrad, 1956.
Findeisen, Nikolai. *Anton Grigorevich Rubinshtein, ocherk evo zhizni i muzykal'noi*. Moscow, 1907.
Keldysh, Yuri. *Istoriia russkoi muzyki*. 3 vols. Moscow: 1947–54.
————. *Russkaia muzyka XVIII veka*. Moscow/Leningrad, 1965.
Orlova, A. *Pyotr Il'ich Chaikovskii*. Moscow: Izdatel'stvo Muzyka, 1980.
Popov, T. V. *Russkoe narodnoe muzykal'noe tvorchestvo*, vol. 1. Moscow, 1955.
Savenko, S. I. *Sergei Ivanovich Taneev*. Moscow: Izdatel'stvo Muzyka, 1984.
Shifman, M. E. *S. M. Liapunov: zhizn' i tvorchestvo*. Moscow, 1960.
Smirnov, M. *Russkaia fortepiannaia muzyka*. Moscow: Izdatel'stvo Muzyka, 1983.
Tsuipin, G. M. *A. S. Arenskii*. Moscow: Izdatel'stvo Muzyka, 1966.
Tyulin, Yuri. *Proizvedeniia Chaikovskii, Strukturnyi analiz*. Moscow, 1973.

PRIMARY SOURCES IN ENGLISH

Liszt, Franz. *Letters*, ed. Constance Bache, vol. 1. London, 1894.
Rimsky-Korsakov, Nikolai. *My Musical Life*. New York: Alfred A. Knopf, 1942.
Rubinstein, Anton. *Autobiography*, supplement compiled by Aline Delano. Boston: Little, Brown and Co., 1890.
————. *Music and Its Masters*, trans. Mrs. John P. Morgan. London: Augener, 1920?
Tchaikovsky, Peter Ilyich. *Diaries*, trans. Vladimir Lakond. New York: Norton, 1945.

SECONDARY SOURCES IN ENGLISH

Abraham, Gerald. "Anton Rubinstein: Russian Composer." In *Slavonic and Romantic Music*. London/New York: Faber, 1968.
————, and Lloyd-Jones, David. Forewords to Eulenburg miniature scores of Tchaikovsky's Piano Concertos, Nos. 1 and 2.
Bakst, James. *A History of Russian-Soviet Music*. New York: Dodd, Mead and Co., 1966.
Bertensson, S., and Leyda, J. *Sergei Rachmaninoff: A Lifetime in Music*. London: George Allen and Unwin, 1956.
Blom, Eric. "Works for Solo Instrument and Orchestra." In *Tchaikovsky: A Symposium*, ed. Gerald Abraham. London: Drummond, 1945.
Bowers, Faubion. *Scriabin*, 2 vols. Tokyo and Palo Alto: Kodansha, 1969.
————. *The New Scriabin*. London: David and Charles, 1974.
Brown, David. *Tchaikovsky: A Biographical and Critical Study*, vol. 1: *The Early Years (1840–1874)*; vol. 2: *The Crisis Years (1874–1878)*; vol. 3: *The Years of Wandering (1878–1885)*. London: Victor Gollancz, 1978, 1982, 1986.
Calvocoressi, M. D., and Abraham, Gerald. *Mussorgsky*. London: Dent, 1946.
————. *Masters of Russian Music*. London: Max Parrish and Co., 1949.
Culshaw, John. *The Concerto*. London: Max Parrish and Co., 1949.
Davis, Richard. "Henselt, Balakirev and the piano." *The Music Review* 28 (August 1967).

Fiske, Roger. "Tchaikovsky's later piano concertos." *Musical Opinion* 62 (1938).
Friskin, James. "The Text of Tchaikovsky's B flat minor Concerto." *Music and Letters* 50/2 (1969).
Garden, Edward. *Balakirev: A Critical Study of His Life and Music.* London: Faber, 1967.
―――. *Tchaikovsky.* London: Dent, 1976.
―――. "Three Russian Piano Concertos." *Music and Letters* 60/2 (1979).
―――. "A Note on Tchaikovsky's First Piano Concerto." *The Musical Times*, April 1982.
―――. "Three Nights on Bare Mountain." *The Musical Times* 129 (July 1988).
Hinson, Maurice. *Music for Piano and Orchestra.* Bloomington: Indiana University Press, 1981.
MacDonald, Hugh. *Skryabin.* London: Oxford University Press, 1978.
Norris, Geoffrey. "Rakhmaninov's Second Thoughts." *The Musical Times* 114 (1973).
―――. *Rakhmaninov.* London: Dent, 1978.
Norris, Jeremy. "The Piano Concertos of Anton Rubinstein." *The Music Review* 46/4 (November 1985).
―――. "A Note on Balakirev's Piano Concerto." *The Musical Times* 131 (July 1990).
Rachmaninov, Sergei. "New Lights on the Art of the Piano." *The Etude*, April/May 1923.
Reilly, Edward R. *Musorgsky. In Memoriam 1881–1981,* ed. Malcolm Hamrick Brown. Ann Arbor: UMI Research Press, 1981.
Seaman, Gerald. "The Rise of Russian Piano Music." *The Music Review* 27 (August 1966).
Stasov, Vladimir. *Essays on Music,* trans. Florence Jonas. London: Barrie and Rockliff, 1968.
Tchaikovsky, Modest. *The Life and Letters of Peter Ilyich Tchaikovsky,* ed. Rosa Newmarch. London: John Lane, the Bodley Head, 1906.
Threlfall, Robert. "Rachmaninoff's Revisions and an Unknown Version of His Fourth Concerto." *Musical Opinion,* 1973, pp.235–37.
Veinus, Abraham. *The Concerto.* New York: Dover, 1964.
Volkoff, Vladimir. *Tchaikovsky: A Self-portrait.* London: Robert Hale and Co., 1975.
Warrack, John. *Tchaikovsky.* London: Hamish Hamilton, 1973.
―――. *Tchaikovsky: Symphonies and Concertos.* London: BBC Publications, 1977.

SOURCES IN OTHER LANGUAGES

Butzbach, Fritz. *Studien zum Klavierkonzert Nr. 1 F♯ moll Op. 1 von S. V. Rachmaninov.* Regensburg, 1979.
Die Musik in Geschichte und Gegenwart, vol. 2. Basel, 1963.
Neibuhr, Ulrich. "Der Einfluss Anton Rubinstein auf die Klavierkonzerte Peter Tchaikovskys." *Musikforschung* 27/4 (1974).
Rattalino, Piero. *Il Concerto per pianoforte e orchestra.* Milan: Ricordi Giunti, 1988.
Rubinstein, Anton. *Die Musik und ihre Meister.* 2d ed. Leipzig, 1892.
―――. *Gedankenkorb.* Leipzig, 1897.
Schumann, Robert. *Gesammelte Schriften über Musik und Musiker,* vol. 4. Leipzig, 1854.
Stengel, Th. *Die Entwicklung des Klavierkonzerts von Liszt bis zur Gegenwart.* Heidelberg, 1931.

Discography

COMPILED BY DAVID A. GRIFFIOEN

The goal of this discography—indeed, of any discography—is not merely to provide eager would-be listeners with a list of available recordings; numerous such sources already exist. Rather, this discography reveals an important aspect of the pieces discussed in the text, namely their performance history. As such, it presents the history of these pieces that begins after the narrative ends. With this goal in mind, every effort was made to include every recording (and subsequent reissues) of the pieces discussed in this book, relying on a number of printed and electronic sources. No arbitrary limits were enforced; the only recordings intentionally excluded are excerpts, condensed or abridged versions, and arrangements for other performance mediums.

To reflect the historical intent, selections are arranged in chronological order of original release date, insofar as that could be determined, with reissues listed at the end of each original entry. Consequently, multiple recordings of a piece by one performer may appear separated by many lines.

These pieces have been released with many different couplings; space limitations preclude including them all. Couplings are therefore indicated (in brackets [ ]) only when they involve other pieces from the discography. Because many of the couplings change from original release to reissue, they are indicated separately for each release and reissue—if the original release includes a coupling, unless it is reiterated for each reissue one can assume that the reissue does not include the same coupling.

Dates are inevitably a problem when dealing with earlier recordings. Only in recent decades have recording companies more consistently included dates on the items themselves, hence much approximation is involved; it is often possible to ascertain only the decade but not the specific year, therefore many of the dates omit the final digit. In the case of 78 rpm records, all that can be safely assumed is that they were issued prior to the 1950s; accordingly, all are dated "19—?" in the discography. The few items that were unable to be dated at all are designated "nd."

Finally, a few words must be said about names. All names appear, whenever possible, in the same form as is found on the recording itself. Spellings have been altered only in cases when consistency demands it; when a newer, more "correct" transliteration of a Russian name has begun to prevail over an earlier English rendition; and in cases of obvious misspelling or typographical error. As a general rule, names of orchestras are presented in their common or familiar anglicized form unless no such form exists.

All selections are 33⅓ rpm long-playing records unless otherwise indicated.

Abbreviations

BPO	Berlin Philharmonic Orchestra
BSO	Boston Symphony Orchestra
CO	Cleveland Orchestra
CSO	Chicago Symphony Orchestra

LAPO   Los Angeles Philharmonic Orchestra
LPO   London Philharmonic Orchestra
LSO   London Symphony Orchestra
MPO   Moscow Philharmonic Orchestra
MSO   Moscow Symphony Orchestra
NYP   New York Philharmonic Orchestra
PO   Philadelphia Orchestra
RPO   Royal Philharmonic Orchestra
VPO   Vienna Philharmonic Orchestra
VSO   Vienna Symphony Orchestra

Anton Arensky, *Piano Concerto in F minor Op. 2.*

Candide 31029. **Maria Littauer** (piano), Berlin Symphony Orchestra, Jörg Faerber (conductor), 196–?
Mezhdunarodnaya Kniga A 9333–9334 and Melodiya D 9333–9334. **Arnold Kaplan** (piano), Moscow State Philharmonic Symphony Orchestra, Boris Khaikin (conductor), 1961. Reissued: EMI His Master's Voice/Melodiya ASD 2607 [Scriabin—Concerto], 1962; Melodiya S 235–236, 1962; Melodiya S 01815–01816 [Arensky—Fantasia], 1969; Melodiya S 11493, 1978.
Auditorium AUD 101. **Felicja Blumental** (piano), Brno Philharmonic Orchestra, Jiri Waldhans (conductor), 1968. Reissued: Turnabout TV-S 34345, 1971?
Everest SDBR 3376. **Felicja Blumental** (piano), Innsbruck Symphony Orchestra, Robert Wagner (conductor), 1974.
Melodiya S 16681–16682 [Arensky—Fantasia]. **Aleksei Cherkasov** (piano), USSR Radio Symphony Orchestra, Aleksandr Alekseev (conductor), 1982. Reissued: Melodiya MCD 107 (CD), 1987; Olympia OCD 107 (CD), 1987.
Hyperion A 66624 (CD). **Stephen Coombs** (piano), BBC Scottish Symphony Orchestra, Jerzy Maksymiuk (conductor), 1993.

Anton Arensky, *Fantasia on themes of I. T. Riabinin Op. 48.*

USSR State Music Trust 015930–015931 (78 rpm). **M. Grünberg** (piano), USSR Radio Symphony Orchestra, Samuil Samosud (conductor), 19—?
Melodiya S 01815–01816 [Arensky—Concerto]. **Arnold Kaplan** (piano), USSR Radio Large Symphony Orchestra, Yuri Ahronovich (conductor), 1969.
EMI His Master's Voice/Melodiya ASD 3505. **Lyubov Timofeyeva** (piano), USSR Radio Large Symphony Orchestra, Algis Zuraitis (conductor), 1978.
Melodiya S 16681–16682 [Arensky—Concerto]. **Aleksei Cherkasov** (piano), USSR Radio Russian National Orchestra, Nikolai Nekrasov (conductor), 1982.
RBM Records 3016 [Rimsky-Korsakov—Concerto]. **Gi-in Wang** (piano), Rheinische Philharmonie, Pierre Stoll (conductor), 1982.
Melodiya SUCD 10-00150 (CD). **Lyubov Timofeyeva** (piano), USSR Radio Symphony Orchestra, Evgeni Svetlanov (conductor), 1991.
Hyperion A 66624 (CD). **Stephen Coombs** (piano), BBC Scottish Symphony Orchestra, Jerzy Maksymiuk (conductor), 1993.

Mily Balakirev, *Concerto Movement in F sharp minor.*

Melodiya D 1324. **B. Shirinsky [Boris Zhilinsky?]** (piano), USSR Radio Symphony Orchestra, Alexander Gauk (conductor), 1953?
Melodiya SM 03557–03558. **Boris Zhilinsky** (piano), USSR Radio Symphony Orchestra, Alexander Gauk (conductor), 1972.

Melodiya S 04993–04994. **Igor Zhukov** (piano), USSR Radio Large Symphony Orchestra, Alexander Dmitriev (conductor), 1974. Reissued: Turnabout TV 34789, 1982.
Hyperion A 66640 (CD) [Balakirev—Concerto; Rimsky-Korsakov—Concerto]. **Malcolm Binns** (piano), English Northern Philharmonic, David Lloyd-Jones (conductor), 1993.

Mily Balakirev, *Piano Concerto in E flat.*

Turnabout QTV-S 34645. **Michael Ponti** (piano), Westphalian Symphony Orchestra, Siegfried Landau (conductor), 1976.
Hyperion A 66640 (CD) [Balakirev—Concerto Movement; Rimsky-Korsakov—Concerto]. **Malcolm Binns** (piano), English Northern Philharmonic, David Lloyd-Jones (conductor), 1993.

Dmitri Bortnyansky, *Sinfonia Concertante.*

Christophorus SCGLX 73 950. **Hans Kann** (piano), Südwestdeutsches Kammerorchester Pforzheim, Paul Angerer (conductor), 197-? Reissued: Christophorus CD 74581 (CD), 1989.
Melodiya S 08697–08698. **Mykhailo Borysovych Stepanenko** (piano), S. Markicheva (harp), A. Bazhenov, B. Skvortsov (violins), IU. Kholodov (viola), L. Krasnoshchek ('cello), V. Prokopovich (bassoon), 1977.
Melodiya S 10-28023. **Dmitri Blagoi** (piano), Olga Erdeli (harp), Marina Yashvili, Aleksei Shalashov (violins), Galina Odinets (viola), Tatiana Priimenko ('cello), Vladimir Vlasenko (bassoon), 1989.
Art & Electronics AED 10370 (CD). **Dmitri Shvedov** (piano), The Chamber Ensemble of the Moscow Philharmonic Society, Andrei Korsakov (conductor), 1991.

Nikolai Rimsky-Korsakov, *Piano Concerto in C sharp minor Op. 30.*

USSR State Music Trust 017956–017959 (2 78 rpm discs). **Sviatoslav Richter** (piano), MSO, Kirill Kondrashin (conductor), 19—? Reissued: Melodiya D 391–392, 1952; Miro MLP-8002, 196-?; Monitor MC 2131, 197-?; Melodiya S 04683–04684, 1974; Everest SDBR 3393, 1976.
MGM E 182. **Fabienne Jacquinot** (piano), Philharmonia Orchestra of London, Anatole Fistoulari (conductor), 195-? Reissued: MGM Classics MCS 7010–7013, 196-?
Westminster WL 5068 [Scriabin—Concerto]. **Paul Badura-Skoda** (piano), Philharmonic Symphony Orchestra of London, Artur Rodzinski (conductor), 1951. Reissued: Westminster XWN 18521 [Scriabin—Concerto], 1957; Westminster W 9724 (monaural) and WST 14521 (stereo) [Scriabin—Concerto], 1968.
Balkanton BCA 2004. **Victor Chuchov** (piano), Simfonichen Orkester na K. T. R., Vasil Stefanov (conductor), 197-?
Melodiya SM 03021–03022. **Igor Zhukov** (piano), USSR Radio Symphony Orchestra, Gennadi Rozhdestvensky (conductor), 1971. Reissued: Melodiya/Angel SR 40188 [Tchaikovsky—Concertos Nos. 2 and 3], 1972; Melodiya/His Master's Voice ASD 2846, 1972; Musical Heritage Society MHS 4946X [Tchaikovsky—Concerto No. 3], 1984.
Candide CE 31056 [Tchaikovsky—Op. 79 and Concerto No. 3]. **Michael Ponti** (piano), Hamburg Symphony, Richard Kapp (conductor), 1972.

RBM Records 3016 [Arensky—Fantasia]. **Gi-in Wang** (piano), Rheinische Philharmonie, Pierre Stoll (conductor), 1982?
Hyperion A 66640 (CD) [Balakirev—Concerto and Concerto Movement]. **Malcolm Binns** (piano), English Northern Philharmonic, David Lloyd-Jones (conductor), 1993.

Anton Rubinstein, *Concertstück in A flat Op. 113.*

Turnabout TV-S 34387. **Felicja Blumental** (piano), Vienna Pro Musica Symphony, Helmuth Froschauer (conductor), 1970?
Marco Polo 8.223190 (CD) [Rubinstein—Fantasy]. **Joseph Banowetz** (piano), Czecho-Slovak Radio Symphony Orchestra, Oliver Dohnányi (conductor), 1990.

Anton Rubinstein, *Fantasy in C major Op. 84.*

Marco Polo 8.223190 (CD) [Rubinstein—Concertstück]. **Joseph Banowetz** (piano), Czecho-Slovak Radio Symphony Orchestra, Oliver Dohnányi (conductor), 1990.

Anton Rubinstein, *Piano Concerto No. 1 in E Minor Op. 25.*

Orion ORS 79347. **Michael Fardink** (piano), RPO, Paul Freeman (conductor), 1979.
Marco Polo 8.223456 (CD) [Rubinstein—Concerto No. 2]. **Joseph Banowetz** (piano), Czecho-Slovak State Philharmonic Orchestra, Alfred Walter (conductor), 1992.

Anton Rubinstein, *Piano Concerto No. 2 in F major Op. 35.*

Marco Polo 8.223456 (CD) [Rubinstein—Concerto No. 1]. **Joseph Banowetz** (piano), Czecho-Slovak State Philharmonic Orchestra, Alfred Walter (conductor), 1992.

Anton Rubinstein, *Piano Concerto No. 3 in G major Op. 45.*

International Piano Archives IPA 500 [Rubinstein—Concerto No. 4]. **Josef Hofmann** (piano), Detroit Symphony Orchestra, Karl Kruger (conductor), 19—?
Orion ORS 74149. **Robert Preston** (piano), Westphalian Symphony Orchestra, Paul Freeman (conductor), 1974.
Marco Polo 8.223382 (CD) [Rubinstein—Concerto No. 4]. **Joseph Banowetz** (piano), Czecho-Slovak State Philharmonic Orchestra, Robert Stankovsky (conductor), 1991.

Anton Rubinstein, *Piano Concerto No. 4 in D minor Op. 70.*

International Piano Archives IPA 500 [Rubinstein—Concerto No. 3]. **Josef Hofmann** (piano), Detroit Symphony Orchestra, Karl Kruger (conductor), 19—? Reissued: International Piano Library IPL 503, 1966.
Columbia ML 4559. **Oscar Levant** (piano), NYP, Dimitri Mitropoulis (conductor), 195-? Reissued: Odyssey 32 16 0169, 1968.
Vox PL 7780. **Friedrich Wührer** (piano), Vienna Philharmonic, Rudolf Moralt (conductor), 195-?
Melodiya D 03596–03597. **Grigori Ginsburg** (piano), USSR State Orchestra, A. Shereshevsky (conductor), 1957. Reissued: Mobile Fidelity MFCD 895, 1989?

Vox/Candide VS 3187. **Michael Ponti** (piano), Philharmonica Hungarica, Othmar Mága (conductor), 1969. Reissued: Candide 31023, 1970; Vox Prima MWCD 7151 (CD), 1987; Vox Unique VU 9014 (CD), 1990.
Columbia MS 7394. **Raymond Lewenthal** (piano), LSO, Eleazar de Carvalho (conductor), 1970.
International Piano Archives IPL 5001–5002. **Josef Hofmann** (piano), Curtis Student Orchestra, Fritz Reiner (conductor), 1977 (rec. 1937).
Melodiya S 09731–09732. **Viktor Bunin** (piano), USSR Radio and Television Symphony Orchestra, Eduard Serov (conductor), 1978. Reissued: Le Chant du Monde LDX 78810–78811, 1985?
Mobile Fidelity/Melodiya MFCD-895 (CD). **Grigori Ginsburg** (piano), USSR Symphony, A. Chershonsky (conductor), 199-?
Marco Polo 8.223382 (CD) [Rubinstein—Concerto No. 3]. **Joseph Banowetz** (piano), Czecho-Slovak State Philharmonic Orchestra, Robert Stankovsky (conductor), 1991.

Anton Rubinstein, *Piano Concerto No. 5 in E flat Op. 94.*

Genesis GS 1012. **Adrian Ruiz** (piano), Nürnberg Symphony, Zsolt Deáky (conductor), 1972. Reissued: Colosseum SM 544, 197-?; Genesis GCD-103 (CD) 1989.

Alexander Scriabin, *Piano Concerto in F sharp minor Op. 20.*

USSR State Music Trust 018864–018869 (3 78 rpm discs). **Samuil Feinberg** (piano), USSR Radio Symphony Orchestra, Alexander Gauk (conductor), 19—? Reissued: Melodiya D 418–419, 1952.
Westminster WL 5068 [Rimsky-Korsakov—Concerto]. **Paul Badura-Skoda** (piano), VSO, Henry Swoboda (conductor), 1951. Reissued: Westminster XWN 18521 [Rimsky-Korsakov—Concerto], 1957; Westminster W 9724 (monaural) and WST 14521 (stereo) [Rimsky-Korsakov—Concerto], 1968.
Melodiya D 5452–5453. **Dmitri Bashkirov** (piano), USSR Radio Symphony Orchestra, Kirill Kondrashin (conductor), 1959. Reissued: Artia ALP-168, 1960.
EMI His Master's Voice/Melodiya ASD 2607 [Arensky—Concerto]. **Arnold Kaplan** (piano), Moscow State Philharmonic Symphony Orchestra, Boris Khaikin (conductor), 1962.
Melodiya D 16311–16312 (monaural) and S 1085–1086 (stereo). **Stanislav Neuhaus** (piano), USSR State Orchestra, Viktor Dubrovsky (conductor), 1965. Reissued: Melodiya SM 03033–03034, 1971.
Melodiya D 019635–019636. **Heinrich Neuhaus** (piano), USSR Radio Symphony Orchestra, Nikolai Golovanov (conductor), 1967.
Candide CE 31040. **Michael Ponti** (piano), Hamburg Symphony Orchestra, Hans Drewanz (conductor), 1971. Reissued: Turnabout TV 34611, 197-?
London CS 6732. **Vladimir Ashkenazy** (piano), LPO, Lorin Maazel (conductor), 1972. Reissued: Decca 6.41 461, 1971; London/Decca SXL 6527, 1972; London 417 252-2 (CD), 1989.
Supraphon CO 2047 (CD). **Garrick Ohlsson** (piano), Czech Philharmonic Orchestra, Libor Pesek (conductor), 1987. Reissued: Supraphon 10 4149 (CD), 199-?
Pantheon D 1032X (CD). **Abbott Ruskin** (piano), M.I.T. Symphony Orchestra, David Epstein (conductor), 1987.
Bis CD-475 (CD). **Roland Pöntinen** (piano), Stockholm Philharmonic Orchestra, Leif Segerstam (conductor), 1990.
Melodiya SUCD 10-00191 (CD). **Aleksei Nasedkin** (piano), USSR Symphony Orchestra, Evgeni Svetlanov (conductor), 1990?

Peter Tchaikovsky, *Andante and Finale Op. 79.*

Candide CE 31056 [Rimsky-Korsakov—Concerto; Tchaikovsky—Concerto No. 3]. **Michael Ponti** (piano), Radio Luxembourg Symphony Orchestra, Louis de Froment (conductor), 1972.

Philips 6703 033 [Op. 79, Complete Concertos, and Fantasia]. **Werner Haas** (piano), National Opera Orchestra of Monte Carlo, Eliahu Inbal (conductor), 1972.

Peter Tchaikovsky, *Concert Fantasia Op. 56.*

Decca SPA 168. **Peter Katin** (piano), LPO, Sir Adrian Boult (conductor), 195-? Reissued: London CS 6055, 1959; London STS 15227 [Tchaikovsky—Concerto No. 1], 1971.

Melodiya D 403–404. **Tatiana Nikolayeva** (piano), USSR State Symphony Orchestra, Kirill Kondrashin (conductor), 1952. Reissued: Classic Editions CE 7, 195-?

Melodiya D 01539–01540. **Oksana Yablonskaya** (piano), USSR Radio Symphony Orchestra, Boris Khaikin (conductor), 1953. Reissued: Melodiya D 21577–21578, 1968.

Philips 6703 033 [Op. 79, Complete Concertos, and Fantasia]. **Werner Haas** (piano), National Opera Orchestra of Monte Carlo, Eliahu Inbal (conductor), 1972.

Vox SVBX 5455, 5459, 5460 [Complete Concertos and Fantasia]. **Michael Ponti** (piano), Prague Symphony Orchestra, Richard Kapp (conductor), 1973. Reissued: Turnabout TV-S 34551 [Tchaikovsky—Complete Concertos Set], 1974; Vox CDX 5024 [Tchaikovsky—Concertos Nos. 1 and 2], 1991.

Melodiya S 06973–06974. **Igor Zhukov** (piano), USSR Symphony Orchestra, Dmitri Kitayenko (conductor), 1976.

EMI CDC 7 47718 [Tchaikovsky—Concerto No. 1]. **Dimitris Sgouros** (piano), LPO, Walter Weller (conductor), 1987.

Arabesque Z6611 (CD) [Tchaikovsky—Concerto No. 1]. **Jerome Lowenthal** (piano), LSO, Sergiu Comissiona (conductor), 1989.

EMI CDC 7 49939–7 49940 (CD) [Complete Concertos and Fantasia]. **Peter Donohoe** (piano), Bournemouth Symphony Orchestra, Rudolf Barshai (conductor), 1990.

Peter Tchaikovsky, *Piano Concerto No. 1 in B flat minor Op. 23.*

Deutsche Grammophon 72129–72131 (3 78 rpm discs). **Shura Cherkassky** (piano), BPO, Leopold Ludwig (conductor), 19—? Reissued: Deutsche Grammophon 18013, 195—?; Decca DL 9605, 195-?

Broadcast Twelve 5118–5121 (4 78 rpm discs). **Maurice Cole** (piano), Metropolitan Symphony Orchestra, Stanley Chapple (conductor), 19—?

Metronome CL 3004–3007 (4 78 rpm discs). **Emil Gilels** (piano), Stockholm Radio Orchestra, Sixten Ehrling (conductor), 19—? Reissued: Regent 5055, 195-?

USSR State Music Trust 014821–014828 (4 78 rpm discs). **Emil Gilels** (piano), USSR State Symphony Orchestra, Samuil Samosud (conductor), 19—? Reissued: Supraphon 40093–40096 (4 78 rpm discs), 19—?; Ultraphon H 24088–24091 (4 78 rpm discs), 19—?; Ultraphon 1658, 1956?; Bruno BR 14005, 1958.

Gramophone D 1130–1133 (4 78 rpm discs). **Mark Hambourg** (piano), Royal Albert Hall Orchestra, Landon Ronald (conductor), 19—? Reissued: Electrola EJ 161–164 (4 78 rpm discs), 19—?; Victor 9055–9058 (4 78 rpm discs), 19—?

Telefunken SK 3092–3095 (4 78 rpm discs). **Conrad Hansen** (piano), BPO, Willem Mengelberg (conductor), 19—? Reissued: Ultraphon G 14273–14276 (4 78 rpm discs), 19—?; Telefunken SK 76–79 (4 78 rpm discs); Capitol P 8097, 195-?

Victor Masterworks 18145–18148 (set M 800—manual sequence and set DM 800—automatic sequence), His Master's Voice DB 5988–5991, and His Master's Voice 8922–8925 (4 78 rpm discs). **Vladimir Horowitz** (piano), NBC Symphony Orchestra, Arturo Toscanini (conductor), 19—? (recorded 1941). Reissued: RCA Victor LCT 1012, 195-?; His Master's Voice AT 103, 195-?; His Master's Voice CSLP 505, 195-?; RCA 26.41018, 1960; RCA Victrola VIC 1554, 1971; RCA Gold Seal 60319-2-RG (CD), 1992.

His Master's Voice RB-16190 and RCA CRM4-0914. **Vladimir Horowitz** (piano), NBC Symphony Orchestra, Arturo Toscanini (conductor), 19—? (recorded live 1943). Reissued: RCA Victor LM 2319, 1959; RCA VL 46016, 1983; RCA Gold Seal 7992-2-RG (CD), 1990; Melodram MEL 18014 (CD), 199-?; RCA Gold Seal 60321-2-RG (CD), 1992.

Columbia LFX 595–598 (4 78 rpm discs). **Kostia Konstantinoff** (piano), Paris Conservatory Orchestra, Charles Munch (conductor), 19—?

Columbia Masterworks 12910–12914 D (set MM 785–5 78 rpm discs). **Oscar Levant** (piano), PO, Eugene Ormandy (conductor), 19—? Reissued: Columbia CL 740, 195-?; Columbia ML 4883, 1954; Columbia ML 4096, 1957?

Gramophone 3466–3470 (set M 399) and His Master's Voice C 7623–7627 (5 78 rpm discs). **Benno Moiseiwitsch** (piano), Philharmonia Orchestra, George Weldon (conductor), 19—?

Decca K 1167–1170 (4 78 rpm discs). **Nicolas Orlov** (piano), National Symphony Orchestra, Anatole Fistoulari (conductor), 19—?

Columbia Masterworks 69134–69137 (Set M 318), Columbia LX 681–684, and Columbia GQX 11060–11063 (4 78 rpm discs). **Egon Petri** (piano), LPO, Walter Goehr (conductor), 19—? Reissued: Columbia Entré RL 3018, 195-?

Victor Masterworks 7802–7805 (set M 180), Gramophone DB 7242–7245, and His Master's Voice DB 1731–1734 (4 78 rpm discs). **Artur Rubinstein** (piano), LSO, Sir John Barbirolli (conductor), 19—?

Victor Masterworks 11-9776–11-9779 (set 1159—manual sequence) and 11-9780–11-9783 (set DM 1159—automatic sequence) (4 78 rpm discs). **Artur Rubinstein** (piano), Minneapolis Symphony Orchestra, Dimitri Mitropoulos (conductor), 19—? Reissued: RCA Victor LM 1028, 195-?

Victor JD 68–70 (3 78 rpm discs). **Artur Rubinstein** (piano), BSO, Erich Leinsdorf (conductor), 19—? Reissued: RCA Victor LM 2681 (monaural) and LSC 2681 (stereo), 1963; RCA Red Seal VCS 7070, 1971; RCA Gold Seal AGL1-4878-A, 1975; RCA Gold Seal AGL1-5217, 1983; RCA Red Seal RCD1-5363 (CD), 1985; RCA Red Seal 6259-2-RC (CD), 1987; RCA Gold Seal 61262-2 (CD), 1992.

Tono X 25051–25054 (4 78 rpm discs). **Victor Schiøler** (piano), Danish Radio Orchestra, Carl Garaguly (conductor), 19—? Reissued: Sonora K 9511–9514 (4 78 rpm discs), 19—?

His Master's Voice DB 5584–5587 (4 78 rpm discs). **Winifred Wolf** (piano), Czech Philharmonic, Václav Talich (conductor), 19—?

Gramophone S 10578–10581 (4 78 rpm discs). **Solomon [Cutner]** (piano), Philharmonia Orchestra, Issay Dobrowen (conductor), 19—? Reissued: Gramophone C 7776–7779 (4 78 rpm discs), 19—?; Gramophone CLP 1001, 195-?; RCA Victor LHMV 1028, 1952; His Master's Voice SLS 5094, 1977.

Columbia LX 19–22 (4 78 rpm discs). **Solomon [Cutner]** (piano), Hallé Orchestra, Hamilton Harty (conductor), 19—? Reissued: Columbia LOX 25–28 (4 78 rpm discs), 19—?; Columbia 67789–67792 (Set M 141—4 78 rpm discs), 19—?; BBC Records BBC CD 71 (CD), 1989.

Angel ANG 35083. **Géza Anda** (piano), Philharmonia Orchestra, Alceo Galliera (conductor), 195-?

Gramophone FALP 102. **Aldo Ciccolini** (piano), Orchestre de la société des concerts du conservatoire, André Cluytens (conductor), 195-? Reissued: Bluebird LBC 1020, 195-?; RCA Victor LBC 1020, 196-?

Westminster XWN 18289 [Tchaikovsky—Concerto No. 2]. **Edith Farnadi** (piano), Vienna State Opera Orchestra, Hermann Scherchen (conductor), 195-?
Angel 35477. **José Iturbi** (piano), Paris Colonne Orchestra, José Iturbi (conductor), 195-?
Decca SPA 168. **Peter Katin** (piano), LSO, Edric Kundell (conductor), 195-? Reissued: London STS 15227 [Tchaikovsky—Fantasia], 1971.
Westminster WST 14014. **Jacob Lateiner** (piano), Vienna State Opera Orchestra, Armando Aliberti (conductor), 195-? Reissued: MCA Classics MCAD2-9829 (CD), 1990.
Philips A 00135L. **Alexander Uninsky** (piano), unnamed orchestra, Willem Van Otterloo (conductor), 195-? Reissued: Epic LC 3010, 196-?
London LLP 276. **Clifford Curzon** (piano), New Symphony Orchestra of London, George Szell (conductor), 1950. Reissued: Decca 6.48112, 1951.
Musical Masterworks Society MMS 12. **Noel Mewton-Wood** (piano), Musical Masterworks Symphony Orchestra, Walter Goehr (conductor), 1950?
Melodiya D 01400–01401. **Pavel Serebryakov** (piano), Leningrad Philharmonic, Evgeni Mravinsky (conductor), 1953.
Supraphon LPV 242. **Sviatoslav Richter** (piano), Czech Philharmonic Orchestra, Karel Ančerl (conductor), 1954. Reissued: Dell'Arte DA 9018, 1985; Supraphon 11 0268-2 (CD), 1992.
RCA Victor LM 1969. **Emil Gilels** (piano), CSO, Fritz Reiner (conductor), 1955. Reissued: RCA Victrola VICS 1039, 1963; RCA Gold Seal AGL1-2908, 1975; RCA VL 89043, 1983.
Capitol P-18007. **Ventsislav Yankoff** (piano), New Symphony Orchestra of London, Rudolf Schwarz (conductor), 1956.
Melodiya D 04328–04329. **Van Cliburn** (piano), Moscow Philharmonic Orchestra, Kirill Kondrashin (conductor), 1958. Reissued: Melodiya SM 03505–03506, 1972; Melodiya SUCD 10-00250 (CD), 198-?
RCA Victor LM 2252. **Van Cliburn** (piano), unnamed orchestra, Kirill Kondrashin (conductor), 1958. Reissued: Franklin Mint Record Society FM 1079–1080, 1981; RCA Red Seal ATL1-4099, 1981; RCA Red Seal ARP1-4441, 1981. (See below, RCA 5912-2-RC, 1987.)
Angel ANG 35543. **Witold Malcuzynski** (piano), Orchestre national de la radiodiffusion française, Nikolai Malko (conductor), 1958.
Capitol PAO 8417. **Leonard Pennario** (piano), LAPO, Erich Leinsdorf (conductor), 1958. Reissued: Paperback Classics SL 9209, 1963; Seraphim S 60316, 1978.
London CS 6100. **Clifford Curzon** (piano), VPO, Sir Georg Solti (conductor), 1959. Reissued: Decca SDD 191, 1969; Decca JB 29, 1979; London STS 15471, 1979; London 417 676-2 (CD), 1987.
Angel ANG 35612. **György Cziffra** (piano), Orchestre national de la radiodiffusion française, Pierre Dervaux (conductor), 1959.
Melodiya D 05470–05471. **Emil Gilels** (piano), USSR State Symphony Orchestra, Konstantin Ivanov (conductor), 1959.
Melodiya D 05468–05469. **Sviatoslav Richter** (piano), Leningrad Philharmonic, Evgeni Mravinsky (conductor), 1959. Reissued: Melodiya SM 02013–02014, 1970; Vox STPL 513.370, 1972.
Columbia MS 6079. **Eugene Istomin** (piano), PO, Eugene Ormandy (conductor), 1959? Reissued: Columbia Odyssey Y 34606, 1977.
Erato EFM 8013. **György Sebök** (piano), Orchestre national de l'opéra de Monte-Carlo, Louis Frémaux (conductor), 196-?
Celebrity UT 149. **Gregory Stockwell** (piano), London Pops Symphony Orchestra, unnamed conductor, 196-?
Mercury SR 90266. **Byron Janis** (piano), LSO, Herbert Menges (conductor), 1960. Reissued: Mercury SR 90448, 1966.

Ducretet Thomson SCC 510. **Raymond Trouard** (piano), Paris Colonne Orchestra, Pierre Dervaux (conductor), 1961.

Melodiya D 010005–010006 (monaural) and S 0307–0308 (stereo). **Vladimir Ashkenazy** (piano), USSR State Symphony Orchestra, Konstantin Ivanov (conductor), 1962.

Columbia ML 5759 (monaural) and MS 6359 (stereo). **Philippe Entremont** (piano), NYP, Leonard Bernstein (conductor), 1962. Reissued: Columbia D3S 715, 1965.

Deutsche Grammophon LPM 18822 (monaural) and SLPM 138822 (stereo). **Sviatoslav Richter** (piano), VSO, Herbert von Karajan (conductor), 1962. Reissued: Deutsche Grammophon 104 922–104 928, 196-?; Deutsche Grammophon 644 107, 1962; Deutsche Grammophon 2862 002, 1962; Melodiya D 011275–011276 (monaural), 1963; Melodiya S 0473–0474 (stereo), 1963; Melodiya SM 04255–04256, 1973; Deutsche Grammophon 419 068-2 (CD), 1986.

Murray Hill Records M 2958 (monaural) and S 2959 (stereo). **Sviatoslav Richter** (piano), unnamed orchestra, unnamed conductor, 1962?

London CS 9360. **Vladimir Ashkenazy** (piano), LSO, Lorin Maazel, (conductor), 1963. Reissued: Decca SXL 6058, 1963; Decca D 62D4, 1977; Decca SXL 6840, 1978; Decca D 271D3, 1982; London 417 750-2 (CD), 1988; London CS 6440, 1988.

Angel S 36142. **John Ogdon** (piano), Philharmonia Orchestra, John Barbirolli (conductor), 1963. Reissued: Arabesque 8012, 1980.

Fabbri TGM 05. **Friedrich Wührer** (piano), Vienna Pro Musica, Heinrich Hollreiser (conductor), 1965. Reissued: Funk & Wagnalls FW 314, 1976.

Melodiya D 018063–018064 (monaural) and S 01331–01332 (stereo). **Grigori Sokolov** (piano), USSR State Symphony Orchestra, Neeme Järvi (conductor), 1966. Reissued: Melodiya/Angel S 40016, 1967.

Seraphim S 60020. **Claudio Arrau** (piano), Philharmonia Orchestra, Alceo Galliera (conductor), 1967. Reissued: Electrola SHZE 161, n.d.

RCA Victor LM 2954 (monaural) and LSC 2954 (stereo). **Misha Dichter** (piano), BSO, Erich Leinsdorf (conductor), 1967. Reissued: RCA 6526-2-RG (CD), 1987.

RCA Red Seal LSC 3069. **John Browning** (piano), LSO, Seigi Ozawa (conductor), 1969.

Columbia MS 7339. **Gary Graffman** (piano), Cleveland Orchestra, George Szell (conductor), 1970. Reissued: Columbia MG 30838 [Complete Concertos Set], 1971; CBS MY 37263, 1982; CBS MYK 37263 (CD), 1982.

Melodiya SM 02115–02116. **Vladimir Krainev** (piano), USSR Radio Symphony Orchestra, Gennadi Rozhdestvensky (conductor), 1970.

Deutsche Grammophon 2530 122. **Martha Argerich** (piano), RPO, Charles Dutoit (conductor), 1971. Reissued: Deutsche Grammophon 2535 295, 1977; Deutsche Grammophon 2543 503, 1983; Deutsche Grammophon 415 062-2 (CD), 1985; Musical Heritage Society MHS 7461, 1986.

Angel S 36755. **Alexis Weissenberg** (piano), Orchestre de Paris, Herbert von Karajan (conductor), 1971.

Philips 6703 033 [Op. 79, Complete Concertos, and Fantasia]. **Werner Haas** (piano), National Opera Orchestra of Monte Carlo, Eliahu Inbal (conductor), 1972.

Angel SB 3798 [Complete Concertos Set]. **Emil Gilels** (piano), New Philharmonia Orchestra, Lorin Maazel (conductor), 1973.

Vox SVBX 5455, 5459, 5460 [Complete Concertos and Fantasia]. **Michael Ponti** (piano), Prague Symphony Orchestra, Richard Kapp (conductor), 1973. Reissued: Turnabout TV-S 34560 [Tchaikovsky—Concerto No. 1], 1974; Vox Box CDX 5024 (CD) [Tchaikovsky—Fantasia and Concerto No. 1] 1991.

Columbia M 33071. **Andre Watts** (piano), NYP, Leonard Bernstein (conductor), 1974.

Deutsche Grammophon 2530 677. **Lazar Berman** (piano), BPO, Herbert von Karajan (conductor), 1976.

Angel SQ 37177. **Horacio Gutierrez** (piano), LSO, André Previn (conductor), 1976. Reissued: Angel AE 34421 (CD), 1985.

Bruno Walter Society BWS-728. **Vladimir Horowitz** (piano), NYP, Bruno Walter (conductor), 1976 (recorded live 1948). Reissued: AS Disc AS-400, 199-?

Melodiya S 06987–06988. **Igor Zhukov** (piano), USSR Symphony Orchestra, Dmitri Kitayenko (conductor), 1976.

Quintessence PMC 7003. **Earl Wild** (piano), RPO, Anatole Fistoulari (conductor), 1977. Reissued: Chesky CD-13 (CD), 199-?

Angel S 37679. **Andrei Gavrilov** (piano), Philharmonia Orchestra, Riccardo Muti (conductor), 1980. Reissued: His Master's Voice OASD 3818, 1980; EMI CDM 7 69125 (CD), 1988.

CBS Masterworks IM 36660 (LP) and MK 36660 (CD). **Emil Gilels** (piano), NYP, Zubin Mehta (conductor), 1980. Reissued: CBS Masterworks MDK 44643 (CD), 1985; Sony Classical SBK 46339 (CD), 1990.

CLS MD-TP 060. **Vladimir Horowitz** (piano), NYP, George Szell (conductor), 1980 (recorded live 1952). Reissued: CLS RPCL 2027, 1981; Movimento musica 01.008, 1981; Movimento musica 011.007 (CD), 1986.

Decca SXL 6955. **Myung-Whun Chung** (piano), LAPO, Charles Dutoit (conductor), 1981.

CBS Masterworks M 36693 (monaural) and MT 36693 (stereo). **Andrei Gavrilov** (piano), USSR Radio Large Symphony Orchestra, Dmitri Kitayenko (conductor), 1981. Reissued: Harmonia Mundi HMC 5166, 1986.

Melodram 302. **Vladimir Horowitz** (piano), Hollywood Bowl Symphony Orchestra, William Steinberg (conductor), 1981 (recorded 1945).

Longanesi Periodici GCL 04. **Van Cliburn** (piano), BPO, Istvan Kertesz (conductor), 1981? (recorded live 1961).

Philips 6514 118 (LP) and 411 057-2 (CD). **Martha Argerich** (piano), Symphonie-Orchester des Bayerischen Rundfunks, Kirill Kondrashin (conductor), 1982.

Erato STU 71451. **Pascal Devoyon** (piano), Philharmonia Orchestra, Charles Dutoit (conductor), 1982. Reissued: RCA Victor Gold Seal 60010-2-RG (CD), 1989.

London 410 112-1 (LP) and 410 112-2 (CD) [Tchaikovsky—Concerto No. 3]. **Victoria Postnikova** (piano), VSO, Gennadi Rozhdestvensky (conductor), 1984.

RCA Red Seal 5708-1-RC (LP) and 5708-2-RC (CD). **Barry Douglas** (piano), LSO, Leonard Slatkin (conductor), 1986.

Telarc CD 80124 (CD). **Jon Kimura Parker** (piano), RPO, André Previn (conductor), 1986.

Deutsche Grammophon 415 122-1 (LP) and 415 122-2 (CD). **Ivo Pogorelich** (piano), LSO, Claudio Abbado (conductor), 1986.

London 417 294-1 (LP) and 417 294-2 (CD). **Andras Schiff** (piano), CSO, Georg Solti (conductor), 1986.

Schwann Musica Mundi CD 11644 (CD). **Lazar Berman** (piano), Berlin Radio Symphony Orchestra, Juri Temirkanov (conductor), 1987.

London 421 181-2 (CD). **Jorge Bolet** (piano), Orchestre symphonique de Montreal, Charles Dutoit (conductor), 1987.

RCA 5912-2-RC (CD). **Van Cliburn** (piano), RCA Symphony Orchestra, Kirill Kondrashin (conductor), 1987.

EMI CDC 7 47718 (CD) [Tchaikovsky—Fantasia]. **Dimitris Sgouros** (piano), LPO, Walter Weller (conductor), 1987.

Naxos 8.550137 (CD). **Joseph Banowetz** (piano), Czecho-Slovak State Radio Symphony Orchestra, Ondrej Lenard (conductor), 1988.

Laserlight/Delta Music 15516. **Jenö Jandó** (piano), Budapest Philharmonic Orchestra, Arpád Joó (conductor), 1988.

MCA Classics MCAD 25216 (CD). **John Lill** (piano), LSO, James Judd (conductor), 1988.

EMI CDC 7 49632 2 (CD) [Tchaikovsky—Concerto No. 3]. **Andrei Gavrilov** (piano), BPO, Vladimir Ashkenazy (conductor), 1989.

Deutsche Grammophon 427 485-2 (CD). **Evgeny Kissin** (piano), BPO, Herbert von Karajan (conductor), 1989.

Arabesque Z6611 (CD) [Tchaikovsky—Fantasia]. **Jerome Lowenthal** (piano), LSO, Sergiu Comissiona (conductor), 1989.

Chandos CHAN 8777 (CD). **Constantine Orbelian** (piano), Philharmonia Orchestra, Neeme Järvi (conductor), 1989.

Arkadia CD-34015 (CD). **Emil Gilels** (piano), Rome Radio and Television Orchestra, Fernando Previtali (conductor), 199-?

AS Disc AS 519. **Artur Rubinstein** (piano), NYP, Artur Rodzinski (conductor), 199-?

EMI CDC 7 49939-2–7 49940-2 (CD) [Complete Concertos and Fantasia]. **Peter Donohoe** (piano), Bournemouth Symphony Orchestra, Rudolf Barshai (conductor), 1990.

Sony Classical SK 45756 (CD) [Tchaikovsky—Concerto No. 3]. **Vladimir Feltsman** (piano), National Symphony Orchestra, Mstislav Rostropovich (conductor), 1990.

CBS Masterworks MBK 46268. **Nelson Freire** (piano), Munich Philharmonic, Rudolf Kempe (conductor), 1990.

Telarc CD 80193 (CD). **Horacio Gutierrez** (piano), Baltimore Symphony Orchestra, David Zinman (conductor), 1990.

Art & Electronics AED 10272. **Sergei Tarasov** (piano), Rostov Philharmonic Symphony Orchestra, Semyon Kogan (conductor), 1991.

Paris Records Album 4. **Conrad Hansen** (piano), Rundfunk in Amerikanischen Sektor Orchester, Wolfgang Sawallisch (conductor), n.d.

Somerset SF 14900. **Ludwig Hoffman** (piano), LPO, Gunnar Staern (conductor), n.d.

Decca VIV 16. **Ilana Vered** (piano), LSO, Kazimierz Kord (conductor), n.d. Reissued: London SPC 21148, 1975.

Peter Tchaikovsky, *Piano Concerto No. 2 in G major Op. 44.*

Concert Hall set AM (4 78 rpm discs). **Shura Cherkassky** (piano), Santa Monica Symphony Orchestra, Jacques Rachmilovich (conductor), 19—?

Decca K 1527–1530 (4 78 rpm discs). **Eileen Joyce** (piano), LPO, Grzegorz Fitelberg (conductor), 19—?

His Master's Voice C 3410–3413 (4 78 rpm discs). **Benno Moiseiwitsch** (piano), Liverpool Philharmonic, George Weldon (conductor), 19—? Reissued: Gramophone C 7607–7610 (4 78 rpm discs), 19—?

Westminster XWN 18289 [Tchaikovsky—Concerto No. 1]. **Edith Farnadi** (piano), Vienna State Opera Orchestra, Hermann Scherchen (conductor), 195-?

Concert Hall Society CHS 1125. **Noel Mewton-Wood** (piano), Winterthur Symphony Orchestra, Walter Goehr (conductor), 195-?

Melodiya D 0749–0750. **Tatiana Nikolayeva** (piano), USSR State Orchestra, Nikolai Anosov (conductor), 1952.

Decca DL 9916. **Shura Cherkassky** (piano), Berlin Philharmonic, Richard Krauss (conductor), 1957.

Columbia ML 6155 (monaural) and MS 6755 (stereo) [Tchaikovsky—Concerto No. 3]. **Gary Graffman** (piano), PO, Eugene Ormandy (conductor), 1965. Reissued: Columbia MG 30838 [Complete Concertos Set], 1971.

Fontana SFL 1141. **Nikita Magaloff** (piano), LSO, Colin Davis (conductor), 1965. Reissued: Philips PHC 9007, 1967.

Baroque Records BU 1865 (monaural) and BUS 2865 (stereo). **Emil Gilels** (piano), Leningrad Philharmonic, Kirill Kondrashin (conductor), 1966.

Melodiya S 01685–01686 (stereo). **Igor Zhukov** (piano), USSR Radio Large Symphony Orchestra, Gennadi Rozhdestvensky (conductor), 1968. Reissued: Melodiya D 024157–024158 (monaural), 1969; Melodiya/Angel SR 40097, 1971; Melodiya/Angel SR 40188 [Rimsky-Korsakov—Concerto; Tchaikovsky—Concerto No. 3], 197-?

Turnabout TW-S 34421. **Friedrich Wührer** (piano), VSO, Heinrich Hollreiser (conductor), 197-?

Philips 6703 033 [Op. 79, Complete Concertos, and Fantasia]. **Werner Haas** (piano), National Opera Orchestra of Monte Carlo, Eliahu Inbal (conductor), 1972.

Angel SB 3798 [Tchaikovsky—Complete Concertos Set]. **Emil Gilels** (piano), New Philharmonia Orchestra, Lorin Maazel (conductor), 1973.

Vox SVBX 5455, 5459, 5460 [Complete Concertos and Fantasia]. **Michael Ponti** (piano), Prague Symphony Orchestra, Richard Kapp (conductor), 1973. Reissued: Turnabout TV-S 34560 [Tchaikovsky—Concerto No. 1], 1974; Vox Box CDX 5024 (CD) [Tchaikovsky—Fantasia and Concerto No. 1] 1991.

Connoisseur Society CSQ 2076. **Sylvia Kersenbaum** (piano), Orchestre national de l'O.R.T.F., Jean Martinon (conductor), 1975.

London 410 113-1 (LP) and 410 133-2 (CD). **Victoria Postnikova** (piano), VSO, Gennadi Rozhdestvensky (conductor), 1984.

EMI CDC 7 49124 (CD). **Peter Donohoe** (piano), Bournemouth Symphony Orchestra, Rudolf Barshai (conductor), 1987. Reissued: EMI CDC 7 49939-2-7 49940-2 (CD) [Complete Concertos and Fantasia], 1990.

Audiofon CD 72030 (CD). **David Bar-Illan** (piano), Orchestre des Concerts Française, Jean-Jacques DuBois (conductor), 1988.

Arabesque Z6583 [Tchaikovsky—Concerto No. 3]. **Jerome Lowenthal** (piano), LSO, Sergiu Comissiona (conductor), 1988.

Peter Tchaikovsky, *Piano Concerto No. 3 in E flat Op. 75.*

Columbia ML 6155 (monaural) and MS 6755 (stereo) [Tchaikovsky—Concerto No. 2]. **Gary Graffman** (piano), PO, Eugene Ormandy (conductor), 1965. Reissued: Columbia MG 30838 [Complete Concertos Set], 1971.

Melodiya SM 03021–03022. **Igor Zhukov** (piano), USSR Radio Large Symphony Orchestra, Gennadi Rozhdestvensky (conductor), 1971. Reissued: Melodiya/Angel SR 40188 [Rimsky-Korsakov—Concerto; Tchaikovsky—Concerto No. 2], 1972; Melodiya S 06973–06974, 1976; Musical Heritage Society MHS 4946X [Rimsky-Korsakov—Concerto], 1984.

Philips 6703 033 [Op. 79, Complete Concertos, and Fantasia]. **Werner Haas** (piano), National Opera Orchestra of Monte Carlo, Eliahu Inbal (conductor), 1972.

Vox SVBX 5455, 5459, 5460 [Complete Concertos and Fantasia]. **Michael Ponti** (piano), Prague Symphony Orchestra, Richard Kapp (conductor), 1973.

Candide CE 31056 [Rimsky-Korsakov—Concerto; Tchaikovsky—op. 79]. **Michael Ponti** (piano), Radio Luxembourg Symphony Orchestra, Louis de Froment (conductor), 1972.

Angel SB 3798 [Complete Concertos Set]. **Emil Gilels** (piano), New Philharmonia Orchestra, Lorin Maazel (conductor), 1973.

London 410 112-1 [Tchaikovsky—Concerto No. 1]. **Victoria Postnikova** (piano), VSO, Gennadi Rozhdestvensky (conductor), 1984.

Arabesque Z6583 [Tchaikovsky—Concerto No. 2]. **Jerome Lowenthal** (piano), LSO, Sergiu Comissiona (conductor), 1988.

EMI CDC 7 49632 (CD) [Tchaikovsky—Concerto No. 1]. **Andrei Gavrilov** (piano), Berlin Philharmonic, Vladimir Ashkenazy (conductor), 1989.

EMI CDC 7 49939-2-7 49940-2 (CD) [Complete Concertos and Fantasia]. **Peter Donohue** (piano), Bournemouth Symphony Orchestra, Rudolf Barshai (conductor), 1990.

Sony Classical SK 45756 [Tchaikovsky—Concerto No. 1]. **Vladimir Feltsman** (piano), National Symphony Orchestra, Mstislav Rostropovich (conductor), 1990.

Albert, Eugen d', 176–7
Alekseev, A.D., 36, 48, 51, 127, 133, 145
Alexander I, Tsar of Russia, 9, 11
Alheim, d', 106
Alkan, Valentin: *Le Festin d'Esope* Op.39 No.12, 27
Alyabev, Alexander A., 7, 10, 16; Concertstück on themes by Steibelt, 12, 17–18
Anna, Duchess of Courland, 5–6
Anonymous: "Akh ne solnyshko zatmilos," 55; "Blow the man down," 65; "Dodo l'enfant do, l'enfant dormira bientôt," 7; "Il faut s'amuser, danser et rire," 130–1, 133, 142, 187; "Iz togo li goroda iz Muromlia," 83; "Oi kriache, kriache, chernyi voron," 127, 133; "Podoydu, podoydu vo Tsar-Gorod," 133; "Sobiraites'-ka, brattsyrebiatushki," 65, 66, 88–92; "Viidi, viidi, Ivanku," 133, 147, 148; "Zhil Sviatoslav debianosto let," 83; "Sredi doliny rovnye," 55; "se zhenikh griadet," 64; "so sviatymi upokoi," 66, 68
Arensky, Anton, 4, 78–84; *Basso Ostinato*, 81; *Fantasia on Themes of I.T. Riabinin* Op.48, 53, 82–4; Piano Concerto Op.2, 78–82, 95, 187, 188
Artôt, Desirée, 127, 146
Asaf'ev, Boris, 51, 82
Asmus, Valentin, 106

Balakirev, Mily, 13–14, 15, 18, 19, 43, 54–69, 77, 85–6, 88, 95–7, 187, 188; *Grande Fantaisie on Russian Folk Songs* Op.4, 54–8; *Islamey*, 3, 14, 58, 125, 178; Mazurka No.5, 59, 92; Octet Op.3, 55; *Overture on Three Russian Folksongs*, 147; Piano Concertos: E-flat, 12, 19, 33, 60–9, 89; F-sharp minor Op.1, 56–60, 70, 80–1; Piano Sonata, B-flat minor, 65, 89, 92; *Russia*, 55, 67; Septet, 55; Symphony No.1, 55
Barenboim, L.A., 37
Beethoven, Ludwig van, 22, 187; Choral Fantasia, 68; Piano Concertos: 14; No.4 Op.58, 25; No.5 Op.73, 19, 33; Piano Sonatas: 25; Op.31 Nos.1 and 2, 32; Op.53 No.21, 13
Beliaev, Mitrofan P., 104, 105, 106, 163, 168, 170
Berlioz, Hector, 20, 49, 60
Bibikov, G.I., 18
Blom, Eric, 126–7, 133, 136, 145, 151, 173, 180–1
Blumenfeld, Feliks M., 3
Bogatyryev, Semeon, 165–6
Borodin, Alexander P., 86; Scherzo, A-flat, 92

Bortnyansky, Dmitri S., 6–8, 16, 18; Piano Concerto, 7; Quintet in C, 7; *Sinfonia Concertante*, 7–8; *Synsopernik*, 8
Bowers, Faubion, 106–7
Brahms, Johannes, 1, 170; Piano Concerto No.1 Op.15, 76–7
Brown, David, 77, 127–8, 134–5, 137, 142, 146
Buini, Giuseppe M., 6
Bülow, Hans von, 50, 115, 117
Byron, George Gordon [Lord], 13

Calvocoressi, Michel-Dimitri, 70, 71, 97
Catherine II, Tsarina of Russia, 5–6
Chaliapin, Fyodor I., 106
Cherlitsky, Ivan G.: Piano Concerto, 12
Chopin, Fryderyk F., 25, 82, 95, 142–5, 187, 188; Etudes: 85; Op.10 No.1, 59; Op.10 No.3, 145; *Fantasia on Polish Airs* Op.13, 17; Piano Concertos: No.1 Op.11, 57; No.2 Op.21, 12, 17, 57, 58, 78, 81, 82; Piano Sonatas: Op.35, 32, 145; Op.58, 32; Scherzo No.3 Op.39, 33, 60, 61–3; Variations on a Theme from *Don Giovanni* Op.2, 17
Clementi, Muzio, 12, 13, 14
Copland, Aaron, 1
Cui, César, 37, 50, 64, 72–3, 74, 86, 94–5, 106
Culshaw, John, 31
Czerny, Carl, 23; *Tägliche Studien*, 85

Dannreuther, Edward, 119, 120, 122, 124, 148, 166
Dargomizhsky, Alexander S., 10, 16, 19
David, Ferdinand, 22
Davidov, Lev V., 72
Debussy, Claude: *Estampes*, *Jardin sous la pluie*, 7–8
Dehn, Siegfried, 23
Diémer, Louis, 2, 163
Dubuque, Alexandre, 13–14, 15, 54
Dussek, Jan L., Piano Concertos: 12, 14; Op.70, 17
Dvořák, Antonin, 1, 2

Ecstedt, A.I. Fitzum von, 10
Eisrich, Charles, 55, 57
Elizabeth I, Queen of England, 5
Engalichev, Parfeni N., 3
Engel, Yuri, 106
Ermannsdörfer, Max von, 177
Esipova, Anna, 50, 51, 53, 177

Falla, Manuel de, 1
Field, John, 9, 10–14, 15, 16, 17, 54, 57; Piano Concertos: No.1, 12, 17; No.2, 12, 16, 32; No.3, 12, 13; No. 5, *L'incendie par l'orage*,

11, 13, 17; No.7, 13; *Variations on a Russian Theme*, 17
Fiske, Roger, 159
Fomin, Evstignei, *Orfeo and Euridice*, 6
Friskin, James, 119, 122–3
Fyodor Ivanovich, Tsar of Russia, 5

Gabrilowitsch, Ossip, 15
Galuppi, Baldassare, 6, 7
Garden, Edward, 33, 65, 84, 127, 131, 147, 149, 156
Genika, R., 78
Genishta, Iosif: Piano Concerto, 12, 13
Gershwin, George, 1
Ginsburg, Grigory, 82
Giordani, Tommaso, 12
Glazunov, Alexander, 4; Piano Concertos: Op.92, 186; Op.100, 186
Glinka, Mikhail I., 2, 3, 7, 10, 13, 16, 18, 19, 37, 50, 56, 58, 86, 142, 187; *Kamarinskaya*, 5, 51, 147; *A Life for the Tsar*, 115; *Ruslan and Lyudmila*, 131
Gluck, Christoph Willibald, 100
Gnessin, Mikhail F., 86
Gogol, Nikolay V., 9
Goldenweizer, Alexander B., 14, 82–3
Grieg, Edvard, 2, 98; Piano Concerto, 3, 81, 100–1, 187; *Symphonic Dances* Op.64, 81
Grinberg, Mariya, 83
Gurilёv, Alexander L'vovich, 13
Gurilёv, Lev Stepanovich, 6

Haydn, Joseph, 8
Henselt, Adolf, 1, 9, 54–5; Piano Concerto Op.16, 57, 95; Variations for Piano and Orchestra Op.11, 55
Herz, Henri, 1, 23
Hofmann, Josef, 14, 15, 50, 98
Hubert, Nikolai, 116
Hummel, Johann Nepomuk, 9, 14, 16, 23; Piano Concertos: Op.85, 13, 16, 54, 57; Op.89, 16
Hünten, Franz, 1

Igumnov, Konstantin, 14, 15, 98
Indy, Vincent d', 1
Iokheles, A., 171
Ippolitov-Ivanov, Mikhail M., 43
Ivan III, Tsar of Russia, 5

Jarrett, Keith, 1
Jurgenson, Pyotr I., 117, 119, 122, 125, 133, 151, 159, 162, 163

Kalkbrenner, Frédéric, 1, 19, 23
Kashin, Daniel N., 6, 9, 18–9
Kashkin, Nikolai, 116
Keldysh, Yuri, 8
Khandoshkin, Ivan Y., "Six Old Russian Songs with Variations . . . ," 6

Klindworth, Karl, 115
Kotek, Joseph, 176
Koussevitzky, Sergei, 102
Koželuch, Leopold, 1
Kreutzer, Leonid, 65
Kross, Gustav, 72
Kruglikov, Semën, 53, 85

Lang, Benjamin Johnson, 115
Laskovsky, Ivan F., 3, 12, 13
Lavrov, N.S., 94
Lhevinne, Josef, 14, 15, 50
Liszt, Franz, 9, 14, 20, 21–2, 25, 26- 30, 33, 51, 68, 86, 122, 170, 187; *Danse macabre*, 70, Hungarian Rhapsody No.6, 76; Paganini Etudes: No.4, 27; No.5, *La Chasse*, 26–7; Piano Concertos: No.1, 19, 60, 68, 76, 78–9, 100, 115; No.2, 19, 25, 27, 60, 83, 86, 95, 123; *Todtentanz*, 70, 71, 115; Transcendental Etudes: No.1, *Preludio*, 79–80; No.4, *Mazeppa*, 26, 157, 178; No.11, *Harmonies du Soir*, 178; No.12, *Chasse-neige*, 27; *Tarantella*, 26
Litolff, Henry: *Concertos Symphoniques*: No.1, 68; No.4, 33, 60–1, 115
Lloyd-Jones, David, 161
Lomakin, Gavriil Y., 19
Lukomsky, L., 171
Lyadov, Anatol K., 3, 105, 106; *Variations on a Theme of Glinka* Op.35, 25
Lyapunov, Sergei, 4, 14, 60, 64–5, 67, 69, 104; Piano Concertos: No.1 Op.4, 95–8; No.2 Op.38, 97; Symphony No.1, 95; *Transcendental Studies*, 97

Margola, Franco, 1
Martini, Padre Giovanni Battista, 6
Martyn, Barrie, 187
Matinsky, Mikhail: *The St. Petersburg Bazaar*, 6
Mattei, Stanislao, 6
Meck, Nadezhda von, 114, 116, 124, 150, 151, 156, 161, 176
Medtner, Nikolai, 14, 15, 74; Piano Concerto Op.33, 186
Mendelssohn, Felix, 1–2, 19, 20, 25, 30, 57, 100; Piano Concerto Op.25, 19; *Songs Without Words* Op.53 No.4, 24–5
Menter, Sophie, 177
Meyerbeer, Giacomo: *Robert le diable*, "Quand je quittai la Normandie," 55
Morozov, Nikita, 101
Moscheles, Ignaz, 1, 23, 31, 33, 104; *Anklänge aus Schottland* Op.75, 17; Piano Concertos, Nos.6–8, 19; *Souvenirs de Danemarc* Op.83, 17; *Souvenirs d'Irlande* Op.69, 17; Variations on "Au clair de la lune" Op.50, 17
Mozart, Wolfgang Amadeus, 1, 8, 19, 54, 57; Piano Concertos, 14; Piano Sonata K.311, 32

Musorgsky, Modest, 70–1, 86; *Boris Godunov*, 66; *Khovanshchina*, 85; *Pictures from an Exhibition*, 3–4, 93, 125; *St. John's Eve (A Night on Bare Mountain)*, 70, 71, 85; *Salammbo*, 70

Napravnik, Eduard: Fantasias on Russian Themes Opp.30 and 39, 78; *Folk Dance*, 89; Piano Concerto Op.27, 78
Niebuhr, Ulrich, 48–9
Nikisch, Arthur, 106
Nikolaev, Alexander A., 48

Odoevsky [Prince], 10

Pabst, Paul, 82
Paderewski, Ignacy Jan, 104
Paganini, Nicolò, 14
Pashkevich, Vasily A.: *The Misfortune of Having a Carriage*, 6
Paul I, Tsar of Russia, 9
Paul Petrovich, Grand Duke, 7
Peter I, Tsar of Russia, 5
Peterson, P.L., 72
Prokofiev, Sergei, 1, 4, 16, 158, 186; Piano Concerto No.1 Op.10, 186
Pushkin, Alexander S., 9

Rachmaninov, Sergei, 1, 3, 14, 15, 16, 17, 93–4, 98–103, 107, 109, 186–7; Capriccio Op.12, 102; *Etudes-tableaux* Op.33 No.5, 89; *Fantaisie-tableaux* Op.5, 4; Nocturne No.3, C minor, 123, 124; Piano Concertos: C minor (sketches), 98; No.1 Op.1, 99–103, 187; No.2 Op.18, 39, 103, 145, 187; No.3 Op.30, 103, 187; No.4 Op.40, 74; Rhapsody on a Theme of Paganini Op.43, 186; Symphony No.1 Op.13, 102
Raff, Joachim, 119
Raphling, Samuel, 1
Ravel, Maurice, 14
Reilly, Edward R., 71
Riabinin, Ivan Trofimovich, 82–3
Ries, Ferdinand: *Variations on a Swedish Air* Op.52, 17
Rimsky-Korsakov, Nikolai, 2, 3, 62, 64, 65, 70, 71, 72, 80, 82, 104–6, 170, 188; Piano Concerto Op.30, 4, 65, 84–95, 183, 186, 187
Rubets, A.V., 133
Rubinstein, Anton, 3, 14, 15, 19–20, 21–53, 54, 71–2, 73, 74, 75, 77, 100, 154, 155–6, 161; Concertstück Op.113, 29–30, 50; *Don Quixote*, 43; Fantasy Op.84, 29–30, 50–1; *Ivan the Terrible*, 43; *The Merchant of Kalashnikov*, 51; *Nero*, 43; Octet Op.9, 22–3, 24, 98; *Ondine*, 24; Piano Concertos: 5; F major, C major (lost), 22; D minor, 13, 22–23, 24; No.1 Op.25, 25–6, 30–1, 32, 34, 40, 76, 80; No.2 Op.35, 30–1, 32, 33, 43, 60; No.3 Op.45, 31, 32, 33, 42, 49, 50, 97, 148, 158; No.4 Op.70, 16, 20, 22, 23, 31–2, 34–7,

45–9, 50, 70, 140, 141, 183, 186, 187, 188; No.5 Op.94, 22, 23, 25, 26, 27, 32, 37, 37–44, 50, 76, 97, 124–5, 157; Russian Capriccio Op.102, 29–30, 42, 50, 51–3, 83; Symphonies: No.2 Op.42 (Ocean), 43; No.4 Op.95, 22; *Tower of Babel*, 43; Violoncello Concerto, 22; Violoncello Sonatas, 43
Rubinstein, Kaleria, 22, 23
Rubinstein, Nikolai, 2, 14, 15, 50, 53, 115, 116, 117, 119, 124, 125–6, 149, 156, 159, 161, 166, 185

Sabeenev, Leonid, 107–8
Safonov, Vasily I., 14, 15, 100, 106
Saint-Saëns, Camille, 20, 49, 100
Salvatore, Giovanni, 5
Sapellnikov, Vasily, 15, 162
Sarti, Giuseppe, 6
Sartori, 6
Sauer, Emil von, 53
Schiller, Madeleine, 161
Schubert, Franz: Quintet, D.667 (Trout), 142
Schulhoff, Ervin, 1
Schumann, Clara, 55
Schumann, Robert, 1–2, 13, 23–4, 54, 98, 170; Piano Concerto Op.54, 65, 128
Scriabin, Alexander, 14, 15, 100; Etude Op.8 No.12, 108–9; Piano Concerto Op.20, 103–13; Piano Sonatas: No.1 Op.6, 4; No.4 Op.30, 108; No.5 Op.53, 108; Prelude Op.11 No.20, 109
Scriabin, Vera Isaakovich, 98, 104
Seaman, Gerald, 7, 18
Senff, Bartholf, 22, 51
Serov, Alexander, 25, 50, 56
Shostakovich, Dmitri, 158
Siloti, Alexander, 14, 43–4, 100, 122, 123, 148–9, 151, 159, 162, 163, 164, 170, 176, 185
Siloti, Kyriena, 123
Skalon, Natalya, 99
Slavinsky, M., 89
Slonov, Mikhail, 99–100
Sokolovsky, Mikhail: *The Miller—Magician, Cheat, and Matchmaker*, 6
Spohr, Louis, 14
Stasov, Vladimir, 33, 55, 60
Steibelt, Daniel, 9, 10–12, 14, 16; *Destruction of Moscow*, 11; *Grand Concerto Militaire*, 11; *Martial Sonata*, 11; *Naval Combat*, 11; Piano Concertos: No.3 Op.33, 17; No.6 (*Voyage sur Mont St. Bernard*), 11
Stoyovsky, S., 163
Stravinsky, Igor, 1

Taneyev, Sergei, 71–8, 82, 105, 135, 149, 151, 157, 159, 161, 162, 163, 164, 168–75, 176–7, 184; Piano Concerto, 71–7
Tchaikovsky, Anatoli, 115, 116, 117
Tchaikovsky, Modest, 43, 115, 116, 168, 170

Tchaikovsky, Peter I., 5, 16, 42–9, 51, 53, 71, 73, 77, 107, 109, 114–85; *Andante and Finale* Op.79, 78, 81, 149, 168–75; *Concert Fantasia* Op.56, 2, 12–13, 149, 175–85; Incidental music for *The Snow Maiden* Op.12, 134, 135; Orchestral Suite No.3 Op.55, 175–6; Piano Concertos: No.1 Op.23, 3, 4, 5, 20, 23, 37, 39, 43–4, 45–9, 75–6, 94, 98, 114–51, 154, 156, 159, 165, 166, 168, 182–3, 185, 186, 187, 188; No.2 Op.44, 2, 44, 98–9, 114, 135–6, 149, 150, 151–62, 164–5, 166, 169, 177–8, 185; No.3 Op.75, 2, 57, 139, 149, 163–8, 175; Piano Sonata Op.37, 83; *Romeo and Juliet*, 115, 182; String quartet No.1 Op.11, 115; Symphonies: E-flat (sketches), 164, 165, 166; No.1 Op.13, 115; No.2 Op.17, 115, 135, 136; No.6 Op.74 (*Pathétique*), 81, 164; *Vakula the Smith*, 114, 128, 135; Variations Op.19, 115; *Voyevoda* Op.78, 164
Thomas, Theodore, 161
Tolstoy, Feofil (Rostislav), 9
Trutovsky, Vasili F., 6
Tsuipin, G.M., 83
Tumenev, G.A., 133

Tyulin, Yuri, 146, 159

Ulybyshev, Alexander, 10, 57

Vanhal, Johann Baptist, 1
Veinus, Abraham, 2, 16, 104
Verstovsky, Alexei N., 10, 16
Villoing, Alexandre, 15, 23, 54; Piano Concerto, 13, 19, 22

Warrack, John, 135, 146, 153, 182
Weber, Carl Maria von, 14; Konzertstück, 50–1
Wielhorski, Mateusz, 10
Wielhorski, Michal, 10
Woelfl, Joseph, 19; Concerto Op.20, 17

Yagolim, B., 73
Yastrebstev, Vasily, 106

Zajazkowski, Henry, 133–4
Zhilin, Alexei D., 18
Zimmermann, J.H., 64
Zverev, Nikolai, 14, 15

JEREMY NORRIS studied at the Royal Northern College of Music, University of Lancaster, and the University of Sheffield. He now makes his home in Italy, where he is Lecturer in the History of Music (Didactics) at the Brescia Conservatoire. He presents lecture-recitals on Russian piano music and also performs regularly with chamber groups. He is author of a monograph on Rachmaninov's piano music and of articles published in *Music Review*, *The Musical Times*, and *Piano Journal*.